COPING WITH TEENAGE DEPRESSION

A PARENT'S GUIDE

COPING WITH TEENAGE DEPRESSION

A PARENT'S GUIDE

by
Kathleen McCoy

With a Foreword by Richard G. MacKenzie, M.D.
DIRECTOR OF THE ADOLESCENT MEDICINE DIVISION
OF CHILDREN'S HOSPITAL, LOS ANGELES

NAL BOOKS
NEW AMERICAN LIBRARY
TIMES MIRROR
NEW YORK AND SCARBOROUGH, ONTARIO

Published simultaneously in Canada by
The New American Library of Canada Limited

Acknowledgment

The excerpt from "On Children" (page 81) has been
reprinted from THE PROPHET by Kahlil Gibran,
with permission of the publisher, Alfred A. Knopf, Inc.,
Copyright 1923 by Kahlil Gibran; renewal copyright
1951 by Administrators C.T.A. of Kahlil Gibran Estate
and Mary G. Gibran.

NAL BOOKS TRADEMARK REG. U.S. PAT. OFF. AND FOREIGN COUNTRIES
REGISTERED TRADEMARK—MARCA REGISTRADA
HECHO EN CRAWFORDSVILLE, INDIANA, U.S.A.

SIGNET, SIGNET CLASSICS, MENTOR, PLUME, MERIDIAN AND NAL BOOKS
are published *in the United States* by The New American Library, Inc.
1633 Broadway, New York, New York 10019,
in Canada by The New American Library of Canada Limited,
81 Mack Avenue, Scarborough, Ontario M1L 1M8

Designed by Alan Steele

Library of Congress Cataloging in Publication Data

McCoy, Kathleen.
Coping with teenage depression.

Bibliography: p.
1. Depression in children.   2. Adolescent
psychopathology.   I. Title.
RJ506.D4M32   616.85′27′0088055   82-2185
ISBN 0-453-00415-6   AACR2

First Printing, April, 1982

1   2   3   4   5   6   7   8   9

PRINTED IN THE UNITED STATES OF AMERICA

DEDICATION

To Aunt Molly . . .
who gave me inspiration and
hope in my teens and a
lifetime of very special joy

Contents

Acknowledgments

Special thanks to . . .

. . . "Tracy," who started it all, giving me painful and personal insights into the problems and challenges that teenage depression can bring.

. . . My agent, Susan Ann Protter, for originating the idea for this book and for her supportiveness throughout my work on the project.

. . . Christine Schillig, my editor at NAL, whose enthusiasm, excellent suggestions and warm support helped me over many rough spots. I am also grateful to Ann Watson, my first editor on the project, who got me off to a good start.

. . . The physicians, mental health professionals and educators whose insights and special knowledge have added so much to this book. I am particularly grateful to the following professionals who were especially generous with their time and expertise: Alan Berman, Ph.D.; Richard C. Brown, M.D.; Elizabeth K. Canfield; Gabrielle Carlson, M.D.; Mary Ann Dan, M.A.; Judith Davenport, M.S.W.; Calvin Frederick, Ph.D.; Lee Robbins Gardner, M.D.; Richard Gardner, M.D.; Sol Gordon, Ph.D.; Randi Gunther, Ph.D.; Shirley Lackey, M.A.; Doris Lion, M.A.; Richard MacKenzie, M.D.; Donald McKnew, M.D.; Marilyn Mehr, Ph.D.; Laurel Moore, M.A.; Sarah Napier, M.A.; Howard Newburger, Ph.D.; Merilee R. Oaks, Ph.D.; Michael Peck, Ph.D.; and Charles Wibbelsman, M.D.

. . . My friends who contributed so much in many ways to this book, especially Jim Alsdurf, Edie Moore, Gene Brissie, Dr. Michael McCoy, Elizabeth McCoy, Michael Polich, Sally Wilson, Mary Soares, Dr. Judith Salz, Dr. Charles Wibbelsman and Mary Connolly.

. . . My husband Bob Stover for his patience and supportiveness during the long months of work on this book, and for his continuing love and belief in me.

xi

. . . All of the teenagers and parents who took the risk of sharing their feelings and their lives with me. Their names have all been changed in the following pages to protect their privacy, but the people and their stories are real.

Foreword

THERE IS NO use for a teenager in American society today. There was a time when a family was valued by society for the number of children it had. Children were assets, assuring the continuity of the family line. When teenagers, they actively participated in maintaining the family through assuming responsibility for a number of tasks in the home, farm, or community. They contributed to the identity of the family. They felt needed and part of the community. Parents would "showcase" their children and teenagers wherever the opportunity arose—at church, picnics, community fairs. They, in general, were proud, and the children were proud!

Teenagers felt needed and built their concept of self around this. They established their future goals, explored their fantasies, and chose their friends within the framework of this identity. Schooling was a means to this end and was, for all practical purposes, a finite experience—finite in the sense that there was a beginning, a middle, and an end; finite in the sense that goals were clear, generally centered around the three R's; finite in the sense that the time commitment was clear and the number of years of involvement, practical. Within a dozen years of concentrated schooling the world was at their feet! The dreams of wealth, respect, power, travel, security, and excitement were the fuel which helped teenagers to value the years of preparation, for one day the world would be theirs!

Today's teenagers are not without their dreams and their fantasies, but somehow they do not seem as attainable. The journey is longer. The educational route now takes decades—high school, college, graduate school—and even then there are many uncertainties. And along the way there is little use for young people, for they are in preparation. They are being molded, without permanent shape. They are not seen for who they are, but for what they can be. And yet they are not that—they are what they are. And who they are is the identity of teenagers today—confronted with the ambiguity of education, the dissolution of family, the hostile commercialism of society, and the insecurity of relationships. And this identity is fragile—threatened by fears of rejection, feelings of failure, and of being different. Panicked by a sense of isolation, teenagers make a commitment to lifestyle, to friends, to sports, to gangs, to music, to fashion. The adult confrontation promotes the isolation, the separateness, the differences, and the "you don't understand me" attitude.

Depression, as Kathleen McCoy points out, is a common concomitant to this struggle, and it is often aggravated by the very things that we think should relieve it. Being with friends may only heighten the fear of eventual rejection. Participation in sports may in the teenager's mind only spell impending failure to live up to the expectations of parents, coaches, teachers, and friends.

The paradox becomes clear—by doing, you undo: undoing in the sense that the teenager now risks losing what identity he or she has attained. With the undoing, the outward spiral of growth and exploration turns inward on itself and involutes. The depressive symptoms begin to manifest themselves. And, like many of the teenagers' messages, they are not direct. It is this indirectness which catches us off guard, both as professionals and as parents trying to help. We fail to recognize, for example, the significance of psychosomatic symptoms, school failure, drug abuse, changed eating patterns, loss of interest in pastimes or sports. That adolescent depression is a great mimicker needs to be underlined in red ink. It can fool even the most astute of professionals and parents, giving rise to the disregard of or the minimizing of complaints. When it is finally recognized, parents often feel a sense of failure and guilt which may immobilize them into a state of inaction. Ms. McCoy, having talked with teenagers, parents, and professionals, has brought together perceptions from all sides of the issue. These insights provide parents with the red ink with which they need to highlight their own teenagers' behavior. The early identification and the use of appropriate remedies within the family—or through professional help—lessens the pain to all and redirects the spiral of adolescent growth outward to excitement and new experience.

Richard G. MacKenzie, M.D., Director
Division of Adolescent Medicine
Children's Hospitals of Los Angeles

Assistant Professor of Pediatrics & Medicine
Departments of Pediatrics & Medicine
University of Southern California School of Medicine

COPING WITH TEENAGE DEPRESSION

A PARENT'S GUIDE

Teenage Depression:
An Introduction

A T FIRST, JANET Anderson's parents were convinced that it was just a stage, just part of being fourteen, as Janet scorned family activities, become increasingly sullen and seemed to lose interest in school.

Even when her grades fell and she started defying curfew rules, her parents were more angered than alarmed. It wasn't until they discovered, via a call from her school counselor, that Janet hadn't attended classes for two weeks that the Andersons began to wonder if anything out of the ordinary might be wrong with their daughter.

After several family therapy sessions, Janet's parents realized that she was severely depressed. "We were shocked," Mrs. Anderson reports. "We kept saying, 'But she didn't *act* depressed! How could she be depressed? *Why* would she be depressed?'"

Janet's story is not an unusual one. Teenage depression is a very real crisis for many families. A number of experts in adolescent development and behavior see such depression as a major contributing factor to serious teen problems such as truancy and trouble at school, drug and alcohol abuse, sexual acting out, pregnancy, running away from home and suicide.

Recent statistics show just how widespread such problems are. For example:

- Every year, more than 1 million teenagers—most under the age of sixteen—run away from home.
- An estimated 1.3 million American teenagers have serious drinking problems.

1

- According to the 1978 High School Senior Survey, one out of every nine seniors reports smoking pot daily, an 80 percent increase in three years.
- Each year, 1 million teenage girls in the United States become pregnant. Thirty thousand of these are under the age of fifteen.
- The suicide rate for teenagers has increased 124 percent in the last twenty years, with close to 10,000 young people killing themselves each year and another 250,000 attempting to take their own lives. Suicide is the second leading cause of death—after accidents—among adolescents. And many accidents may, in fact, be disguised suicides.

These statistics are startling, but the individual stories behind the statistics are even more alarming, for the young people figuring into these statistics come from all communities, all economic levels, a myriad of home situations, anyone's family. What they have in common is depression. Feeling helpless and hopeless, many teenagers are using alcohol and drugs as self-medication. Pregnancy and/or sexual acting out become an antidote to the loneliness and isolation they feel. Truancy, running away, self-imposed starvation, and attempted suicide are often desperate cries for help.

When a teenager in your own family is experiencing such a crisis, the statistics become relatively meaningless. Trapped in a cycle of anger, confusion, fright and despair, parents and teen may all feel increasingly helpless and terribly alone.

During my years as an editor and advice columnist for *TEEN* Magazine, I met many troubled teenagers and their parents, in person and by mail. A number stand out in my memory.

There was Beth, thirteen, a shy, quiet eighth-grader who was expecting a baby in two months. Her pregnancy was intentional, Beth admitted, and she planned to keep her baby "because then I'll have someone of my own who will love me for sure. I won't be alone any more."

There was Ann, a newly divorced mother of a fourteen-year-old boy. Ann wrote to me agonizing over her son's sudden truancy and drug use, feeling angry, scared and guilty. "I don't know what to do," she wrote. "I'm afraid for him and upset for me. I know it's hard for him right now with his Dad moving out, but it's an awful time for me. How can I help him when my first reaction is, 'How could he do this to me right now?'"

There was Wendy, fourteen, whom I interviewed in a shelter for teenage runaways in St. Louis. Drawing her blanket around her like a cocoon, Wendy tried to explain why she had run away from home four times in the past two months. "I'm no good to anyone," she said quietly, staring at the floor. "I get upset and fuss at home and it causes trouble for everyone. I had to run away to save my parents' marriage."

And there was Tracy who, perhaps more than any other, touched my life and my understanding of teenage depression in a new and special way. Bright, talented and personable, Tracy was an "A" student, a promising ballet dancer and a model child. Even as she approached adolescence, her episodes of moodiness and rebellion were mild and only occasional. But everything changed for Tracy during the second semester of her freshman year of high school. Her best friend moved away. Her mother was injured in an auto accident and, soon after that, her beloved thirteen-year-old pet cat died. Initially Tracy seemed to cope well. She wrote to her friend, took on more household responsibilities and never said much about the cat. But she gradually began spending more time alone and was increasingly sullen and snappish. She saw less and less of her friends. By May she was refusing to go to school, sleeping all day and staying up all night, pacing and crying. She lost twenty pounds, quit ballet and started talking about suicide.

Unfortunately, Tracy's story is another that is not unusual. What made Tracy unique for me was the fact that she is a close relative of mine. During Tracy's crisis, I began to see teenage depression from a new perspective: not as an objective professional, but as a concerned, sometimes despairing, family member. I watched, alarmed, and tried to help as Tracy slipped further into deep depression and as her parents became more and more frightened and bewildered. They were completely at a loss to understand and cope with this child who had suddenly become a stranger.

With time and skilled counseling help, Tracy recovered. But her long bout with depression proved costly in many ways. She never went back to high school, although she did pass an equivalency exam. Her dream of becoming a classical ballet dancer is as yet unrealized. Although she is working hard to make up for lost time in her dance classes, some pain lingers. She feels that if she had been more in touch with her feelings and if her parents had recognized the early warning signs of her depression and had acted appropriately, she might not have had to endure so much pain for so long.

Tracy's parents also have regrets: that they didn't see trouble coming, that they couldn't face the facts about the seriousness of Tracy's depression until she was in a life-threatening crisis, that they didn't—at least initially—know how to help.

Their initial denial, confusion and helplessness, however, are common and understandable parental reactions to teenage depression. After all, this problem is often not easily identifiable as depression. In many instances a depressed teenager will seem much like any normal moody, rebellious adolescent. How can a parent tell what is a temporary stage and what is a crisis? Why do so many teenagers suffer from depression? Can it be prevented? How can the parents of a depressed teen deal with their own feelings of shock, fright, anger and guilt? And how can a parent help a deeply depressed adolescent? When is it time to seek outside help?

This book—with insights and guidelines from a variety of experts including psychiatrists, psychologists, adolescent medicine specialists, school and family counselors, social workers, parents and teenagers—is designed to help the concerned parents who may be asking such questions.

Parents are of vital importance to a depressed teenager. As a parent, you can be your child's best initial source of help if you understand the dynamics, the causes, the symptoms and the most constructive ways of coping with teenage depression. By taking early and appropriate action, you may help your son or daughter to avoid or overcome serious depression and prevent him or her from becoming yet another tragic statistic.

PART I

Facing Facts About Teenage Depression

CHAPTER 1

Teenage Depression: What Is It?

"**W**HY LIVE? WHY die? To keep on living an empty life takes patience from an empty person. . . ."*

These words are taken from the diary of Vivienne Loomis, a bright, attractive, well-loved fourteen-year-old whose suicide in 1973 shocked and bewildered both family and friends. And yet Vivienne *had* given warning signals for months. She had confided her feelings to close friends. She had written letters to her teachers.

Yet her signals were not taken seriously. How can you determine if the signals *are* serious, or if they are just the everyday frustrations of a sensitive adolescent? What exactly is teenage depression?

Take the case of Ron Wells, a seventeen-year-old high school senior who seems blessed with all things bright and beautiful. He is smart, popular, handsome and athletic. He has just been accepted at the college of his choice, a highly competitive Ivy League school.

Ron's parents are proud—and puzzled. They have not yet realized that Ron is seriously depressed. During the past few weeks, he has become reclusive, moody and apathetic about his classes. He recently received his first "C" ever in an English test. His appetite has diminished. He is irritable and snappish with his parents and close friends. He sometimes talks about life being an incredible burden.

* From *Vivienne: The Life and Suicide of an Adolescent Girl* by John Mack and Holly Hickler (Little, Brown, 1981).

This is so unlike Ron, and it is a frame of mind seemingly so at odds with the happy realities of his life.

In a rare open moment, Ron tries to explain his feelings to his parents. "I've been feeling empty, down and kind of depressed lately," he tells them.

"Depressed?" Mr. Wells replies with more than a hint of impatience. "What do you possibly have to be depressed about? We've given you everything. You're smart. You have friends. You got into college. What more could you want? How could you be depressed?"

Ron shrugs and stares at the floor.

If you have a depressed teenager—or know one—this scenario may have some familiar elements. Once you realize that your teenager might be depressed, your first question is likely to be "Why?"

It seems incredible that someone with youth, vitality and a myriad of life opportunities could be depressed. Granted, adolescence is no breeze. Friends can be fickle. Growing bodies can be awkward at times. There is that constant baffling mixture of yearning for security and pressure toward independence. But to an adult these conflicts seem minor in comparison with the advantages of youth, vitality, and opportunity.

And so, despite your own memories and your best intentions, you feel tempted to echo the old myth, "But these are the best years of your life," when you see your own teenager moping around the house or lashing out angrily for reasons that are hard to understand. Depression and youth seem utterly incongruous.

Parents have not been the only ones to question the validity of depression in the young. Until recent years, mental health professionals were also skeptical about the existence of true depression in young people. In the past, traditional analytic dogma held that serious, ongoing depression in children and young adults was rare. The prevailing view was that true depression could not exist before the formation of the idealized self-image (also called the superego), a developmental stage usually not reached until well into adolescence. A youngster's personality was not deemed sufficiently mature enough to suffer serious depression.

To the great misfortune of many unhappy teenagers, serious study of childhood and adolescent depression was postponed. But times are changing. In the last few decades, more and more professionals have recognized that young people, even infants, can become depressed.

In a pioneering study some thirty years ago, researchers discovered and documented symptoms of depression in infants who had been separated from their mothers. More recently, a report from the National Institute of Mental Health (NIMH) examined a number of psychiatric studies and concluded that as many as one in five children may suffer from depression.

Even suicide in preadolescent children is not unknown. Dr. Gabrielle Carlson, a psychiatrist at the UCLA Neuropsychiatric Institute and a nationally known expert on the subject of childhood and adolescent depression, has seen children as young as seven or eight who are suicidal and seriously depressed. And Dr. Lee Robbins Gardner, a psychiatrist and assistant clinical professor of psychiatry at Columbia University's College of Physicians and Surgeons, notes that one young girl cited in a recent study suffered from frequent crying spells, overeating, self-destructive behavior and progressively dangerous episodes of tripping and falling after her mother's suicide. When referred for treatment, the girl was four years old.

Among mental health professionals there is growing acceptance of the fact that children and teenagers can and often *do* feel genuine—sometimes profound—depression.

But the question in many minds is still, "Why?" Why does depression strike some young people who have so much potential, so many options and such great advantages?

CHAPTER 2

What Can Trigger
Adolescent Depression?

TERRI WAS A week away from her fourteenth birthday when her
father died suddenly of a heart attack. She cried continually,
refused to go to school and lost ten pounds in three weeks following
his death. She also started picking fights with her mother and
younger brother, alternating between bouts of despair and bursts
of anger. Finally, her worried and exhausted mother took her to the
family doctor.

When the doctor gently asked Terri what she was feeling and
how losing her father was affecting her feelings, she began to cry.
"We didn't get to say 'goodbye' because he died at work," she
sobbed. "I can't stand it. I didn't get a chance to tell him I loved
him. We always got along great until this year when I started wanting to be on my own more and I mouthed off to him a lot. I had a
fight with him the night before he died about something that was
just dumb. I feel like a terrible person. Now he'll never know I loved
him. It's like nothing matters anymore. And I'm mad at God, too.
Why did my Dad have to die anyway, when I loved him and needed
him so much?"

Terri's feelings of grief, guilt and anger are far from unusual.
While many teens are not as verbal about their feelings as Terri,
those same conflicts are often there.

While the death of a parent is obviously enough to cause the
onset of severe depression in many children, experts agree that

teenagers usually become depressed in reaction to a combination of stresses.

"Factors such as a parental divorce or a family relocation can be significant losses to a teenager, but they are not usually enough *in isolation* to bring about severe depression in a teen," contends Dr. Calvin Frederick, chief of Emergency Mental Health at the National Institute of Mental Health and professor of psychiatry at George Washington University.

The following stressors are the most commonly cited in connection with teen depression. If your child is experiencing several of these in combination, he or she could be at risk for serious depression.

A Significant Loss

Loss can be due to death, divorce, separation, or loss of an important friend or romantic interest. Loss can also be more subtle— the loss of childhood, of a familiar way of being, loss of goals through achievement or of boundaries and guidelines. These and other typical "loss traumas" that can trigger depression in teenagers are discussed below.

The Death of a Loved One

The death of a parent or close family member is a major trauma for an adolescent. He or she may feel temporarily devastated by grief, guilt, panic and anger. If the young person is not able to express these feelings in a supportive atmosphere, depression may set in.

When John's twelve-year-old brother David died of cancer, he never shed a tear or showed any other outward signs of grieving. But in the weeks following his brother's death John, who was thirteen, began getting into fights at school, withdrew from his friends and became alternately distant and angry with his parents. Bewildered, his parents took him to see the hospital social worker who had counseled the family throughout David's illness. It took several sessions both alone with John and with the family together to help John begin to voice his feelings. He had not been able to cry, even though he was devastated by the loss of his brother, "Because I'm walking around with a big, hurting lump inside me. I tried to pound it out by fighting but it didn't work."

Finally, with support from his parents and counselor, John was able to cry and to voice other feelings like guilt over his jealousy of David, who had received the lion's share of parental attention during his long illness. He was also able to voice his anger and grief over his brother's death and his fear that his parents sometimes wished that he, not David, had died.

Grief over the death of a friend can be especially painful at a time when friends are so important. A friend's death is also a reminder of our own mortality. Guilt can take its toll, too. If the friend died in an accident, or by suicide, the teenager may be plagued by "If only's . . . ," asking over and over why he or she wasn't there when needed. These "if only's" are a way of denying helplessness in the face of death. Denial, rather than acceptance, is often a forerunner of depression.

The death of a pet is frequently a major crisis for a young adolescent—one that is too often minimized. Some youngsters become very close to their pets even as they begin to pull away from the family in their quest for independence.

The death of Tracy's cat, for example, was a major factor in triggering her long bout of depression. She had been feeling essentially alone for a long time as her parents struggled with marital problems and as she began her own adolescent push toward autonomy. Her only invariably faithful companion was Emmy, a cat she had had since she was a toddler.

"I used to talk my problems over with Emmy all the time," Tracy recalls. "I know it sounds dumb, but it helped. At least *she* seemed to listen. She would put her paws around my neck, lick my face and purr. She always loved me no matter what."

When Emmy died, Tracy felt that she had lost her only real friend. Her feelings of loss and desperation were heightened by the fact that she was afraid and embarrassed to tell anyone how much the cat had meant to her and the fact that her family and friends seemed to take the death rather casually. Although there were other losses and pressures in Tracy's life—her best friend had moved away and her mother had been seriously injured in an accident and needed special care at home—Emmy's death proved to be the final, unbearable loss. She never said much to anyone about Emmy. But Tracy's behavior began to change abruptly after she lost her pet. She became even more isolated, refusing to go to school and sleeping all day. She lost interest in her beloved ballet lessons and then stopped eating and started hinting about suicide.

"Things had been bad for a while," Tracy remembers. "But to me, losing Emmy was the worst thing that could have happened and what was terrible was that no one really understood. I felt more alone than ever before."

Separation from a Loved One

Death, of course, is not the only loss that causes depression. Separation from an important person can also be a factor in adolescent depression. This separation often comes about as the result of divorce, when a parent moves out of the house and, in some sense, out of the child's life. But such separations also occur as the result of constant business travel, long tours of duty in the service or a parental jail term. In some ways, a separation can be even more painful than the death of a loved one.

"Separation from a vital love object is an important stress factor," says Dr. Donald McKnew, a child psychiatrist on the staff of the National Institute of Mental Health, who, along with his colleague Dr. Leon Cytryn, is one of the nation's best-known and most respected researchers on the subject of childhood and adolescent depression. "We have found that the damage seems to be greater in a coming and going situation—when the loved one drops in and out of a child's life—than it is in the single, final separation that death brings."

The fact of death, after all, is nonnegotiable. It must be faced and life must go on without the lost loved one. But when an important person drops in and out of a youngster's life, the teen may suffer from an ongoing cycle of hope, disappointment, rejection and despair.

After her parents' divorce, for example, Tammy began running away to the homes of friends for a day or two at a time. Her grades dropped and she spent a lot of time alone in her room, sulking and crying. During a conference with Tammy's teacher, her mother observed that these episodes were often linked with her father's behavior. Despite liberal visitation rights, Tammy's father had almost dropped out of her life. He seldom called and almost never visited. It was usually Tammy who initiated most of the contact with her father. She felt terribly rejected by his long silences, coming to the conclusion that she was no longer loved or valued. But just when she was beginning to adjust to the fact that her father was gone, he would reappear with presents and promises of a closer, ongoing relationship and more frequent fun times together. Tammy's hopes would soar once again. She would make all kinds of plans for future get-togethers, only to be disappointed again as her father totally disappeared from her life for months at a time. This cycle of hope, rejection and continual loss was, as subsequent counseling revealed, a major contributing factor to Tammy's depression.

Separation from friends and from one's roots due to a family move is a loss that can also be a major stressor and produce reactive depression.

Fourteen-year-old Melanie, for example, lost interest in hobbies and school and started sleeping a lot after her family moved from New Jersey to the San Francisco Bay Area. Her mother, worried that something might be physically wrong with Melanie, took her to see Dr. Charles Wibbelsman, an adolescent medicine specialist with the Northern California Permanente Medical Group.

"There was nothing physically wrong with Melanie, but in talking with her I discovered that the family move had separated her from her best friend—a very significant person in her life—and she was greatly affected by this," says Dr. Wibbelsman. "Adults may tend to minimize such a loss. After all, we have more experience in coping with such separation. We know we can keep in touch, meet new friends and take care of ourselves. But these facts aren't obvious to the inexperienced teenager. A close friend is a salient part of his or her life. Also, such partings are usually the result of a parental choice or transfer. When someone else makes the decision to move, the teenager suffers not only the loss of a friend, but also the sense of lacking control over his or her destiny. Some kids who have no roots and whose parents move frequently have problems with peer relationships—and are subject to periodic or chronic depression."

A romantic breakup, too, can be particularly devastating to a teenager, whose feelings are so new and intense and who does not yet know that one can survive the loss of a love, learn and grow from the experience and someday love again.

Loss of a Familiar Way of Being

Adolescence brings a number of physical and psychosocial changes, all of which mean growth and loss.

"Depression is, to some extent, a part of normal adolescent development because in growing and developing the young person experiences loss," says Dr. Richard C. Brown, director of Adolescent Health Services at San Francisco General Hospital and assistant clinical professor at the University of California, San Francisco Medical School. "This involves loss of childhood and a family-centered life. In forming strong new ties with their friends and questioning family values and traditions, teens begin to separate from their families. They are making new commitments to new friends, feeling love and affection outside the family and seeing themselves as separate from the parents. Their bodies are changing, too, and these internal changes combined with social changes can make this a time of disequilibrium. The teenager is losing the comfort of dependence and the simplicity of being a child. As a result, the teenagers (and their parents, too) may be in a state of mourning."

Thirteen-year-old Kyra, for example, was distressed to find that even though she was growing to prefer the company of her friends most of the time, her parents were also becoming a bit more distant. She had always been especially close to her father, enjoying outings, games and wrestling matches with him. As she began to develop physically, however, her father stopped the wrestling matches and, in fact, stopped touching her at all. He seemed a little uncomfortable around Kyra now that she was no longer physically a child.

Kyra saw this distance as a rejection and as a huge loss. Her sadness and anger were evident when she told her school nurse, "I feel like either killing myself or tearing up the photography book Dad gave me for Christmas—just to show him how I feel!"

Loss of Self-Esteem

Depreciation, rejection and the inability to live up to high parental expectations can cause significant loss of self-esteem and trigger reactive depression in adolescents.

Teenagers, who are living through so many physical, social and emotional changes, are newly aware of their shortcomings and limitations and may be especially sensitive to criticism or rejection— obvious or implied, real or imagined. And teens' testing of boundaries, rules, ideas and behaviors may tax parental tolerance to the breaking point, making them easy targets for criticism.

"Teenagers are masters (often perceptive and accurate) at criticizing and expressing contempt," says Dr. Gardner. "However, they are simultaneously super-sensitive to criticism, from parents especially. They need a lot of tact and small doses of criticism."

Also, certain patterns of rejection may escalate when a child reaches adolescence.

"Rejection often comes in the form of a blunt statement stressing the child's inadequacy," says Dr. McKnew. "Parents may be unaware of their own rejecting behavior. They may reject a fault or handicap in the child that they despise in themselves. A woman who doesn't feel good about her femininity may reject her daughter. A man may, for the same reasons, reject a son. Age can be a problem. Some parents are very good with infants, but reject their children as they get older and more independent. In this instance the child can become very depressed and feel that he or she has let the parent down by growing up."

As Ken, a fourteen-year-old whose father died six months after Ken's birth, grew to prefer the company of his peers, his mother became angry and rejecting. He found himself torn between wanting to please his mother and wanting to please himself. His mother's labels, like "selfish" and "ungrateful," have increased his confusion and subsequent depression.

Dana was her father's favorite when she was little, cute and compliant. But when she began to develop her own interests and her own point of view, her father seemed to lose interest in her, favoring her younger brother. Dana is now struggling with feelings that she is a bad, unlovable person—even though no harsh or angry words have ever been spoken.

Jason, referred to a youth and family therapist by his school counselor, has grown up with poor self-esteem. "Nothing I've ever done has ever been enough," he tells the counselor. "If I rake the leaves, Dad wants to know why I didn't clean the garage while I was at it. If I make an 'A minus' in school, my folks want to know why it wasn't an 'A' and tell me I'm a failure. I'm getting interested in computers and am thinking about a college major in computer science or maybe engineering. But my parents have their hearts set on my being a doctor. Anything less makes me a second-class citizen or something. Nothing I accomplish is ever enough."

After speaking with Jason's parents, his counselor noted that their excessively high expectations for their son reflected their own feelings of inadequacy and their disappointment with their own career choices and financial status. Most parents, of course, want the best for their children. But Jason's parents felt that unless he was the best as *they* defined it, he was a failure.

Sometimes the patterns are less obvious. Dr. Carlson notes that in her practice at UCLA she recently encountered a teenage boy who was severely depressed and chronically suicidal, with very low self-esteem. "His father was a brain surgeon and his mother was a psychiatric social worker," she says. "I made the comment that I have never seen a chronically suicidal kid who didn't have family problems. They denied any problems. Yet as I watched the family talk with each other, I noticed that every time the boy said something his mother would contradict him or discount what he was saying with a comment like, 'It *wasn't* that way. You misunderstood.' Nobody was listening to what the boy was saying."

The parent who doesn't listen is implying that what his or her child feels, thinks and says is not particularly important. Such a message can be a blow to a teen's often shaky self-esteem.

A crisis in self-esteem can also occur when a teenager is not allowed autonomy, is not trusted and is given little power over his or her own destiny. This saps self-esteem.

Loss of Boundaries and Guidelines

Social and economic turbulence have affected family life-styles a great deal in recent years. The growing incidence of divorce and the impact of inflation on the average family have meant the rise of two-career families. Parents have less time to spend with their children than they did a generation ago. In particular, the last decade has been a time of increased emphasis on self-discovery and self-fulfillment, at the cost of traditional values and life-styles. Many of these changes, of course, have been for the better. But others have meant more conflict within the family and often less time spent together. As a result, many of today's teens feel a loss of support, a lack of caring.

Dr. Calvin Frederick contends that a number of factors related to social and economic changes contribute to teenage depression and suicidal behavior. "Some of the key factors we have found in adolescent depression and suicide include breakdown in the nuclear family, lack of purpose and guideposts and connection with others in this do-your-own-thing society," he says. "Young people today find it much more difficult to fit into the family unit. They don't have the stable guideposts that earlier generations had."

Loss of Normality

Depression can be triggered by an illness or injury that sets a teenager apart from peers—temporarily or forever.

"Physical illness is a particular problem in adolescence because teenagers are so aware of and concerned with body image," says Dr. Gardner. "There is an extra emphasis on body image at this time and great emphasis, too, on all the changes the body is experiencing. Most teenagers are disturbed about at least one physical thing. It may be height, testicle size, breast development or even one pimple. There is a preoccupation with the body and any insult to it—even if it *seems* minor—may cause an overreaction."

Life is especially difficult for an adolescent with a chronic disease like diabetes or epilepsy.

"We see quite a lot of depression in chronically ill adolescents," says Dr. Richard MacKenzie, director of the Division of Adolescent Medicine at Children's Hospital of Los Angeles and president of the Society for Adolescent Medicine. "Teenagers with a chronic disease may feel inner turmoil about a disorder that separates them from their peers. There may be conflicts with parents about treatment routines and allowed activities. Parents may not trust the child's judgment. A chronic illness can also impede a teenager's emancipation from the family. All this sets the scene for serious depression. The teen's self-esteem is endangered tremendously."

Gayle's diabetes was diagnosed when she was ten, but the major conflicts about it and Gayle's serious depression over her illness didn't begin until she was in her early teens.

"I just got sick of having to be different," Gayle, now seventeen, remembers. "I couldn't eat everything my friends ate. I had to follow—and still do—a strict meal schedule, which has always made my life less spontaneous than those of my friends. And my parents drove me nuts with their concern. They kept asking me— in front of my friends even—'Have you eaten?' and 'Did you test your urine?' And if we ate out, it was such a big deal. My mom would always make sure the chef knew that I was diabetic! It made me feel like a weirdo—and furious. I stopped trying to take responsibility for myself for a long time. I figured, 'If my parents are going to live life for me, I give up.' I felt for a long time like my parents sometimes used my diabetes to control me, to keep me from doing things I wanted to do. I was *so* depressed!"

A frightening health crisis and a sensitive yet strong-willed new doctor helped Gayle and her parents find a balance of power. From then on, Gayle has taken an increasing amount of responsibility for her own health and her life in general. At seventeen, Gayle reports that taking control of her medical condition has been a growing experience and a weapon against depression. "Now I feel like a normal person who just happens to have a medical problem that I can control," she says. "I don't feel strange, out-of-it and depressed that much anymore."

Loss of Goals Through Achievement

This sense of loss may be difficult to understand when it happens. The feeling strikes when things are going well, when a teenager has won a prize, made the team, met a challenge, finished a project, graduated or accomplished some other long-term goal. The fact behind this reaction to positive stress is that in achieving a goal one loses that goal. For a time, the teen may wonder "What now?" and feel a deep sense of loss.

"The senior year of high school can be a special problem for teenagers," Dr. Gardner observes. "There is a letdown. Bright kids who have fulfilled their dreams of admission to college are especially vulnerable. For years, they've talked about and planned for college. Now they're in and feel frightened and conflicted when confronted with the fact that their dreams are becoming reality."

Ron Wells, whose personal story was discussed in the preceding chapter, is an example of a teenager afflicted with depression in the wake of achievement.

The reactions of others to the teen's achievement may heighten the youngster's sense of loss and confusion.

Two weeks after she won the "Best Actress" award in a state-wide drama festival, Carole confided tearfully to a favorite teacher that winning the award meant more separateness than ever from her classmates. Some were obviously jealous and made cutting remarks. Others seemed a bit in awe of her. This separateness—and the letdown involved in getting back to her regular routine after all the excitement of winning—added up to depression for Carole.

Jim, a math whiz, was elated when he was admitted to MIT. His excitement over college and his upcoming graduation gave way to confusion, disappointment and finally depression when he noticed the sudden coolness of Mr. Jackson, his math teacher and mentor for the past two years.

"This is not an unusual situation," says Dr. Gardner. "Teachers put a lot into the success of their students. Graduation can be a tremendous loss for a teacher, especially when kids express happiness at leaving and put down the school. The teacher may feel that kids today have it easier and there may be some role reversal as the kids overtake the teacher in certain ways. Physically, this may have happened earlier, but now the student may pass the teacher intellectually or in terms of achievement and so teachers may be less than sympathetic."

All of these factors may combine to make some victories bittersweet, and depression in the wake of triumph a real possibility.

Parental Depression

Depressed teenagers often have depressed parents. Some researchers feel that there may be a genetic link to chronic depression, but serious depression in the parent can also trigger reactive depression in a teenager. "The youngster's depression may be the result of identification with the parent or an altered relationship due to the parent's depression," says Dr. McKnew.

Lack of emotional support from parents may be a vital factor in an adolescent's depression. "Often we find parents who are so depressed themselves that they can't see beyond their own needs," Dr. Carlson points out. "They may have a chronic 'Who cares?' or 'Oh, shut up!' attitude toward their children. From a common-sense point of view, this has to have an impact on the child, especially if he or she has no other resources to turn to."

Limited Inner Resources for Coping with Frustration and Loss

This is a common problem, especially among young adolescents.

"These young adolescents can be very fragile," observes Dr. Wibbelsman. "Life experience is so limited that the youngster has a great deal of difficulty finding workable solutions to a problem or crisis. Often, teenagers don't have the experience and memories of coping constructively, or maybe even growing, through a difficult time."

The resulting sense of helplessness can lead to severe depression, even suicide. "When a teenager is suicidal, the three H's—helplessness, haplessness and hopelessness—are usually present," says Dr. Frederick. "Events seem to be conspiring against the child, who feels helpless to deal with the problem. There seems to be no hope that things can be different. It is this loss of hope which can lead to suicide."

Other Stresses That Can Trigger Teenage Depression

Family Conflicts

These range from parent and step-parent quarrels and marriage problems to sibling battles, alcoholism or drug abuse by a family member.

Poor Communication Within the Family Unit

When family members don't communicate well, teens have a lack of emotional support in crises.

High Parental Expectations

The teen may feel a sense of hopelessness in never measuring up to parental expectations. Parental love becomes conditional on achievement.

Learning Disabilities

Experts have found that a number of teenagers with learning disabilities are depressed. This may be due to low self-esteem or teasing from peers.

The inability to cope or feelings of helplessness and hopelessness can render adolescent depression potentially very dangerous. That is why it is so important for parents and other adults to understand the dangers and the nature of teenage depression well enough to recognize or suspect it when it strikes a young son, daughter, relative or friend. It is imperative to realize that depression *does* happen to teenagers, even those who have everything going for them. It is vital to admit that it could even happen to your child, that it might very well be part of the growing pains your son or daughter experiences during adolescence. And it may be comforting to know that recognition of these facts and the causes and sometimes unique symptoms of teenage depression is an important first step in helping your teenager find his or her way back from hopelessness.

PART II

Identifying Teenage Depression— The Signs and Symptoms

CHAPTER 3

Teen Depression
Is Different from
Adult Depression

TEENAGE DEPRESSION IS elementally different in a number of ways from adult depression. These differences can be quite important. They make it difficult for parents or even health professionals to recognize depression in a teenager and to offer appropriate help and support.

What are some of the ways that teen depression is different?

Teenagers Have Different Ways of
Showing Depression

A depressed adult usually feels and looks sad and lethargic. A depressed teenager, on the other hand, may seem extremely angry and rebellious, with "acting out" behavior such as school problems, truancy, sexual promiscuity, drinking, drug abuse, running away from home or other risk-taking behavior and psychosomatic symptoms quite common. These behavioral problems, which can mask depression, are not always indicative of underlying depression. But in many instances, they are.

"I believe that whenever you see an adolescent who has a constellation of symptoms and problems not fitting into a medical disorder or disease, depression should be considered as a cause," says Dr. Richard MacKenzie. "In so many instances, it is."

25

Dr. Richard Brown points out that it is the sometimes frenetic quality of teen depression that can be so misleading. "Hyperactivity, which can be a phobic reaction against depression, is often one of the characteristics of adolescent depression," he says. "The teen may *look* very nondepressed, but if you prick the surface of this hyperactivity, you will find, in many instances, that the young person *is* depressed."

Why do teenagers deal with their depression in these ways? Therapists treating teenagers have a number of theories.

"Teenagers are being hit with so much so fast in the many hormonal, physical and social changes and tasks they face," says Shirley Lackey, a family therapist with the La Mirada (California) Family Service Association. "As a result, they may develop an intolerance of feeling and their emotions will only get discharged through actions."

Some of this acting out is learned behavior.

"Drug abuse, for example, is a very common acting out behavior for a depressed teenager," says Dr. Marilyn Mehr, a psychologist and director of Behavioral Science at the Family Practice Center in Glendale, California. "This behavior is actually taught to our kids. Use of alcohol and of prescription drugs such as tranquilizers is widespread among adults, so kids have a model for drug use and abuse. They get the message, 'If you feel bad, *take* something instead of *doing* something to help yourself.'"

A number of mental health professionals believe that lack of verbal skills can be a major factor in a teen's acting out behavior.

"One is not likely to see anything that looks like adult depression in an early or mid-adolescent—someone twelve to seventeen," contends Judith Davenport, a clinical social worker and psychotherapist in private practice at the Center for Counseling and Psychotherapy in Santa Monica, California. "I feel this is so because, cognitively, most kids' minds are not fully developed at this point. They can't intellectually pinpoint and express what they are feeling. It's rare to hear a teenager come out and say, 'I feel depressed.' When this happens, it means, 'I need help.' But generally teenagers have a great deal of ambivalence about their dependency needs versus their growing need for independence. For a teenager to admit that he or she needs help feels like regressing back to childhood."

And so depressed teens may cry for help indirectly through troublesome, even destructive, behavior and through physical symptoms.

Teenagers Elicit Different Responses to Their Depression

At least initially, an adult's sadness may bring sympathy from family and friends. A teenager's acting out behavior tends to provoke alarm, anger, fear and frustration in those close to him or her.

"When Val was going through her crisis, depression was the last thing we thought of," admits her mother, Barbara. "She defied us constantly, took drugs and drank too much. At first, we figured it was all because she had fallen in with the wrong crowd. Then, many crises later, we decided she was a spoiled, ungrateful, rotten kid. Only after she ran away and we finally threw up our hands and got professional counseling did we realize that Val was seriously depressed. If we had only realized that, we would have tried to be more supportive and get help for her sooner. But how were we to know? It's so hard. There were some days I just couldn't help yelling at her and wanting to wring her neck. It was an absolutely impossible time at our house."

Teen Depression Can Be Extremely Intense

This intensity is often due to physical or hormonal changes, the developmental tasks of adolescence (which include alienation as a part of growing away from parents), shaky self-esteem and a great need for peer acceptance coupled with a lack of social experience.

While these changes and tasks don't invariably spell crisis for the adolescent (a recent survey of adolescents by Chicago psychiatrist Dr. Daniel Offer and psychologists Eric Ostrov and Kenneth Howard revealed that 85 percent of the healthy, school-attending teenagers surveyed reported that they were happy most of the time), depression is a fact of life some of the time for most teenagers, and for those who are troubled, the tasks and pressures of adolescence can lead to intense bouts of depression.

"Basically, all teens are depressed to some degree," says Judith Davenport. "They are suffering a great loss. They have to lose the image of their parents as perfect in order to grow up, so many adolescents are in a mourning process and feel quite alone. This depression is also cultural. In some societies, breaking away from parents is not encouraged or expected, but in this society it's essential."

This essential breaking away is complicated by the complex variety of skills and prolonged education often required in our industrialized society. Independence is prized, but adolescence prolonged. Many teens are hungry for independence, but they know that, realistically speaking, full personal freedom may be years away. This realization may deepen a young person's feeling of hopelessness if he or she is caught in a difficult home situation.

The changes of adolescence bring unique pressures. "At times, adolescents are overwhelmed with physical, cognitive and emotional changes," says Dr. Brown. "Life looks like a scary and immense undertaking as they confront all the changes in feelings, life tasks and a peer-oriented social world."

Because of these tasks and pressures, Dr. Gardner adds, "There are mood fluctuations, and it's hard to tell at times what is 'normal' depression and mood changes and what may be depressive illness."

In this framework of tumult and separation from parents, a teen's reactions to negative experiences—a lost love, a correction by a teacher or family problems—can be intense. All too often, depressed teenagers don't have the experience to know that time heals, that there is always hope, that they can survive a crisis and perhaps even learn from it. Life is often seen in absolutes—intensifying any crisis.

Teen Depression Is Often Minimized by Adults

Part of this problem may be due to the fact that parents, too, are going through different life stages.

"Usually, the teen has parents in middle age who are going through their own developmental changes, their own sense of loss, and who perhaps feel that they are losing just what the adolescent is gaining," Dr. Mehr points out. "So the parent may react to the adolescent with some anger, jealousy and hurt."

At this stage, it's extremely easy to look at a teenager and say, "My God, you're young! You have your whole life ahead of you. What could you possibly have to be depressed about?"

The experience gap can also be a factor. As an adult, you have a much broader perspective and are not as likely to react so intensely to every setback, slight, loss or stressor in your life. It's an understandable temptation to say, "You'll get over it . . . it's not really such a big deal . . . wait until you're grown up and face *real* problems!" At times, our generational chauvinism leads to invalidation of all adolescent feelings and experiences.

Poet Peter McWilliams, author of a number of books, remembers the fan mail he received when his first book of poetry, written around the theme of loss of a love, was published. At the time, McWilliams was only seventeen, a fact that was not revealed in his book jacket biography or in any publicity releases about the book. "I got all these letters from adults of all ages saying how they could really identify with my feelings and how I really touched their lives and their experiences through my poetry," he says. "But I'm afraid that if they had known I was only seventeen, the reaction would have been, 'What would *you* know about love?' or 'It was just puppy love. You'll get over it,' instead of, 'I understand, I've been there, too.'"

It's important to know that despite their lack of life experience and perspective, teen feelings and problems are real. The grim statistics on teen suicide, alcoholism and drug abuse bear this out.

The Acting Out Behavior of Teenage Depression Can Have a Lifelong Impact

While adult lives can be severely affected by bouts with depression, the destructive potential of serious teenage depression is even greater, with more long-lasting aftereffects. Dropping out of high school, having and keeping a baby, getting into trouble with the law, sustaining a serious injury as the result of risk-taking behavior or stunting one's emotional growth by anesthetizing painful feelings with drugs or alcohol can have a great impact on one's future, preventing a young adult from having a full, healthy, productive life—or making it considerably more difficult to do so.

Of course, there are success stories—teens who weather a stormy, troubled adolescence and emerge as strong, resourceful, productive and happy adults. But many times it's difficult or even impossible to undo the damage that destructive choices bring and to make a new start.

For example, Norman Fleishman, director of the Population Institute in Los Angeles, laments the fact that "when a young teenage girl gets pregnant and decides to keep and raise the baby herself (as most seem to be doing these days) about 90 percent of her life-script is already written for her. Freedom is curtailed just when it should be increasing. Dreams go unrealized, often forever. The young teen mother is more likely than others her age to spend a lifetime undereducated, unskilled and living in poverty."

Darryl, whose depression caused him to drop out of high school, keeps wanting to try for a second chance, but his low self-esteem holds him back. "I have these feelings sometimes that I'm not as good as the next person," he says. "My brother just graduated from medical school. My sisters are both college graduates and have great jobs. Me, I'm just a flunky, trapped in boring, dead-end jobs when I have a job at all. I keep wanting to go back to school at night and get my diploma, but I'm so tired after work and it's a drag to think about studying. I know I have to do it to get ahead, but I keep thinking, 'Next year I'll do it for sure. . . .'"

If a teenager has the benefit of early intervention and help in coping with his or her depression, however, the life script can be quite different.

"We're finding that adolescence can be a very useful time, and the idea of the die being cast permanently at an earlier age is in error," says Dr. Lee Robbins Gardner. "Adolescence is a time for reworking ways of coping and finding ways of reorganizing the self in the area of socialization. Many teens who have problems in junior high, for instance, can be much more successful in high school."

What Are the Different Types of Depression?

Depression is often used as a sort of catch-all phrase to describe a variety of symptoms. Sigmund Freud saw depression as a reaction to early losses and separations, a result of rage and guilt turned inward. Today, we might describe depression as the result of a complex mix of social, psychological and/or physical factors that can act on a person's nervous system, triggering sadness, hopelessness and self-deprecating thinking and behavior. For some people, depression comes in the wake of a major loss or setback. For others, the reasons are not so clear-cut. For some, depression can be a lifelong illness that comes and goes in an endless cycle of misery.

While we often talk about depression as a singular psychological disorder, there are actually several major kinds of depression. These include reactive (or acute) depression, endogenous (or chronic) depression, manic-depressive illness and psychotic depression.

Reactive Depression

Reactive depression usually comes about as the result of a specific event in a person's life—particularly a significant loss or trauma. Grief over the death of a loved one, the loss of daily contact with a parent through divorce, a romantic breakup or even the death of a beloved pet are some of the more obvious losses that can cause a teenager's depression. The achievement of a long-term goal or other positive life stresses are also occasionally linked with reactive depression. A complete discussion of various traumas that can trigger reactive depression is included in chapter 2.

In many instances, the beginning of a reactive depression is sudden and quite clearly linked with a loss or life stress. Usually this depression lingers only while the young person is working through his or her grief and diminishes as the teenager learns to cope with the loss. In other instances, however, reactive depression continues long after the initial trauma or, in some cases, first becomes apparent after the initial trauma as a delayed reaction.

Endogenous Depression

While most teenage depression appears to be reactive, there are instances when an actual cause of a young person's depressed mood is elusive. In such instances, the youngster may be suffering from *endogenous* depression. The depression appears to be internally generated with no obvious external causes. Endogenous depression is seen as a physiological disturbance, possibly as the result of changes in the brain's biochemistry.

Researchers are currently studying the roles of biochemistry, genetics and various toxins in producing endogenous depression.

The Biochemical Factor. Research into brain functioning has revealed that vital information regulating feelings, thoughts and behavior is transmitted to the brain cells by the nervous system through the release of chemical substances called neurotransmitters. Released at nerve terminals, these chemicals cause an electrical chain reaction of sorts from one nerve ending to another.

In the part of the brain that is associated with emotions, the brain function neurotransmitters are amino acid compounds called biogenic amines; they include serotonin, norepinephrine and dopamine. Some scientists theorize that an imbalance of these chemicals in the brain might be linked to endogenous depression. Some frequently prescribed antidepressant drugs alter the action of amines in the brain and are believed to correct existing chemical imbalances.

There are some new tests available that show promise of differentiating between endogenous and reactive depression—that is, determining whether the depression comes from within or is a reaction to external causes—based on chemical/hormonal actions and levels in the body.

In one test, the dexamethasone suppression test (DST), a blood sample combined with a dexamethasone tablet can allegedly identify endogenous depression in much the same way that a glucose test can identify diabetes. The test measures the functioning of the limbic system of the brain, which influences the adrenal glands, which in turn secrete a hormone called cortisol.

Dexamethasone, which mimics cortisol, shuts off the production of this hormone for a time in nondepressed people. In those with major depression, however, cortisol production continues, indicating a malfunction of the limbic system, which also involves parts of the brain controlling mood states and emotions.

This test is seen by psychiatrists as a useful additional method of pinpointing endogenous depression and of determining which patients may need drug therapy in addition to psychotherapy. It is also considered useful in diagnosing depression in children and teens when the depression may be masked by behavior problems rather than classical adult symptoms of depression.

Another test, the thyrotropin releasing hormone (TRH) test, was developed some years ago by endocrinologists to diagnose thyroid gland disease and has proved useful in diagnosing endogenous depression as well in recent years. TRH is manufactured by the hypothalamus gland in the brain, which signals the pituitary gland to make TSH (thyroid stimulating hormone). In this test, the patient is given an injection of TRH to stimulate production of TSH, which in turn is measured in a blood sample from the patient. Researchers have found that people with severe depressions tend to produce a lower-than-normal level of TSH in response to the test injection. This is thought to be because chemical systems regulating the thyroid also regulate moods. Researchers at Fair Oaks Hospital in

Summit, New Jersey, have found that the TRH test correctly identified cases of major depression 92 percent of the time.

Much still needs to be learned about the function of brain chemicals and the role they may play in depression. And it is difficult to view the biochemistry of the brain in isolation from environmental and genetic factors.

Dr. Donald McKnew says, "It is possible that hormones produced in adolescence can effect disturbances. This is usually the case when a young person has a psychological predisposition to get depressed."

The Genetic Factor. Recent research indicates that heredity may have a considerable impact on behavior. While the extent of genetic influence, especially on depressive disorders, is not yet clear, recent studies have revealed some fascinating evidence.

Studies of twins raised apart have provided particularly interesting comparisons of genetic versus environmental influences. It has been found that if one identical twin suffers from a depressive disorder, the other twin has a 60 to 70 percent chance of sharing the disorder—even when the two were raised separately.

In his study of the brains of people who had committed suicide, Dr. David E. Comings of the City of Hope National Medical Center in Duarte, California, discovered an especially high concentration of an abnormal protein, which he named Pc1 Duarte and which is present in about one-third of all brains he examined. He eventually realized that the protein was present in an unusually large proportion of brains of suicide victims, and he theorizes that some people may carry a gene that makes them particularly susceptible to depression. Dr. Comings is quick to point out that it is too early in his study to say with certainty that there is a cause-and-effect relationship between the protein and depression. He feels that there is a possibility that this protein has a genetic link, predisposing some people to depression. This genetic vulnerability, added to environmental factors, may result in serious depression.

Dr. Donald McKnew and Dr. Leon Cytryn have been studying the children of manic-depressive parents for some years now, most recently doing a four-year follow-up study on the children, many of whom are now adolescents. "In the control group—children whose parents are *not* manic-depressive—the incidence of affective disturbance is about 10 percent at any given moment," says Dr.

McKnew. "In the children of manic-depressive adults, 30 to 50 percent were found to be depressed."

The 30 percent figure remained constant when the children were studied again four years later. "Those who were depressed in the latency period [ages six to twelve] were 50 percent less depressed four years later," says Dr. McKnew. "But every one of these had some *other* mental illness such as phobias or hysteria. So 30 percent of the children of manic-depressives continued to be disturbed, though not all of these were specifically depressed."

With the children of depressed parents, environmental factors such as lack of emotional support and other stressors connected with living under the same roof with a disturbed person must be considered. But a number of researchers suggest that genetic factors can increase susceptibility. In his studies of the genetic roots of depression, Dr. George Winokur, chairman of the psychiatry department at the University of Iowa, has found that a group of patients with a family history of depression consistently scored highest on hormone tests revealing endocrine abnormality. These abnormalities, he points out, may well be symptoms if not causes of brain dysfunction.

Toxic Factors. Alcohol, drugs, viral infections, glandular disorders and serious injuries can trigger depression. Although an adolescent's use or abuse of alcohol or drugs (like barbiturates) can *signal* depression, use of these may deepen existing depressed feelings. Viral infections such as mononucleosis can cause a secondary depression, as can glandular disorders such as high or low thyroid function. With serious injuries shock often sets in, altering body chemicals and affecting the function of the nervous system for a time, possibly bringing on depression.

Again, environmental factors must also be considered in combination with the physical. An adolescent whose normal routine is curtailed because of illness or injury may be suffering, too, from a reactive depression.

Manic-Depressive Illness

Manic-depressive illness is also called *bipolar* depression, because it brings strongly contrasting, recurring moods ranging from high excitement and energy to deep depression. With other, *unipolar*, types of depression, the depressed mood is relatively constant.

Bipolar depression usually appears in adulthood and its origin has been linked to a possible physical/metabolic disturbance of the nervous system. Manic-depressive illness is said to afflict approximately 1.2 percent of the U.S. population.

Psychotic Depression

Psychotic depression occurs as the result of a mental disorder such as schizophrenia, a brain tumor or disease or, in some instances, from extreme exhaustion. Although it may appear to be like some of the other types of depression—with feelings of despair, sleep disturbances and the like—psychotic depression can also bring hallucinations, strange fantasies and a complete lack of contact with the outside world. Delusions of grandeur fluctuate with low self-esteem and feelings of deep despair.

Which Type of Depression Is Most Common in Teenagers?

"Our experience with several hundred young people ranging in age from six to sixteen who have affective disorders has been that psychotic depression is not frequent in childhood," says Dr. McKnew. "Manic-depressive illness and chronic depression are also equally rare in the young, particularly prior to adolescence."

Mental health professionals who treat teenagers indicate that most adolescent depression is of the reactive variety. The major challenge, then, is to help the young person discover, explore and work through feelings about the losses and life stresses that have brought about his or her depression.

Another category of depression, masked depression, is often mentioned in relation to adolescents. But this has become somewhat controversial as a separate category in recent years. In the past, the term *masked depression* was used to describe depression that might be mistaken for rebellion, recklessness or simply "bad" behavior: depression accompanied by acting out behavior instead of the more familiar depressive symptoms of sadness, listlessness and low energy.

More recently, however, experts have discovered that acting out behavior can occur in *all* types of depression, especially among adolescents. For this reason and because not all acting out behavior signals depression, many mental health professionals no longer see masked depression as a distinct category. Instead, an adolescent may be seen as having a reactive (or endogenous) depression with or without acting out behavior. Or he may exhibit acting out behavior as his primary problem.

"Depression may or may not be the predominant factor in acting out behavior," says Dr. McKnew. "The acting out may predominate and any depression, if present, is secondary. Instead, the problem might be diagnosed as a conduct disturbance. But if the patient fits established criteria for depressive disorders, then the acting out symptoms are part of the integral picture."

Acting out behavior is always an important clue that something is wrong, and often it is a symptom rather than a separate category of depression. This is especially true in young adolescents who lack the insight and the verbal skills to identify and express their painful feelings more directly.

CHAPTER 4

Early Warning Signs

How Can You Tell If It's Normal Rebellion or Dangerous Depression?

As you flip through the family photo album, a child smiles back at you. With a wave of nostalgia, you remember the adorable baby, the inquisitive toddler, the curious, companionable school-age child who loved to share time, interests and activities with you, a child who was affectionate and reasonably compliant.

Now, however, if your experience parallels that of many parents today, that lovely child has become something of a stranger. It may be difficult to pinpoint when things started changing. Perhaps it was when your child began to refer to you consistently in the third person (*"He* won't let me—naturally!" or—to a friend over the telephone—"I can't talk now. *She* just came in the room!").

From then on, perhaps, you haven't been able to do anything right as your child has attacked your life-style, ideals, activities and goals, becoming increasingly hard to reach, moody and given to outbursts of anger. When via coaxing, cajoling or vicious threats your teen can be persuaded to join a family outing to Grandma's, the movies or a local amusement park, he or she is likely to lag sullenly behind the rest of the family, ashamed to be seen with you. Those old interests and passions—dancing lessons, astronomy, soccer or stamp collecting—have faded and as far as you can tell your teenager spends an inordinate amount of time doing absolutely nothing. You suspect that he or she skips school occasionally and you know that interest in school is waning. Suddenly, there seem to be battles over everything—rules, responsibilities, curfews, attitudes and opinions.

And sometimes you may wonder what is happening here. Is this the way it's supposed to be? Is your teenager going through normal adolescent rebellion or is his or her behavior indicative of more serious problems? Is this just a phase or not?

"Maybe it's just a phase" is an expression of hope uttered by many a beleaguered parent and in many cases they are correct. Rebellion is often part and parcel of being a teenager.

"Oppositional behavior is a common way of separating from parents," says Dr. Marilyn Mehr. "For example, if parents expect a lot from their kids academically, poor grades can show that the child is different. He may need to define himself in this way. Also, a lot of adolescents go through a period of disorganization due to body changes, and this can affect moods, school performance and the like. Very commonly this is nothing more than a phase."

Before you face an empty nest, Dr. Lee Robbins Gardner observes, you may well experience what she calls "the battered nest." "The kids have to make it comfortable for themselves to leave," she says. "They need to feel that they're not leaving so much."

During this time of rebellion and separation, quite often you may find yourself in no-win situations.

"I've heard teenagers say, 'My mother doesn't care about me. She doesn't even tell me when to come home,'" says family therapist Shirley Lackey. "Yet if the mother *does* set curfew rules, there's a fight. This is simply part of adolescence. You have to count on some ongoing tension for awhile. The best advice I can give to parents during this phase is 'Hang in there!'"

Rebellion, then, is a difficult but usually temporary phase. In the same way, a transient episode of depression over something specific such as a romantic breakup, a classmate's cruel remark or a setback or major disappointment like failure to make the team can also cause a teenager to go through a phase of anger, moodiness and withdrawal or mild acting out behavior.

Yet such behavior can also be symptomatic of serious depression. How do you tell the difference? It can be difficult. "A typical teen runs from troubling feelings with rebellion. So it's hard to tell what is serious depressive disease," says Dr. Gardner.

The difference between "normal" adolescent rebellion and transient depression and serious depression is based on the time, the degree and the amount of deviation from the child's usual personality and behavior.

In evaluating your teen's behavior, it may be helpful to ask yourself the following questions.

How Frequent and Intense Is This Rebellious Behavior?

When a teenager is going through a rebellious phase, there are usually moments of calm between stormy outbursts and challenges to your authority. There may be surprising moments of sweetness and cooperation and some ability to get along with various family members at least sporadically. While acting out behavior such as withdrawal from the family, temper outbursts and experimentation with cigarettes, alcohol or marijuana may be part of this rebellion, it is usually temporary and experimental in nature. Cutting classes on occasion is also a temporary gesture of rebellion.

The key word is *temporary*. If a teenager regularly cuts classes, is often drunk or stoned, is constantly angry and unable to get along with anyone in the family, he or she may be suffering from serious depression.

How Long Has This Been Going On?

The acting out that teenagers do to express rebellion and some transient depression is limited in time as well as scope.

"Normally, episodes of transient depression last no longer than a few days or a week or so," says Dr. Donald McKnew. "In the case of bereavement, if a parent, sibling, relative, friend or beloved pet dies it may take up to six months for the teen to work through his grief. Generally, though, it is when the depressive reaction is intense, lengthy and, as far as you can see, not related to obvious stresses, that your child may have serious depressive illness."

If acting out behavior is consistent, intense and continues over a period of weeks or months, it is a danger sign.

Is the Behavior Change Drastic for My Child?

While the changes that regular teen rebellion bring seem like overnight transformations, they probably started developing over a period of time as your child began preferring to be with peers, differed with you on increasingly frequent occasions and became less involved in family activities. The changes are usually not drastic. An excellent student's grades may fall a bit in the tumult of early adolescence, but it is unlikely that he or she will fail a class.

However, it is an obvious sign of trouble when behavior changes come with little or no warning and when they are drastically out of character. When an "A" student refuses to go to school or starts failing classes, it may be a sign of a depressive crisis.

How Vulnerable Is My Teen to Depression?

Fourteen-year-old Lisa's behavior, life-style, friends and general outlook on life have changed drastically during the past few months. Her parents realize that Lisa needs help, but they aren't sure what is wrong or what kind of help she might need.

You may identify with this situation. Perhaps your child refuses to verbalize his or her feelings and is afraid to ask for help directly. There is often an unspoken code among teenagers: "You don't tell an adult." They may confide feelings of anger or sadness to friends, who are not equipped to help. How can you begin to identify the root causes of a child's depression and steer him or her toward help? Because a great deal of adolescent depression is a reaction to a combination of stress factors, you can begin by considering the following questions. Be alert to the fact that *several "yes" answers in combination over the past year can indicate that your child is especially vulnerable to depression.*

1. Has anyone in your immediate or close extended family died during the past year?
2. Has a family pet died or been lost?
3. Has your child lost a friend through death in the past year?
4. Have you and your spouse had significant marital problems recently with an increase in the number of arguments and tensions?
5. Have you and your spouse separated or divorced this past year?
6. If you are divorced, has your child seen a great deal less of you or your spouse during the past year?
7. Has your family moved within the past twelve months?

8. Has your child changed schools this year—either due to a move or due to progressing on to junior high or high school?

9. Has another child in your family left home for college, marriage or independent living?

10. Has a friend or romantic interest of your teenager's moved away recently?

11. Have you or your spouse experienced serious depression recently?

12. Do you or your spouse have a drinking or drug abuse problem?

13. Has anyone in your family had a serious illness or injury during the past year?

14. Does your teenager have a chronic illness such as diabetes or epilepsy which sometimes limits his or her participation in normal teenage activity or which is a source of conflict between you and your teenager?

15. Has your teen had a serious or prolonged illness this past year?

16. Has your child sustained an injury that required curtailment of his or her normal routine and activities recently?

17. Has your child experienced significant physical changes in the past year, for example, a growth spurt, breast development, voice change, beginning of menstruation?

18. Is your child lagging behind peers in physical development and is he or she possibly the object of teasing because of this?

19. Has anyone in your extended families including parents, grandparents, siblings, aunts, uncles ever suffered from significant depressive illness?

20. Has your family had a significant change of life-style recently, for example, financial hardships, a parental job loss, a parent reentering the job market?

21. Does your child seem to have low self-esteem and be highly self-critical?

22. Do you have high expectations of your child and find yourself extremely disappointed—showing this disappointment openly—when your child's performance falls somewhat short of these expectations?

23. Is someone in your family, especially a parent, extremely critical of this particular child? Is this teen regarded as the family misfit or seen to be the focus of a lot of family conflict?

24. Have you felt distance growing between you and your teen during the past year? Is it difficult or impossible to communicate these days?

25. Do you find yourself increasingly unable to spend as much time with your child as you or he or she might like?
26. Are you quite permissive, with few rules and regulations for your teenager?
27. Are you a strict parent, with many rules and a low tolerance for conflict or disagreements? Do you hear yourself saying, "Because I said so!" or "Don't you dare talk back!" quite often?
28. Is openly expressed anger taboo in your home?
29. Do you have trouble trusting or expressing trust in your teenager?
30. Has your teen suffered through a significant romantic breakup recently?
31. Has he or she experienced estrangement from an important friend?
32. Does it seem to you that your teenager is often the target of teasing and ridicule from peers?
33. Does your teen seem unusually sensitive to teasing, criticism or indifference from peers, teachers, relatives or friends?
34. Does your teenager seem to have difficulty making and keeping friends?
35. Is your child prone to either-or, black-and-white thinking, such as feeling like a failure if he or she isn't always the best?
36. Does your child have a learning disability?
37. Is your child having difficulty with a particular teacher this year? Does he or she feel picked on, intimidated or put down by this teacher and complain more than usual about difficulties at school?
38. Has your family had an addition—birth of a baby or adoption of a child, grandparents or other relatives moving in—that have increased your teen's responsibilities or decreased his or her privacy?
39. Has another child in your family made significant achievements in the past year or so? Have there been any comparisons made between siblings, always in favor of the achiever?
40. Has your teenager achieved a significant goal recently, for example, graduated, won an award, made a team, perfected a skill or otherwise achieved unusual positive recognition?

CHAPTER 5

What Are the Symptoms of Adolescent Depression?

THE SYMPTOMS OF adolescent depression are many and varied. They are most significant when several occur in combination. These symptoms may include the following.

Disphoric Moods

An increase in sadness, anxiety and expressed hopelessness may indicate depression. A depressed teen may seem bored, listless, disenchanted with life in general, and exhibit little interest and pleasure in the things he or she used to enjoy.

Changes in Eating and Sleeping Habits

Lack of interest in food with a major or rapid weight loss is often a clue to depression. Compulsive overeating and sudden weight gain can also be danger signals. A major change in sleeping habits is also a symptom of depression. Among the sleep disorders to watch for: insomnia, early awakening that is uncharacteristic of your child, confused sleeping patterns (e.g., sleeping all day and staying up all night) or sleeping too much.

For example, when fifteen-year-old Maggie lost her appetite, dropped twenty pounds in several weeks and started staying up all night and sleeping all day, it was an unmistakable red flag to her family that something was terribly the matter.

Social Isolation

If your teenager has no friends or has lost interest in or broken ties with close friends, he or she may be immobilized by depression. Social contact and the effort involved in maintaining close friendships might have become too difficult, or perhaps your child's friends have "deserted" him or her. This can be a valuable clue, since peers, even more readily than parents, sense when something is seriously the matter.

"Peers serve many crucial functions in adolescence," says Dr. Lee Robbins Gardner. "Teenagers need to talk with each other, to feel part of a group. They use peers to flesh out their own identity and try themselves out within the peer group. However, the dependency needs of the troubled adolescent may be so intense that others feel threatened and reject the adolescent, isolating him further."

Sudden Change in Behavior

If an "A" student suddenly starts failing or regularly skipping classes, if a quiet, cooperative son or daughter is suddenly belligerent, angry and taking uncharacteristic risks, if a teen with passionate interests suddenly loses all motivation, inclination and momentum to pursue these, depression could be the cause. While behavior usually changes somewhat during adolescence, the developmental changes (including oppositional behavior) are more gradual, less intense and more intermittent than behavioral changes of depressed teenagers.

Acting Out Behavior

Conflicts at home, running away, cutting classes, becoming sexually promiscuous, shoplifting or drug abuse: all can indicate serious depression.

"Acting out behavior is often a response to the discomfort a teenager feels, a discomfort he or she may be unable to identify or cope with," says Dr. Richard MacKenzie. "When I was in medical school, it was said that when a teenage girl was depressed she got sexually active and when a teenage boy was depressed he stole cars. Now we know so much more about the symptoms and signs of depression. I believe that *any* kind of behavior that is unusual for your child should be thought of as possible depression until proven otherwise."

Hyperactivity

Many adolescents signal their distress by hyperactivity. They pace restlessly, get overinvolved in a frenzy of activities, act up in class, are nervous, anxious and irritable and find themselves unable to relax.

This hyperactivity is quite common in depressed adolescents. It is considered by many mental health professionals to be a phobic reaction against depression. The depression itself remains, though masked, just under the surface.

Excessive Self-Criticism

If your teen is suddenly extremely self-critical and is of the opinion that he or she is a complete failure, ugly, unpopular and incompetent, even when facts show otherwise, he or she may be depressed.

"Look for inappropriate guilt," says Dr. Donald McKnew. "For example, the teen may express feelings that he or she is a failure despite excellent school grades or feel that he or she is to blame for parents' quarrels." Such self-criticism reflects low self-esteem and hopelessness, which are often associated with depression.

Extreme Passivity

Loss of interest in hobbies and other active pursuits is a common symptom of depression. Withdrawal from activities, interests and friends, sulking and lying around the house or constantly watching television, are also common symptoms of depression.

"Constant TV watching is often tied in with depression," says Dr. Richard Brown. "It becomes a vicious cyclical relationship. The depressed teenager watches more TV and becomes more vegetative and thus more depressed. It's important for parents to know that excessive TV watching can be a major indication of depression."

Psychologist Marilyn Mehr feels that such TV watching can also indicate possible factors contributing to a young person's depression. "It is my feeling that extreme TV watching means that there is not much family interaction," she says. "And this can be a factor in depression."

Psychosomatic Complaints

Rick's parents are concerned because their son has been complaining of stomach pains and seems extremely tired. Yet an examination by the family doctor has revealed that there is no obvious disease or disorder present.

Kara has been suffering from severe headaches lately, often missing classes and spending a great deal of time sleeping. Her parents are afraid that something is seriously wrong with her physically and are insisting that she see a doctor.

In some instances, symptoms like the above *can* signal physical disease or disorders, so a thorough examination by a physician is a sensible first step. If the exam reveals no organic disease or disorder, however, depression may be the culprit.

Among the common psychosomatic symptoms often associated with depression are: headaches, stomach-aches, low back pain, increased sensitivity to aches and pains and general fatigue, a feeling of being tired regardless of how much sleep one has had.

These symptoms, particularly if frequent and disruptive of a teenager's normal routine of school and activities, are strong indications that the young person is depressed.

Substance Abuse

Abuse of drugs, alcohol or other substances can be at once a symptom and a cause of depression.

Heavy and frequent use of alcohol is in many instances self-medication for depression, but at the same time, it can deepen the problem. Sometimes use of alcohol or other substances for social reasons brings on depression in young people. Caffeine, another commonly used substance found in coffee, tea, colas and chocolate, can also cause physical and psychological symptoms when it is used to excess. For example, Patti Haley's headaches, anxiety and depression alarmed both Patti and her parents until Mrs. Haley happened to spot an item in the newspaper about caffeine abuse and its symptoms. Patti had been drinking two six-packs of cola a day as well as several cups of coffee. When she cut down on her intake of caffeine, the symptoms diminished. Recent medical findings have identified excessive use of caffeine as a causative factor in some instances of gastrointestinal problems, anxiety, headaches and depression.

So it can be helpful to consider your teenager's substance use habits—whether you know what they are or simply suspect what they may be—in evaluating his or her possible depression.

Risk-Taking Behavior

Driving too fast, a sudden interest in risky pursuits (like motorcycle racing), carelessness in using safety precautions and restraint, participating in a dangerous sport or activity or running away from home are all forms of risk-taking behavior that may be a sign of depression. Especially if the onset of this behavior is sudden and quite uncharacteristic for your child, depression may be the underlying cause.

Accidents

Constant accidents—from falling to automobile or bicycle mishaps—can be a result of depression. "This is a form of self-destructive behavior," says Dr. Gardner. "Of course, it's an erroneous oversimplification to say that all accidents are intentional. It could be that your child is simply clumsy or that he or she is more active and thus more exposed to the possibility of accidents than most. But keep in mind that when someone is upset, poor judgment and impulsivity are often present and can make accidents more of a possibility."

School Problems

Some of the most common symptoms of depression are related to school. These include a sudden drop in grades, a loss of interest and motivation in studies or school activities and social events, fights with teachers and classmates and habitual truancy.

Acting out in the school setting may be particularly frequent because school is a primary focus and possible stress factor in a teen's life. It is also one of the most obvious calls for help. Observes Mary Ann Dan, a special education teacher in the Los Angeles area, "Kids often use school as a stage and can put on quite an attention-getting act."

School is the focal point of a great deal of rebellion, since parents and teachers often have high expectations in this area. Failure to meet those expectations is noticed promptly and with great concern.

Sexual Acting Out

This behavior can also be a symptom of depression, especially when it occurs in teenage girls, and it is particularly distressing to parents. Adolescents may become sexually active in contrast to long-held beliefs; they may become promiscuous and indulge in indiscriminate sex leading to pregnancy. Promiscuity, in both adults and teens, is usually a desperate attempt to banish feelings of depression, to increase self-esteem (by feeling wanted), to achieve intimacy and, with pregnancy, to gain the love and unquestioning acceptance of another human being—a baby.

"A girl may feel important while pregnant and needed once the baby is born," says Dr. Mehr. "Some pregnant teen girls express the desire to have someone all their own to love them."

This illusion of unconditional love, coupled with lack of insight into the unrelenting demands that the complete dependence of an infant brings, leads a number of teen girls to seek pregnancy—either consciously or subconsciously—through deliberate sexual activity

and contraceptive carelessness. A great number of teenage pregnancies are *not* unwanted nor unplanned. Some teens see parenthood
as a way to recapture the joy of the childhood they are losing, as a
way to be loved and important to at least one other person, or as
an antidote to depression.

Suicidal Talk or Behavior

If your teenager talks or muses about various methods of suicide
or observes, "I'd be better off dead!", the possibility of serious
depression should be considered immediately. A number of people
believe the myth that those who talk about suicide never attempt
it. But statistics show that many suicides are, in fact, preceded by
attempts or verbal hints and warnings.

When your teenager even hints about suicidal thoughts, it's time
to pay close attention and possibly seek professional help. And if
your child has made an active suicide attempt—even a half-hearted
one—it should be viewed as a warning of serious depression and
a cry for help. In such instances, professional help is vital. Whether
your teen talks about suicide or tries to do something about these
feelings, this is a symptom that should *never* be ignored.

If you have recognized any of these symptoms—particularly several
in combination—your child is probably suffering from depression.

But now that you know that depression is a strong possibility, what
do you do?

PART III

How to Cope with Teenage Depression

CHAPTER 6

The Ideal Way to Cope with Teenage Depression

IDEALLY, COPING WITH teenage depression means being alert to the symptoms, investigating your teen's feelings, listening, giving loving support, helping as much as you can and assisting your teen in finding outside help if it seems to be needed.

Your actions should follow a pattern similar to the steps described below.

Communicate Your Observations and Concerns to Your Teenager

"'If your teenager shows symptoms of depression, try asking him or her if he or she is depressed," advises Dr. Merilee Oaks, a clinical psychologist in private practice and on the staff of the Adolescent Unit at Children's Hospital, Los Angeles.

Some other approaches suggested by Dr. Oaks include:

"We haven't had a chance to talk much lately. You've seemed angry and have had some changes in your behavior. I've noticed that you've been crying a lot, honey. What is it? Can I help you?"

"I've seen you crying a lot lately and I'm worried. Can you tell me what it is? If you can't, can we think about finding someone else to help you?"

Listen Carefully to What Your Teenager Says

You get important information and clues to your child's feelings if you know how to listen. If you're a poor listener—constantly interrupting, judging and contradicting—it's likely that your child won't tell you anything or, even if he or she tries, you won't really hear his or her thoughts or feelings.

"Keep back the 'but's,' the excuses, the attacks and the judgments," says Judith Davenport. "If you're serious about expressing the sentiment 'I love you no matter what' this is the chance to prove it—by listening to what your teenager has to say."

If you communicate your love and caring with active, nonjudgmental listening, you are really saying, "We're in this together and you have our support. We want to help you. There is hope."

Help As Much As You Can, Then Be Open to Help from Others

As a parent, you give your teenager unique and vital help by showing unconditional love and support, by offering firm guidance, by making honest attempts to communicate and by modifying the home environment to relieve stress on the teenager. For example, examine and try to change any of your own behavior that causes needless stress, such as excessive criticism, nagging, scapegoating and the like.

"My advice in the initial stages of a teen's depression is to be supportive and wait and see," says Dr. Donald McKnew. "The depression may be self-limiting. If symptoms persist, visit your physician, school counselor or clergyman for assistance in deciding what further help may be needed for your child."

Dr. Lee Robbins Gardner suggests that it might be particularly helpful to discuss your situation with a mental health professional. "There are no pat answers for a parent who is having problems with an adolescent who is acting out and who is possibly depressed," she says. "Each situation is a highly individual one and it may be most useful to discuss this with a mental health professional who can try to help your teenager understand his or her own feelings and to develop better coping mechanisms."

Realizing the limitations of your ability to help your child is difficult, but important to your teenager.

"It may be that you, as a parent, can't help your child right now because he or she is going through a period of devaluing you as a way of growing toward independence," says Dr. Marilyn Mehr. "Be open to the idea of having another significant adult person step in to help. This may be a relative, minister, teacher or friend who is better able to help right now. It may be a physician or other health professional. It can be difficult for you, as a parent, to feel secure enough to accept such help. Instead of feeling hurt, angry or jealous, see these people as complementary parents. They're helping your child—not replacing you."

Why the Ideal Is So Elusive

Communication, warm support, compassionate listening and openness to outside help—the techniques are easy to enumerate but difficult to implement on a day-to-day basis. No matter how great your concern and your commitment to help your child, you are human, too, and the ideal is often hard to achieve, for the following reasons:

You and Your Teenager Don't Communicate Well

Your caring questions may be met with silence, anger and rejection. Or you may not be able to ask the questions at all. It may well be that before you begin to communicate your love and concern for your child with maximum effectiveness, some of the communication blocks between you will have to be diminished or eliminated. As we will see in chapter 8, this can take time, effort and a great deal of patience and commitment on your part, but it is well worth your efforts. It can change your child's life.

Your Teenager's Problems Seem Too Complicated and Overwhelming

If your teenager is having symptoms in combination—trouble at school, conflicts with friends, drinking or taking drugs or becoming sexually active in addition to wreaking havoc at home—you may be uncertain about where to begin in sorting out these problems and seeking outside help. The challenge of dealing with your child's combination of problems as well as the underlying depression, and of finding the best help you can (a necessity when symptoms are serious and in combination like this) may immobilize you. If you find yourself in this situation, you can discover special help in chapters 7 through 30. These are constructive action plans for specific problem situations and ideas for finding help that will be best for your child.

Your Negative Feelings Come Between You and Your Teenager

It is not easy to live with a depressed person of any age. It is even more difficult to be the parent of a depressed teenager. You may find that, before you are able to help your teenager directly, you will need to help *yourself*. This is almost inevitably the best starting point.

CHAPTER 7

Help Yourself First: Negative Feelings and How to Deal with Them

CYNTHIA AND STEVE Bachman seem to be living symbols of the American Dream. She is an award-winning educational film producer and he is a successful attorney. They have two bright, beautiful children: Rachel, a seventeen-year-old high school senior, and Adam, thirteen, an eighth-grader. They are well traveled, affluent and live in a lovely home in the hills overlooking West Los Angeles.

But there are flashes of anguish, anger and concern in Cynthia's eyes as she lingers over coffee, talking about Rachel. For Rachel's problems have become the focus of family concerns and conflicts over the past few years.

"Our worries over Rachel go back quite a few years actually," Cynthia says, lighting her fifth cigarette in ten minutes. "When she was in grade school, she developed cancer and had over three years of radiation and chemotherapy before being given a clean bill of health at the age of ten. It was about that time—when she was ten or eleven—that I noticed her compulsiveness about cleanliness and the fact that she seemed to have trouble relating to people. I took her to a psychologist and he told me she was fine, that I should be proud to have such a bright, achieving child."

Cynthia admits that it was tempting to believe the optimistic diagnosis despite her nagging doubts. For a time it seemed to be justified. Rachel kept on achieving and not making waves for the next few years. It wasn't until her family moved from New York to Los Angeles when Rachel was sixteen that more obvious problems began to surface.

"The move was quite a change for Rachel," Cynthia recalls. "She transferred from her small private school to a large public school with 2,300 students. She got into the honors classes, worked hard and got all 'A's' her first semester there. She also made an effort to make friends and joined a temple youth group. But something didn't seem right with her. Then, just before semester exams, she had a sort of crack-up. She got hysterical and started screaming. I tried to talk with her and comfort her but nothing helped. I didn't realize that she was in a serious depression. She seemed better the next day and so I let it go."

Rachel's apparent recovery was destined to be brief, however.

"The real trouble came a few months after her one-day crack-up," Cynthia says, lighting yet another cigarette. "Suddenly, she didn't want to go to school, started dressing in a random and sloppy way and was unable to make decisions of any kind. She was deeply depressed, complaining about her lack of friends, yet she was doing a good job of alienating the friends she did have. Our moment of truth came when her math teacher called to say that Rachel was not doing well and seemed disturbed. Soon after that, at a parents' open house at her school, all of her teachers mentioned that something seemed to be very wrong with Rachel. I immediately sought professional help after that."

This point in the story, rather than being a quick, happy ending, was only the beginning of the family's trials, despite the fact that Rachel's psychiatrist is one of the best available in the area, that Rachel is responding to therapy and that her family is cooperating fully in ongoing treatment and therapy.

"Rachel's depression has been harder for us to cope with than her cancer, as strange as that may sound," Cynthia says. "This is because it involves all the intricate family relationships and has such an uncertain prognosis. We have no idea when or if she might really start feeling better. With her cancer, we knew that after a chemotherapy treatment on Wednesday, she would feel better on Friday. And then, too, her surgeon had been careful to say, 'Don't feel guilty about Rachel's illness. There is no genetic link, no link with lack of care. It just happened.' Depression is another story, though. When your child is depressed you *do* feel guilty and no one can tell you any different. You keep wondering, 'Where did we go wrong? Where was the turning point? How did *I* contribute to this?' "

Guilt is only one of the troubling feelings that Cynthia and Steve have encountered as parents of a severely depressed teenager.

"My husband was devastated and didn't know how to handle the situation when it first became obvious," Cynthia reports. "He still can't cope with the ups and downs and irrationalities of Rachel's moods. I'm . . . so many things. I'm concerned, scared, hostile, angry and exhausted—for starters. As the parent of a depressed teenager, I walk an emotional tightrope. You have to be so careful about what you say and do, what you take over and what you let go. It's so hard not to catch your child's depression as you might catch a bad cold or the flu. It's so hard to deal with the anxiety and the anger. I feel emotionally battered. My daughter seems to yo-yo me back and forth between a lot of feelings. She can be very removed at one point and then hostile and angry the next. It gets to the point where you don't know how to find your center."

Although life circumstances differ, many parents know what an emotional roller coaster living with a depressed teenager is. Like Cynthia you may have a number of troubling and conflicting feelings: love, anger, anxiety, grief, guilt, fear and depression. There is no sure cure, no easy way out in coping with and resolving these feelings. It's important to realize, however, that you're not alone, that these feelings are not strange or unusual and that, before you can help your teenager, you must begin to understand and come to terms with your own feelings.

Admittedly, this is no simple task. As Cynthia relates, these feelings come in combination and are difficult to isolate. And there are no simple 1-2-3 solutions to what's troubling you. But that fact should not be grounds for pessimism.

"It's important to recognize the fact that for every difficult problem, there is usually a simple solution that is wrong," Dr. Lee Robbins Gardner points out. This means, in part, that you should take time to explore your feelings and the active alternatives you may have, sorting out your situation and considering constructive coping ideas. Some common feelings reported in parents of depressed teenagers are discussed below.

Denial

Bonnie Salazar is divorced, in her late thirties and the mother of an obviously troubled fourteen-year-old. Her son's problems are obvious, that is, to everyone but his mother. When a school counselor called her at work to say that Joe has had a number of unexcused absences in the past few weeks, that he is failing three classes and getting into fights when he does come to school, Bonnie shrugged it off as "just a phase." Later, when she discovered drug paraphernalia in their home, Bonnie readily believed her son's story that he was just keeping the stuff for a friend.

"My son and I are very close and I know he isn't a bad person," she says. "I think people over-react to a lot of teenage phases. Sure, he's having problems at school and I feel bad about it, but I really believe it will pass. Joe knows he's free to come talk to me at any time if anything is *really* bothering him."

Bonnie's denial of her son's combination of symptoms is a common and understandable occurrence among parents of troubled teens. Denial, after all, functions as a self-protective emotional reflex when a person is faced with the unthinkable and the unbearable. It is the initial coping mechanism in the face of disaster ("This isn't happening. Not really. Not to *me!*"). We may deny any of a number of things—including the harsh realities of death, serious illness, psychological and family problems. When the trouble is focused on your child, denial is a particularly common reaction.

Why Parents Deny

Why do parents so often deny problems in their children? Rod Casey, the father of a deeply depressed fifteen-year-old boy who acts out at school and has been picked up by the police for occasional shoplifting and vandalism, says that his initial reaction was denial. His son's problems hit too close to home. "I kept saying to myself 'Oh, well, I was wild as a teenager, too.' I was. I was also very troubled and needed help which I didn't get until years later. I've spent my life being hounded by bouts of depression. It's very hard for me to see my son suffering from the same thing essentially. As a parent, you always want and hope that things will be better for your kid. I get mad at myself for being depressed. I feel guilty, like I've passed on my problems to Terry. All in all, that's a heavy burden to face and, until I got some help myself, I just couldn't face the fact that Terry had real emotional problems."

If the reality of a child's problems is frightening, parents deny the seriousness of the situation. To admit it would be admitting failure as a parent. This seems synonymous with being a "bad person."

"We see a lot of denial from parents with depressed teenagers," says Dr. Richard MacKenzie. "This is because so many parents feel that the teen's problems reflect negatively on them, on their qualifications to be parents and on the family well-being in general. Often we need to reassure parents that they are really good people who have weathered a lot of storms."

Many parents deny their children's problems on the premise that this, too, shall pass. Or they attribute problems to a simpler identifiable cause. Perhaps, they feel, a physician or mental health professional holds the key to an easy and complete solution, fixing the problem child and thus transforming the troubled family scenario as if by magic.

"I had a case not long ago where there were obvious problems in the entire family," says Dr. Charles Wibbelsman. "The father was an alcoholic and was also abusive to his wife and son. The mother was preoccupied with marital problems and exhausted from holding two jobs to keep things together financially. The teenage son had fluctuating moods and mild acting out behavior. The mother came into my office complaining about the boy, labeling him as the family's major problem. The boy was pretty O.K., albeit depressed over his home situation. The mother was shocked at my suggestion that family therapy might be in order. She wanted her son to have all kinds of medical tests because she was convinced that his behavior was due to low blood sugar. She didn't want to face the fact that something was wrong with the family. She wanted to feel that something simple was wrong, something I could find and fix with tests and treatment."

Minimizing and misinterpreting symptoms is another form of denial.

Family counselor Shirley Lackey recalls a joint mother-daughter counseling session recently where the thirteen-year-old girl said that she felt like killing herself. The mother's immediate reaction was, "See? She's trying to manipulate me!"

"While it is true that such statements can be used in a manipulative way, as a weapon and a way of saying, 'Look what you've done to me—I don't want to live!,' you simply can't dismiss a suicide threat as manipulative," Mrs. Lackey points out. "Kids *do* kill themselves. If you ignore these threats, the kid may feel he or she is out on a limb and then will go ahead and commit suicide."

How to Cope with Denial

While facing the reality of a child's or family's problems is extremely painful, it is the necessary first step toward resolving conflicts and issues, exploring alternatives and making the situation less overwhelming and unbearable.

"It is much more constructive to ask yourself, 'How can I help?' rather than, 'How can I deny that I contributed to this in any way?' " says Dr. Marilyn Mehr.

And Dr. Richard MacKenzie adds, "It's better to admit, 'We're in trouble. Let's see what we can do about it.' Families and the people in them are in a constant state of change. In fact, life might be boring without the challenge of occasional troubled waters."

Guilt

Guilt is practically a universal feeling among parents of troubled teenagers. Many could identify with Cheri Koppel, the mother of a depressed fifteen-year-old girl, who says that "every time I see Jenny in trouble again, every time she looks angry or unhappy—which is often—I wonder to myself what I did wrong. Is it because I've worked outside the home since Jenny was three? Is it because we didn't give her ballet lessons? Maybe I should have been more involved in her activities, been a Scout leader or something. But as a working mother I never had time. If I had spent more time with her, asked less of her, been a more nurturing mother, would she be having all these problems now? Sometimes I almost drive myself crazy with the guilt. And when I don't, Jenny does. She says that her problems *are* my fault, that I can't understand her and that I'm not like other kids' mothers. It makes me feel rotten and leaves me wondering what to do."

Why Parents Feel Guilty

Parents are particularly vulnerable to guilt because most feel very much responsible for their children. Some, in fact, tend to regard themselves and their children as a single unit. When parent and child don't see each other as separate people, one or both may feel the successes and failures of the other in an intense and highly personal way.

"So many parents see the child as a reflection of themselves," says Mrs. Sarah Napier, an educational psychologist with the Glendale, California, Unified School District. "I tell them 'You're a separate person. When a child is fifteen you can't be responsible for all his or her choices or activities.'"

Dr. Calvin Frederick adds that, "It's important to remember that a lot of things impact on teenagers besides parents. School and peers, for example, can be very important and what parents are contributing at this point—at least in terms of time—may be relatively little. . . ."

Still, it's difficult *not* to feel guilty when your child is in trouble, when you wonder what might have gone wrong in the teen's upbringing and how things might have been different. It is especially difficult not to feel guilty when others seem to focus all the blame on you for your child's problems.

"Too often, parents are an easy target," says Dr. Frederick. "It's easy to blame parents immediately for a problem. Teenagers themselves do this a lot. But it doesn't begin to solve the problem. Both teenager and parent must take responsibility for his or her own actions."

Sometimes the lines of responsibility are difficult to discern. Sue Riley, a newly divorced mother of two (including thirteen-year-old Debbie) recently moved her family from the big, comfortable suburban home they had shared for a decade to a smaller condominium close to the city. It meant a change of school and friends for the kids but was affordable and convenient to Sue's new job. Ten-year-old Matt seemed to adjust quickly, but Debbie became hostile and morose. She has been having difficulties at school, says she has no friends and constantly blames her mother for this negative turn of events.

Sue sighs as she relates the story of their almost daily battles. "We *had* to move. I *have* to work and the divorce just couldn't be helped," she says, her eyes brimming with tears. "It's all very logical and reasonable, yet I feel I've done something terrible to my daughter by getting divorced and moving. But then when she starts in on me I get so mad. I always end up saying something like 'I had to move, so shut up!' Then I feel worse than ever."

This situation is not uncommon, family counselor Shirley Lackey observes. "Keep in mind that you the parent have a right to your own feelings and choices," she says. "You did the best you could, made the best possible choices you could make at the time. When you feel you have a right to your own feelings, you can accept your children's negative feelings with some understanding and without being consumed by guilt."

How to Cope with Guilt

An important part of dealing with and resolving your guilt is realizing the scope and limitations of your responsibility. You are not responsible for anything and everything that is amiss in your children's lives. If you take such responsibility you can become immobilized, depressed and powerless, overwhelmed by guilt. You might then slip into denial, hoping that your child's problems would go away magically with time.

A constructive plan of action is to examine your relationship with your teenager, trying to pinpoint ways you may have contributed to his or her problems as well as things you've done right. It is also useful to explore ways you have *not* contributed to the present situation.

"This self-examination can be painful, but it can also be reassuring and can bring about growth," says Dr. Frederick. "You may find that you haven't contributed as much to the problems as you initially thought. You may find yourself feeling less guilty and more able to help yourself and your child."

Marital conflicts, financial insecurities, necessary relocations and the like are inevitabilities of everyday life. You can forgive yourself for not being perfect. No family or parent can possibly be perfect. No home situation, however troubled, is the sole source of a teenager's depression. Many factors, including inborn temperament and outside influences, also impact on your child emotionally and influence his or her choices and responses.

"I used to feel just terrible about being divorced and the single mother of a teenage son," says Gail Smith. "Every time Scott had a problem, I'd think, 'Oh, it's because of the divorce. It's because he doesn't have a day-to-day Dad. It's because I don't do enough for him or with him.' Then I started looking around and, hey, guess what? Some of my friends with reasonably happy marriages have problems with their kids, too. Now I realize that neither myself nor the divorce are totally responsible for Scott's moods."

If a teenager tries to transfer all the blame for problems to you, point out firmly that while mistakes were made in the past, making the best of a difficult situation and finding constructive ways to cope are part of growing toward maturity. Blaming another takes away much of one's own power to act, and heightens the sense of helplessness that contributes strongly to depression.

"Both you and your teenager must take responsibility for your own actions," says Dr. Frederick. "When I'm with a teenager who is complaining endlessly about a parent and blaming him or her for all existing problems, I say, in effect, 'O.K. You've convinced me that your parent is a real s.o.b. Now what?' The point, of course, isn't whether the parent really is or isn't an s.o.b., but the fact that the teenager must take responsibility for his or her own life, to go on to set his or her own house in order."

Families Anonymous, a nation-wide organization of self-help groups for parents with problem teenagers, encourages members to "release with love," to let their children take an increasing amount of responsibility for dealing with problems that are properly theirs. This does not mean that the parents don't ever offer help or guidance, but that they set firm limits on their own responsibility for the problem, encouraging their teens to cope with and learn from their own mistakes. These parents, in releasing with love, are working to avoid the trap of overwhelming guilt and a lifelong role as rescuer.

Fear

Fear has become something of a way of life for Ted and Joyce Howe. Their sixteen-year-old son Mark, who has had diabetes for five years, has been sullen, depressed, rebellious and reckless for months. He is careless about eating on time, has started drinking occasionally with some new friends and has experienced episodes of insulin shock more frequently than usual. In the past Ted and Joyce were able to control what Mark ate and keep his meals and insulin injections tied to a strict schedule. Recently Mark has rejected this structured regimen. He is upset because his health needs make him different from his peers, and so he is denying his disease. His parents are understandably frightened—for Mark and over their sudden loss of control.

While circumstances differ greatly from family to family, parental fears over loss of control are very common. In some instances, relinquishing some control or the notion of regaining total control of your child eases fear and tension.

How to Cope with Fear and Anxiety

"Sometimes you get further with a teenager by giving up some control," says Dr. Marilyn Mehr. "In an instance like Mark's it is important to put the responsibility for both treatment and control of the diabetes Mark and his doctor so that the disease is no longer an issue between the teenager and the parents."

While stepping back and allowing your teenager to take more control and responsibility for his or her own life can be scary initially, it pays off by defusing the impact of rebellion in a certain area of the teen's life.

In giving up the expectation of retaining total control over your teenager's actions, you must clarify what really matters and what doesn't. If you find yourself nose-to-nose with your adolescent over all issues—major and minor—you are helping to create a stressful, anxiety-producing situation that erodes your ability to take control when you must.

"If you find yourself setting down a lot of rules, it could be because of your own fears," says Dr. Lee Robbins Gardner. "Save your fights for the important things."

Beverly Sanders, the mother of a depressed fifteen-year-old daughter with a spotty attendance record at school, is afraid of many things. "I worry that Suzi misses school a lot, dresses in sloppy clothes when she does go and that she isn't popular," she says. "I keep on her about school, clothes and her relationships with others and she keeps telling me to get off her back. I want the best for her and I'm so afraid she won't have it."

Beverly may be able to reduce her anxiety and her stress level by concerning herself with one major issue—her daughter's attendance at school—and letting the peripheral issues go. She might decide, for example, that as long as Suzi goes to school, she can wear whatever she chooses. Letting go of control in minor ways while providing firm guidelines over major issues can reduce your fears and increase your effectiveness as a parent.

Some parents feel fearful of their adolescents as the children grow and change and as horror stories of how bad adolescents are seem to abound.

"I felt so sure of myself when Gina and Ty were small," says Gianna Morelli. "I could count on their being a certain way. Now they're both so unpredictable, especially Ty. He's almost six feet tall. I tell him to do something and he looks down at me and says no. John and I can set all kinds of rules and curfews but we can't always enforce them. The kids are suddenly like strangers in this house. I don't know how they think or feel or why they act the way they do."

Fear of your own adolescent escalates anxiety and conflicts at home.

"Many parents end up bargaining with the teenager and trying to make deals," observes psychotherapist Judith Davenport. "But kids have enormous contempt for parents who do this. They realize that they're in charge and they know that they shouldn't be. They get scared and wonder, 'Who's going to care for me? Who's going to take me seriously?' "

Remember that your teenager is still, in many ways, a child who needs guidance on major issues. Resolving to be firm when it counts will help reduce your fears and the frequency of confrontations with your teen.

A number of parents, quite understandably, are fearful over the possible consequences of their children's acting out behavior. If you have a teenager who is not going to school or who is taking drugs, abusing alcohol or who may be sexually promiscuous, you are likely to be frightened about the consequences, envisioning a lifetime for your child of un- or underemployment, unrealized potential, legal problems, damaged health or early death or life-option-reducing developments such as early pregnancy and parenthood. There are no easy answers for reducing these fears and no instant solutions to these situations. Communicating concern, insisting that the teenager try some type of professional help, and perhaps seeking professional help for the entire family are steps in the right direction.

Sharing Vulnerability

Even when a teenager is wreaking havoc on their lives and their emotions, some parents are fearful of sharing their vulnerability, letting the teenager know how his or her acting out is affecting them.

"Many parents have a need to be seen as perfect," says Ms. Davenport. "They don't want their kids to see their vulnerability. But it may help to let your teens know they can affect you, even hurt you. When you express your vulnerability and feelings, your child may allow his or her own feelings to surface."

Special education teacher Mary Ann Dan often uses her own vulnerability to reach difficult, depressed, rebellious teenagers. "A lot of these kids can't find their feelings," she says. "So they just act out in bizarre ways. The way I reach them is through a very personal relationship. They are allowed to know me and my vulnerability. Until you get past the facades and relate to each other on a personal level there is no real communication and no resolution."

Judith Davenport, who counsels a number of teenage clients, agrees. "I use my own reactions a great deal when I work with teenagers," she says. "I let them know how they affect me. They are often shocked to realize that they can have an impact, that they can hurt me, make me feel good or make me angry by what they say. This gives them permission to find and to have their own feelings."

Sharing vulnerability can be the start of a new and better level of communication between you and your teenager. Being able to express both positive and negative feelings will defuse tension, decrease depression and let all parties blow off steam. In many instances, too, it will decrease a teen's need for the acting out behavior that has brought such fear and anxiety into your life.

Anger

Cynthia Bachman, whose story about her depressed seventeen-year-old daughter Rachel began this chapter, has become well acquainted with feelings of anger and frustration during the past year. "I've felt terrible anger and hostility toward Rachel during all this trouble," she says. "It probably sounds terrible, saying that I'm angry with a girl who is so troubled and who needs so much help. But let's face it, I am and I don't think I'm at all unusual. I've been known to get furious at Rachel when she acts like a five year old, even though I know *why* she acts that way. I'm angry at the way this has disrupted all our lives and how long it has been going on."

Cynthia's feelings parallel those of a number of beleaguered parents. When you have a child in trouble, you worry. But you also feel very angry about the situation in general.

Why Parents Feel Angry

This anger is triggered by a combination of factors. You see your teenager, poised on the threshold of so many choices and so many opportunities, ignoring, canceling out or not realizing his or her good fortune—and you feel angry. You may have invested many of your hopes, dreams and feelings of self-worth into your child and feel furious when he or she doesn't come through as expected. You may feel victimized, your life invaded. You are likely to feel frustrated when, even with your own and outside efforts and intervention, the situation may show no signs of quick change or resolution.

Faced with such anger, most parents feel guilty and try to deny and repress the feelings they consider unacceptable and inappropriate. But anger is inevitable. The question is how to deal with it. "Most people cannot tolerate anger very well—and teens can be very angry and insulting to parents," Judith Davenport points out.

The Dangers of Unexpressed Anger

The problem is, of course, that unexpressed anger doesn't simply go away. It comes back to haunt us in a number of ways.

Joy and Ken Jones, frustrated and furious over problems with their son Rick, have displaced their anger at him onto each other, with resulting marital conflicts.

Joan Peters, a single working mother, traces some on-the-job problems back to her anger and frustration over her troubled thirteen-year-old son Larry. "I'm an office manager and try to be fair," she says. "But lately I haven't been succeeding too well. I've been so upset over Larry that I find myself blowing up at some of the people I supervise, sometimes over the smallest things and sometimes without real cause."

There are times when unrecognized, unexpressed anger takes its toll in other ways. Sally McFarlane, a single parent whose fourteen-year-old daughter is severely depressed, complains that she has been having more migraine headaches than usual during the past few months and that she feels exhausted no matter how much sleep she gets. It could be that the anger buried deep inside Sally over being alone and responsible for the day-to-day care of a troubled child is depleting her energy and hope for the future, making Sally vulnerable to depression, too.

One of the major disadvantages of denying or repressing a strong emotion like anger is that denial becomes a way of life. You begin to repress all feelings—love, joy and happiness as well as anger and despair. You numb yourself, and in the process lose some vital coping aids. After all, when you face a troubling situation memories of having weathered other crises, of sharing closeness and good times and love with your child in the past, can sustain you. But if you devote your energies to burying your feelings, you may bury these memories and the capacity to recapture the joy and hope you once had as well.

How to Cope with Anger

It's natural—even necessary—for you to feel angry right now. There is no quick or easy way out. But if you can get in touch with your angry feelings and use them constructively, there is hope. For anger is an opportunity, an energizer, when vented in constructive ways. It can inspire you to take action, to seek some solutions, to break the cycle of inertia into which you and your teenager may have fallen.

Try to pinpoint your angry feelings and their source. What can you do about your anger right now? Communicate your feelings to your teenager. Sharing your feelings in a constructive way will help both you and your teen blow off steam. Explore ways to deal with conflicts and decrease your child's needs to express his or her painful feelings with acting out behavior.

"If you say, 'I feel angry when you stay out past midnight and don't even call,' and state your own limits about what you can tolerate, you are taking a step in the right direction," says Ms. Davenport. "It is actually more difficult to respond this way than to scream, 'You're doing this to drive me crazy!' But it is also a much more effective catalyst in changing a troublesome situation."

If you express your anger, you are giving your child the message that it's O.K. to feel angry, and there are better ways to express anger than by hurting oneself or others. Serving as a constructive model for your teen is crucial in building a more positive relationship.

If you can't get through to your teenager right now, expressing your anger to your spouse, a friend, relative or counselor is also a helpful way to release yourself and explore action alternatives. You might keep a diary. Testing your responses on paper first is a good way to find the most appropriate plan of action for the next challenge you face with your teenager.

Physical exercise—particularly vigorous sports involving hitting motions (like tennis and racquetball)—also helps to reduce some of your pent-up tensions and frustration. All this will leave you better equipped to cope with your ongoing problems.

Depression/Despair

When sixteen-year-old Tom Black's depression—signaled by drug use, falling grades, stomach-aches and reckless driving—became evident, it was only the beginning of his family's trials. After two months, many crises and countless confrontations, his fourteen-year-old sister Ann is having severe headaches, Dale Black is finding himself increasingly impatient and short-tempered at home and at work and Lucy Black has slipped into a serious depression of her own.

"I don't see anything to look forward to and this is the first time in my life that I can remember feeling that way," she says. "We've tried and tried to help Tom and nothing works. We tried to get him to see a counselor. He won't go. Tom and his problems have taken over our lives. We have no free time, no fun, no relaxation. We've stopped entertaining and seeing friends and Dale and I never go out anymore. It's very hard not to resent Tom for that. After two months of trying to handle my own feelings and Tom, too, I don't have any energy left. It's terribly discouraging to try so hard and accomplish so little."

Unfortunately, Lucy Black's plight is quite common among parents of depressed teenagers. Some experts estimate that if you live with a depressed person, your own chances of developing depression may be as high as 80 percent.

Why Depression Can Be Contagious

Depression tends to strike parents who are most concerned about their depressed child, parents who want very much to do the right thing, to take the best possible care of the troubled teen.

The problem is that extending such care and concern is often an exhausting, ungratifying endurance test, at least initially. The depressed teenager is not likely to thank you for your help and may even actively resent it. He or she may try to block your efforts at communication, may continue to blame you for his or her pain, may refuse helpful alternatives and remain generally unresponsive to your sacrifices, love and pain.

Under such circumstances, it would be a bit unusual if you didn't feel flashes of resentment, anger and exhaustion and despair, feelings you might push aside because your energies are focused on helping your child. When you're under such constant pressure with no immediate happy ending in sight and a myriad of buried feelings, depression often results. In some ways, then, depression can be catching. Unfortunately, it can become a constantly reinforced cycle of despair, impairing the quality of your life, your marriage and your ability to be an effective, loving parent.

How to Prevent or Cope with Your Own Depression

The key to preventing or combating your own depression is *self-care*. When you have a troubled teenager, it is common to become so focused on him or her that you lose sight of your own needs. But taking good care of yourself is a vital part of being an effective helper. How can you begin to take better care of yourself? The following suggestions might give you some ideas.

Keep Your Own Life and Routines As Normal As Possible. When a child is depressed and needs a lot of attention and extra help, or when the young person is acting out in destructive ways that keep you constantly worried, it is easy to slip into a pattern of having your life revolve around the child and his or her problems. This sets up a vicious cycle of resentment and despair.

It is important that you keep your own separate life as normal as possible. Resist the temptation to stop seeing friends, cancel vacation plans or drop hobbies and other pursuits you enjoy, particularly if you feel yourself slipping into depression. These outside interests and pleasures can be uplifting and energizing. Get out of the house —away from the problem situation. Give yourself opportunities to step back, blow off steam, distract yourself and seek some necessary relaxation and support. Keeping regular routines will give some semblance of order and normality in your life, even in the midst of a crisis.

In spite of their daughter's problems, Linda and Steve Harrison kept to their long-established routine of Sunday afternoons alone together—browsing through bookstores, taking leisurely drives or enjoying a brunch for two at a favorite French café. "We started to get away from this when the problems with our daughter Angie started," says Linda. "But we found that we couldn't just sit around worrying and watching her twenty-four hours a day, seven days a week. It was impossible. We give her a lot of time and care, but we need time for us, too. When we gave up our precious time alone together, we found that we missed each other *and* we had more trouble communicating in general. Now Sunday afternoons are a sort of mini-vacation for us, a way to relax, get back in touch with each other, share feelings and regroup our strength and our forces for the week ahead."

Develop a Support System and Use It. This is especially important if you're a single parent. "Many single parents are so very much alone," says educational psychologist Sarah Napier. "They don't belong to groups or churches and have no close friends or family who will help them. They have nobody to fall back on, no release from the constant stress and responsibility they face—and they need this occasional release so much!"

If you find yourself in this situation, taking steps to change it will help a great deal. Enlisting the aid of ex-spouses, other parents of teenagers, grandparents, friends, neighbors and co-op child care groups (if you have younger children) will help relieve you from your responsibilities from time to time. Even an occasional few hours of freedom—to get away, be by yourself or to spend time with friends—will do a great deal for your own mental health and your ability to cope. Since support systems are so vital to your well-being (and that of your family), don't be reluctant or shy about seeking them out.

It is important, too, to encourage any constructive support systems your teenager develops. Involvement with a youth group, church activities, time with friends or sharing confidences with another adult—a favorite teacher, relative, youth worker, counselor, neighbor or family friend—will help a depressed teen tremendously and take some of the pressure off you. But it may not be easy for you to accept such help.

"One of the hardest tasks of parenthood is to let go and allow your child to develop intimate relationships elsewhere," says Judith

Davenport. "But in order to grow up, a child must do this. It helps if you both have other meaningful people and activities in your lives."

Other significant people in your child's life will never replace you, but will help your teen grow in ways he or she must. They ultimately help improve the quality of your own relationship with each other by aiding your child's personal growth and the development of new insights.

If you are married, it's important to develop a strong support system with your spouse if at all possible. This means taking turns coping with your teenager, giving each other time to rest. It means being unified in the face of crisis, without blaming each other or allowing your teenager to play one of you against the other. Of course this is easier said than done, but even if you succeed in unifying and supporting each other *part* of the time, it goes a long way in reducing some of the stresses you face daily.

Do Good Things for Yourself. Taking good care of yourself means taking time out to do whatever you need to do to stay healthy, fit and reasonably satisfied with life in general. This means eating well (even when you don't feel like it), getting some regular physical exercise at least three times a week (this can be a great stress-reducer, whether you take long walks, run, swim, play tennis or bicycle) and making space in your life for things you enjoy. This might mean dinner out alone with your spouse or a friend, involvement in a worthy cause, a solitary afternoon of window-shopping or a long, hot, uninterrupted bath. Particularly when you're under pressure, you need all the healthy habits, events to anticipate and satisfying or comforting outside pursuits you can get!

Restructure Your Priorities. Make an effort to sort out what is a crisis in your life and what isn't. Then let the less important issues go to give yourself more time and strength to deal with what really matters, whether these issues relate to your teenager or to someone else.

Resolve to take each day as it comes so you don't put added stress on yourself by agonizing over the past or dreading the future. When you're in the midst of a crisis, getting through each day—one at a time—is a manageable goal. Your current situation realistically is something that will probably not be resolved quickly or easily. Don't subject yourself to the added strain of expecting instant results from counseling or therapy or your own efforts to help. Major problems generally take some time to develop *and* to resolve.

Make Use of Professional Help When You Need It. Many people who need help from a psychologist, psychiatrist, family or marriage counselor or other mental health professional avoid seeking such help out of shame. It is no disgrace to need a helping hand, but it *is* a shame to suffer needlessly or longer than necessary because you're too afraid or embarrassed to seek professional help. (See chapter 29 for information on types of help available.) Professional counseling may involve your entire family, your teen, you and your spouse or you as an individual. Even if your teenager or your spouse refuse to seek help, don't hesitate to look for it yourself if you're having trouble finding your way out of the present crisis on your own. Seeking and making good use of professional help in resolving the crisis will do a great deal for you and your family. It will give you support, relief, new insights and added strength and help to rebuild your self-esteem and hope that life will be better.

Be Gentle with Yourself. It is tempting—but ultimately hurtful—to be extremely self-critical when you face a family crisis. Resist the temptation and be gentle with yourself instead. You deserve gentleness. More to the point, you need it during this time. No one is superparent—*always* patient, understanding, compassionate, strong, wise and nurturing. Learn to let go of the need to be perfect. Even when you fall short of a goal or make a mistake, remind yourself that you did the best you could.

Learning to be gentle with yourself, to make time for yourself and your own needs is vital. You must be your own nurturing parent in order to be the person—and the parent—you want to be. You will be more in touch with your feelings and better able to communicate your concern and your love to your child.

CHAPTER 8

Barriers That Block Family Communication

IT'S HARD TO say when the sullen silences and the angry confrontations began for Julie Fraser and her parents. Julie's early years had been tranquil enough. She had always been quiet, cooperative, a bit timid and never talked back to her parents. In the past two years, however, there has been a change.

"It started the summer she was thirteen," Mrs. Fraser remembers. "She started defying us, crying a lot, arguing about everything and became highly sensitive to any criticism. She is moody and withdrawn these days. I don't know what she's thinking. I have no ideas what her goals are or *if* she has any goals for now or the future."

"We never talk but to yell at each other," Mr. Fraser observes.

And Julie later confides that "every time my parents talk to me, it's to criticize. They don't like anything I do. I'm never good enough. In between, we don't have much to say to each other. I'd say we don't know each other at all anymore. They're my parents, but they don't know *anything* about who I am."

A growing number of parents and teenagers are strangers to each other. They hide feelings and endure long silences punctuated by misunderstandings, angry words, mounting frustration and more silences. The communication gap between generations is so common that it has become something of a cliché, and it is particularly common when a teenager suffers from depression.

Why do so many parents and teenagers fail to communicate?

One factor in the parent-teen communication gap is developmental. Adolescents experience a myriad of physical, emotional and social changes, and during this time they really begin the task of separating from their parents, developing a separate, individual point of view and becoming close to others outside the family. Teens feel pressure not only to please their parents and themselves but also to please their friends who are now so important in their lives. It can be a tough balancing act with many painful conflicts.

Parents and teens who enjoy open communication have a better chance to compromise and agree on how much freedom and responsibility the young person can assume at any given time. But those with a history of minimal communication and poor communication skills are at a distinct disadvantage during this trying time of upheaval and conflict. These are the families of strangers who argue to no avail, who experience crisis after crisis with no resolution. Family members are caught in a perpetual no-win situation. Low self-esteem and poor communication become a self-perpetuating way of life.

Many families fall somewhere in the middle of all this. They're able to share (or at least remember) some good times together. They find themselves able to agree or compromise in some cases, but are unable to resolve major conflicts in a satisfying, constructive way. They have trouble showing vulnerability, sharing thoughts and feelings openly.

Both teens and parents in this type of family feel some sadness, anger or regret over the fact that they seem to be losing touch. But they lack skills to break the barriers that have grown between them. Communication blocks and barriers are practically universal, and incredibly varied. You and your teenager may be caught in a communication-blocking cycle where philosophies, habits and the words you use keep you from really hearing and getting through to each other.

Communication-Blocking Philosophies

There are two common viewpoints that block good communication: generational chauvinism and the concept of parental ownership of children.

Generational Chauvinism

This destructive philosophy afflicts both parents and teenagers. What it means is that each generation is convinced that the other, whether older or younger, has little of value to offer in terms of wisdom, wit or companionship.

Generational chauvinists are inclined to make sweeping generalizations such as:

"What does she know? She's only fifteen—just a silly kid!"

or

"Older people are *so* out of it! My parents are *really* thick!"

or

"Kids today are totally irresponsible. They don't know how to work and take responsibility. Now when *I* was young . . ."

or

"Adults don't know how to have fun. They're dull, dull, *dull!*"

or

"Kids shouldn't even be *thinking* about sex!"

or

"Sex? *My* parents???? You've got to be kidding!"

Both teens and adults who embrace generational chauvinism feel that they have all the answers for the other generation, if the other would only have the brains to listen. But because each cancels out the other's credibility, nobody listens and communication is blocked.

Parental Ownership

More common and much more potentially destructive is the concept of parental ownership. Many parents feel they should have total control over their children's lives and choices, that children should accept and embrace all their parents' values, wishes, goals and dreams. In conflicts, these parents use power rather than reason and are intent on winning. They seem to "win" consistently, especially when their children are small. However, when the children reach their teens, and begin to grow physically and put more emphasis on the opinions and values of their peers, parental power diminishes. Lacking other skills to work through problems, such families find themselves locked into a continuing round of disputes and disappointments. The parents see their children as rebellious, ungrateful and unruly. The teens see their parents as tyrannical and uncaring. Neither side listens to the other and communication is impossible.

"Failure to value the autonomy of family members sets the stage for conflict," says Dr. Saul Brown, chief of the department of psychiatry and the Thebians Community Health Center at Cedars-Sinai Medical Center in Los Angeles. "Parents may lack the ability to value each other and their children as separate and treasured people. They may not value autonomy, or take pleasure in one another's competence. There is no validation, there are silences when there should be compliments; teasing when there should be encouragement and crossed arms when there should be reaching out."

Dr. Brown's comments describe quite accurately the home situation of Sherry Newman, fifteen, and her brother John, thirteen. Both have been seeing a family counselor for depression after their parents became concerned over a variety of changes. John was sleeping too much, Sherry cried a lot and both had little energy, were falling behind at school and seemed unable or unwilling to communicate with their parents.

As their counseling progressed, it was clear that Mr. and Mrs. Newman were concerned parents, determined to give their children the best possible start in life. They were so alarmed about the prevalence of drugs, alcohol abuse, premarital sex and, as Mr. Newman puts it, "general teenage shiftlessness" in their community that they had forbidden their children to socialize with friends after school or on weekends. Sherry and John were not allowed to date. In an effort to instill a sense of pride and the value of hard work, Mr. Newman insisted that his children not only take over many household chores but also work part time for their five-dollar-a-week allowances in his manufacturer's representative business. Despite their good intentions, the Newmans have alienated their depressed children.

"We don't have any time to ourselves," John complains. "Dad will give me a list of things to do on a Saturday and say, 'When you finish all that, come to me and I'll give you another list of things to do.' I never get a chance to decide what *I* want to do. I never get to do *anything* I want to do. Sometimes I feel like running away or sleeping for a week. You can't talk to my parents about this either or they think you're being a smart-mouth."

"It's like what we want for ourselves or what we think doesn't count at all," Sherry says. "I've stopped trying to talk with my parents because they never listen anyway. We're hoping things will change now that we're all seeing a counselor, but so far not much has."

While the Newmans have carried the idea of parental control to an extreme, misuse of power is present to lesser degrees in many other families. In such instances there is little discussion over issues, no room for teenagers to make decisions or choices on their own (at least not without risking considerable conflict with their parents), and the question "why?" is often answered with "Because I said so!"

As a result of their lack of autonomy, or the lack of parental approval when they do show signs of growing competence and independence, the teenagers lose hope that trying to communicate with their parents will accomplish anything constructive. They also begin to question their ability to cope with life and to make independent decisions. Deprived of the pride that constructive coping and decision making bring, these teenagers tend to have low self-esteem.

It is necessary for the sake of a child's healthy development to let go gradually as he or she grows, to give him or her the power to make decisions about some aspects of life and a voice in deciding major issues. It is also vital to recognize and accept your teenagers separateness.

"It may be difficult to accept this separateness," says Dr. Richard MacKenzie. "But there *are* parts of your nearly grown child that you don't know any more—aspects of him or her that you may *never* know."

Psychotherapist Judith Davenport says that she often hears parents lamenting the fact that while they used to be so close to their children, things have changed now that these children are adolescents. And they're wondering what went wrong.

"I often reply, 'What makes you think that something is wrong?' " says Ms. Davenport. "Growing apart, sharing closeness with others outside one's immediate family and becoming one's own person is an important part of growing up."

As a parent, you watch your child grow away from the moment he or she takes his first step, acquires the skills to feed and dress himself and learns to say no. Adolescence is simply another series of steps along the way to adulthood and full independence. Throughout this time of growth and learning, parents must keep a delicate balance between firm guidance and loving encouragement. It is painful to see your child grow away, although you feel pride and a sense of accomplishment in this growth. A parent's ability to love, to guide and then to let go gradually as the child's competence increases is essential to his growth and to good parent-teen communication.

When a parent clings too tightly, wields power too heavily, focuses on winning a battle rather than resolving differences with mutual respect and consideration, power and control become the major household issue, causing rebellion, resentment and added stress for all and blocking communication.

If you find yourself in this position on occasion—unwilling to listen, to discuss differences constructively, to compromise and to let go, even in little ways—remember that while you helped to create your child's life, he or she owns it and must live it. Kahlil Gibran expressed this concept in his famous essay "On Children" in *The Prophet*:

> *Your children are not your children.*
> *They are the sons and daughters of Life's longing for itself.*
> *They come through you but not from you,*
> *And though they are with you, yet they belong not to you.*
> *You may give them your love but not your thoughts,*
> *For they have their own thoughts. . . .*
> *You may strive to be like them, but seek not to make them like you.*
> *For life goes not backward nor tarries with yesterday.*

Letting go, of course, does not mean ceasing to care or be an important part of each other's lives. In a very real sense it can allow you to become close to your teenager in a new way, communicating more openly and effectively than ever before.

Communication-Blocking Habits

What follows are some of the more common communication-blocking habits that occur among parents. These habits become a special problem when children reach adolescence, and they also hinder your ability to help a teenager in distress.

Labeling and Belittling

When problems develop, putting a "label" on the teen can be a big temptation. It seems to be a way to pinpoint what is wrong so that the teenager can see it and change. It can also be a way for the parent to get some distance and deny any responsibility for the problem. A parent may say something like:

"You're just a spoiled brat! That's your basic problem."
"You're being very immature."
"You don't know what you're talking about."
"You've always been the problem in this family. If it weren't for you . . ."
"You're a tramp . . ."
"You're a disappointment to me . . ."
"Why do you say and do such dumb things? You make your own problems, you know."
"You always put your foot in your mouth, don't you?"

This approach obviously erodes a teen's self-esteem and destroys the motivation and ability to make changes. It disclaims any parental responsibility for contributing to the problem and cancels out any chance that the parent will try to help the situation by modifying his or her behavior in any way. Above all, it destroys the trust and confidence a teenager needs to be open with a parent.

"I went through a time of feeling very alone last year," says Monica Blake, sixteen. "My parents were so caught up in their own friends and activities and things weren't going well for me at school. I started getting down on myself and really felt like I needed to get close to someone. Finally, I met this guy who listened to me and really seemed to care. He helped me a lot, but my parents kept criticizing him because of his hair and the way he dressed. I tried to share my good feelings and tell Mom how much Joe had helped me find myself and she said, 'Oh, what does *he* know about anything! You're both just kids! I wish you'd see less of him. You're getting too close.'"

A few months later, after Monica's mother found birth control pills in Monica's purse, there was an emotion-filled showdown.

"I had only just started taking them and Joe and I had had sex only a few times," Monica says. "He was the first—and to this day —the *only* guy I've been to bed with. But to hear my parents, you'd never know that! They screamed and yelled and called me a tramp and lots of other names, plus I got grounded for six months and forbidden to see Joe ever again—or so *they* say. I tried to tell them how Joe and I got close in the first place and how I felt like I needed someone to talk with and be important to, but they were too busy yelling to listen. They'd say things like 'Don't talk back!' or 'Don't try to pin the blame on us!' They acted like I was taking on every guy at school. It made me feel like I can't talk to them at all because they don't care about who I really am."

If Monica's parents had been willing to listen and to *share* feelings with their daughter, they could have communicated their displeasure over her behavior and might also have learned something important about their daughter and themselves. By labeling Monica in such a hurtful way, they may have lost the chance to be close to her.

Not all labeling and belittling is so obvious, but even in less dramatic instances it can erode both self-esteem and communication.

Alan Adams, fifteen, has become increasingly interested in politics over the past year. Full of excitement over his discoveries, ideas and opinions, he has tried repeatedly to share them with his parents. Instead of listening, his parents are prone to interrupt and invalidate his ideas with comments like:

"That's wrong. You don't know what you're talking about."
"How can you say that? You're incredibly naive."
"Don't get on that 'I'm going to save the world!' bandwagon again."

Lately Alan has become more and more withdrawn, feeling angry, shut out and uncertain about his own abilities. His parents complain that he won't talk to them anymore.

When Katie Lee broke up with her boyfriend recently, she was distraught and tried to share her feelings with her mother. Unfortunately, her mother chose to respond in a belittling way: "You're overreacting. Besides, he was a bum. You always choose the wrong type of guy and then get hysterical when the inevitable happens. You never seem to learn."

"I made some wrong choices and had some bad luck," Katie admits. "But I just wanted to talk and cry a little with someone who would listen. I know my mom has heard all this before, but it would have helped if she could have listened instead of putting me down. It's not real tempting to try to confide in her when I only feel worse afterward."

Often, such communication blocks are not due to premeditated cruelty but to hurtful habits developed within the family. In many instances, such habits create serious problems.

"There was a study done a few years ago comparing communication patterns in two-child families, each with one female teenager," says Dr. Alan Berman, professor of psychology at American University and a partner with the Washington Psychological Center. "Six of these teenage girls had attempted suicide. The other six had no history of suicide attempts. The families were observed conversing. In the families with suicidal teenagers, that child was constantly ignored and put down in conversations. The presumption was that this had been going on prior to the suicide attempt."

Another hurtful and belittling pattern of behavior is the "What will people think?" reaction to a teenager's problem.

Janet Zelig, for example, is fourteen years old, five feet two inches tall and weighs over two hundred pounds. The issue of her obesity has become a major family crisis. Her slim, socially active and sports-minded parents are bewildered and humiliated by Janet's eating habits and appearance. They have begged, nagged and yelled, withheld food and marched her to a succession of diet and nutrition experts, but to no avail. Janet is unimpressed by their concern over her weight and is not willing to cooperate or to talk about her problems with them. "They're just upset about my weight because of themselves," she says bitterly. "They're just concerned about what people around here think about them, having a daughter who's overweight. They don't care about me."

Dr. Merilee Oaks, a liscensed clinical psychologist in private practice and on the staff of the Adolescent Unit at Children's Hospital of Los Angeles, observes that this "What will people think?" syndrome is a fairly common belittling communication block.

"Families get caught up in the issue of community standing, agonizing over what others will think, worrying about a child's obesity, for example, largely because others might think that they are bad parents," she says. "At that point, the child simply can't relate to this way of thinking. He or she gets the feeling that he or she is being treated as an object."

Even in relatively problem-free families, a habit of labeling and belittling can create problems.

Jenny Sullivan, for example, is finding it difficult to talk with her parents because they seem to focus on her physical flaws instead of her growth as a person. "I try to tell them how something went well or about an idea I have that I'm really excited about and they cut me off," she reports sadly. "I get comments from them like 'Ummm . . . that's nice. Why don't you *do* something with your hair?' or 'Gee, is that a pimple on your nose?' They don't like to hear me feeling good about myself. If I say how proud I am about something I did it's always, 'Don't get big-headed now!' It isn't worth talking with them most of the time. We aren't on the same wave length and it just gets me upset and mad."

These communication-blocking habits, by the way, are certainly not a parental exclusive. Teenagers can and often do fall into it themselves with comments like:

"Oh, *Mother*, what do *you* know about it?"
"You're too old to understand."
"How can I talk to you? You don't know what's going on."
"You're unfair!"
"You always blame me for everything!"

In some instances labeling and belittling are a cyclical habit—indulged in by parents and teenagers alike. They pave the way for a total lack of communication.

Ordering, Prescribing and Lecturing

As a parent, you may find yourself falling into verbal habits like ordering ("Do it because I say so!" or "Stop feeling sorry for yourself. Just snap out of it—now!"), prescribing ("The trouble with you is that you're lazy" or "What you need is . . .") and lecturing ("What you have to understand is this . . ." or "Don't you know that . . . a stitch in time saves nine, Rome wasn't built in a day and it's not wise to count your chickens before they're hatched?").

What these conversational tactics do is to communicate the idea that the teenager has no voice in decision making, that you don't trust his or her judgment, are not interested in anything he or she might have to say, that you the parent have all the power and that there is no room for discussion and compromise. As a result the teenager stops trying to communicate, with the rationale that "they never listen to me anyway, so what's the use?"

The teenager stops listening, too. When he or she hears you winding up for another order, prescription, lecture or combination of the above, the adolescent is likely to tune you out and add to your frustration with eye rolls, deep sighs and expressions of long-suffering tolerance wearing thin ("Yes, *mother!*" or "O.K., I will—*in a minute!*" or "Oh, just forget it . . .").

And so no one gets heard, everyone feels angry and nothing is solved.

Filibustering

When some of us attempt to answer a question, make an observation or give what we feel might be helpful advice—especially if it is to our child—we unwittingly launch a filibuster than could stun a Congressional veteran. It is tempting to take an idea and run with it, to give your teen all the benefits of your experience, your insights and your accumulated wisdom. The problem with such monologues, however well meant, is that they stop conversation, exasperate instead of fascinate your listener and often make your teenager less likely to seek your help and advice.

"I like to be able to ask my Dad about things that bother me," says sixteen-year-old Jason Ryder. "But I figure it's not worth it if I have to sit around listening to all the stories about when *he* was my age and how well he handled everything and how he has all the answers. He does know a lot and I want to have a discussion and tell him some of the things I'm feeling, but he never gives me a chance. It's like my feelings don't matter or else he forgets I'm there."

After all, the essence of communication is sharing, so taking the floor and refusing to relinquish it for a little give-and-take is an excellent communication stopper.

Taking Over the Problem

When something is amiss with your child, you feel his or her hurt acutely. You may also feel a huge temptation to take over and make his problem yours. Or you may do this automatically without much thought.

"If I have a problem, I don't let my parents know if I can help it," says Ron Daniels, sixteen. "My mom's usual reaction is to get all upset, even cry. The last time she cried was when I didn't make the varsity basketball team. I was feeling down and wanted to talk about it, but the way she reacted made me feel worse. I felt guilty for making her feel bad and got into telling her, 'Oh, well, it's O.K. Don't get too upset, Mom,' when *I* wanted to be comforted myself. My dad is worse. Tell him a problem and before you're finished talking, he has ninety-two solutions that *he* wants to act on—like 'Why don't I call and talk to the coach?' and things like that. It's easier to talk with my friends or just figure things out on my own."

Another way of taking over a problem is by seeing it as a personal affront, as something your child does *to* you.

"When I was feeling real depressed last year and couldn't stand to go to school unless I had a drink first, I knew I was in trouble," says Diana Leonard, fourteen. "I felt like my parents had all these expectations about me being the perfect daughter and the top student in my class. These were things I couldn't be no matter how hard I tried. I felt like a failure. I talked to a counselor at my school and she suggested that I share my feelings with my folks. Well, I tried and told them that I felt so depressed and bad that I was developing a drinking problem. You know what their reaction was? 'How could you do this to us? We trusted you and you've let us down.' It was like I was a horrible person because I had this problem. My parents eventually got us into counseling together, but that first reaction from them hurt a lot. It did *not* make me glad I confided in them—at least, not at first."

The key to avoiding this communication-blocking habit is to determine who *owns* the problem. This requires that you see your child as a separate person with his or her own life and own set of problems which may or may not be problems for you.

Determining ownership of a problem is a major skill taught in Parent Effectiveness Training (PET) classes, which are held in cities and towns across the nation. PET's founder, clinical psychologist Dr. Thomas Gordon, explains that when a person's needs are not being met or he or she is not satisfied with his behavior, he owns the problem.

For example, if a teenager fails to make a team, feels rejected by a friend, gets into trouble at school, or feels embarrassed about a comparative lack of physical development, he or she owns the problem. Any of these will naturally be of concern to you, the parent, but when you see them as your teenager's problems, then you are in a better position to help your son or daughter cope. You will not be as likely to feel victimized or immobilized by problems that are not really your own. You will be better able to listen and to help your teen work through the problem, thus acquiring a valuable life skill. On the other hand, when you take over and try to solve your child's problems for him, he will feel loss of self-esteem, suspect that you don't trust his ability to come up with effective ideas and solutions of his own and may angrily reject your advice with the accusation, "You're treating me like a baby!"

If some aspect of your teen's behavior is a problem for *you* but not for him, it's important to make this clear. If, for example, your daughter has been coming in half an hour after curfew for the last several weeks, that extra thirty minutes out may be fine with her but worrisome and irritating for you. Approaching the problem in the spirit of "I get very upset and worried when you come in late" may open the door to communication—helping her see *your* side of the situation.

Giving Mixed Messages

We don't always say what we mean—or mean quite what we say—and the result is confusion, misunderstandings and blocked communication.

"Some parents give subtle encouragement to their children's conflicts," says Dr. Lee Robbins Gardner. "This comes from fear of the child and encourages acting out behavior. For example, when a boy cuts school, his father might say, 'I never had the guts to do that,' or 'I did that too.' "

When such encouragement occurs, mixed with prohibitions against the behavior, it results in a great deal of confusion and conflict.

Strict and constantly repeated prohibitions also carry a mixed message. "By constantly voicing strict prohibitions against certain behavior, one subconsciously encourages a child to act out in these ways, maybe as a means of fulfilling one's own needs," says Doris Lion, a family therapist in Los Angeles. "For example, a parent may tell a thirteen-year-old daughter over and over 'Don't you *dare* have sex! Don't you *dare* get pregnant!' On one level, the parent means this. On another, by focusing so strongly on sex the parent is subconsciously encouraging the child to act out sexually, maybe as a way to make up for lost opportunities in the parent's own youth. It is helpful to examine your own childhood and feelings behind every very strong prohibition you voice. It is important, of course, to convey what behavior is acceptable to you and what isn't and which values you cherish and hope your child will at least respect. It may be quite another matter, however, if all your concern is focused on one area and expressed in such strongly prohibitive terms."

Subtle or not so subtle put-downs are also contained in some mixed messages. In many instances, a parent's original intent is to encourage, and he or she may not realize how clearly negative implications ring out to the teenager.

"My personal bias is against the word 'potential,' " says Dr. Randi Gunther, a psychologist in Palos Verdes, California. "Telling a child 'You have such potential' *seems* to be encouragement, but it also means 'You're not so hot now.' It is much more constructive to focus on special qualities, abilities and talents the teenager has now that can be developed and used now and in later life."

Sandra Shelton, seventeen, says that she tunes out whenever her mother says, "You have a beautifully shaped face." Why? "Because it's a lead-in to her standard beauty lecture and critique," Sandra says. "What it *really* means is 'The shape of your face is great, but everything else about you is the pits.' That's always the way it goes. It makes me feel so bad I stop listening. I know some of her advice might do me some good, but I get too hurt and mad to follow it. I feel like unless I look perfect she won't accept me as a worthwhile person."

Saying things like "I'll be so proud of you when you graduate from college!" communicates to the teenager that you aren't proud of him or happy for him now. And the sweetness of some successes are soured by mixed messages when the teenager tries to share the news with you. Saying things like:

"That's nice, but don't get a big head about it."
"Second prize? Gee, why didn't you come in first?"
"Of course you did well. You always do. You're our son!"
"Oh, fantastic! Wait until I tell my friends!"

can sabotage a young person's enjoyment of his achievement in a number of ways. What the above messages are really saying is: to talk about achievement shows conceit; second prize is an occasion for disappointment; the achievement was nothing important, simply expected behavior; and the achievement is *yours* and your greatest joy is in sharing it with friends, not your teenager. In each case the child is left feeling inadequate.

Another category of mixed messages is comprised of "yes" messages that really mean no. For example, instead of telling your teenager that he or she can't go scuba diving for the first time with a group of equally inexperienced and unsupervised friends, you might find yourself saying, "I guess you can go if everyone else goes, but I don't think it's safe and I'll worry about you every minute you're gone. Have a good time!"

This puts the teenager in a no-win situation. If he goes, he feels guilty. If he stays home, he feels deprived. It is much more constructive to make your feelings clear—for example, "I feel that you would be taking unnecessary risks in this situation and I can't give you my permission to do this. If you and your friends took a course in scuba diving or were under the supervision of an experienced diver and instructor, I might change my mind. Until then, I have to say no."

Mixed messages that put your teenager down, place him or her in a no-win situation or that imply that he or she is not trusted are very effective communication blocks, creating a great deal of distance between parent and teenager.

Dishonesty

In many cases parents say dishonest things or deny reality, hoping to encourage their teenagers. But the teen often sees the essential dishonesty and feels worse because of it.

"I saw a fifteen-year-old boy in counseling recently," says family therapist Shirley Lackey. "He was depressed because he was too short and small to make the football team. He told me, 'My parents have been promising me I'd grow since I was thirteen. When is it going to happen? Being short really bothers me.' It is a real mistake to say something like 'It doesn't matter. You'll grow' to a kid when there is a possibility that he or she will *not* grow enough to meet a goal like getting on the football or basketball team. It is more constructive to help your teenager explore ways to feel good about himself or herself and find other interests to pursue."

If, in an effort to encourage a child's interests, you tell him or her that he is the greatest writer, singer, artist or athlete you've ever seen (when he or she is actually just good, average or fair or simply learning a skill) the teen may immediately pick up on the difference between your judgment and reality and promptly lose faith in your opinions.

"My mother thinks that every essay I write is the greatest," says Beverly Brown, fourteen. "That's kind of nice of her, but it doesn't mean much. If I want constructive criticism or to share something *I* really like and am proud of, I go to Dad. When he says something is good or not good he is sincere and often right. I trust his judgment. He's honest and fair."

Another form of dishonest noncommunication is hiding feelings and insisting that something doesn't bother you when it does, avoiding confrontations with the person directly involved in your conflicts.

"My mother has this little habit of not telling me when she's bugged about something," says fifteen-year-old Mike Saunders.

"She'll act like everything is O.K., then run to Dad and complain about me doing this or not doing that when she never told me it was a problem. Then Dad comes down on me like a ton of bricks and she plays the innocent martyr. It's disgusting."

Dishonesty—which can be seen as lack of understanding, trust and caring—is a highly effective communication block.

Interrogation

Asking too many questions can create distance and block communication, especially when you're dealing with teenagers. While it's important to ask for and have certain information like where your teenager is going and with whom, a barrage of questions when the teen is trying to tell you about a problem or some troubling feelings interrupts the flow of his or her thoughts, gets the conversation off on unwanted tangents and, if such questions are worded in a negative way, sets you up as a judge, making the teen less inclined to try to communicate.

Trying too hard to get your child to open up can also have a blocking effect.

"When I get home from school I'm tired," says Patti Reine, sixteen. "Usually, it has been just another boring day, you know. But my mom meets me at the door practically and goes, 'What happened today? What's new and exciting? What did you do? Who did you eat lunch with? How is Spanish class coming along?' I know she's real interested in me and all and I appreciate it to a point, but I get turned off by all her questions, especially her 'What's new and exciting?' Usually *nothing* new or exciting happens at school and that's bad enough, but when I feel mom expects me to bring home exciting news every day it just makes it worse. I'd like to talk more to her but she runs at me with all these questions and I just feel like running the other way. Usually, I just say, 'Nothing happened!' and run to my room and shut the door fast."

It would be more effective to create an atmosphere of warmth and openness and to keep the questions to a well-thought-out minimum.

Getting Stuck in the "Old Information" Rut

If you're like most parents, you find yourself bringing up certain observations again and again while your teenager reacts with anger, resentment and begins to tune you out. If you don't want to be tuned out, take care not to linger over and rehash information your teenager already knows. Old information sounds a lot like nagging or put-downs. Statements like "This is the third 'C' you've made in geometry this year!" or "You're only fourteen. You're just a kid!" does not give your teen any new insights into his or her problems. Keep observations current ("You seem to be having some trouble in geometry class" or "I feel that you're not quite ready emotionally for that kind of responsibility") and focus on things that can be changed within a relatively short period of time. This will prevent some communication blocks.

Minimizing the Situation

What seems trivial to you from an adult's perspective may be a major problem for a teenager, who may feel a great need to talk over feelings of anger, loss and grief over a rejection by a friend, a broken romance, the loss of a pet or failure to reach a goal like making a team. Such sharing will be short-circuited, however, if you try to console the teenager by saying that it doesn't matter.

"I tried to tell my dad about how crushed I was when Ben dropped me for my best girlfriend," says Jana Weisman, thirteen. "He didn't take it seriously. He acted like it didn't matter that my world was falling apart. He just said, 'Don't worry, sweetheart. Men are like subway trains—there's another one along every few minutes. Next week you'll be in love with someone else and won't even remember Ben!' But that's not true! Getting dumped hurts a lot and Dad just doesn't understand."

Telling a teenager that he or she shouldn't feel a certain way also sabotages communication. Saying, "You shouldn't be so upset. It isn't that important" or "You're getting mad for nothing" minimizes the problem and denies feelings that the teen is trying to share. The teenager, feeling unaccepted, unheard and frustrated, withdraws or reacts in anger. It is far more constructive to say things like "That really hurts, doesn't it?" or "I know it's really hard for you right now."

Withdrawing

Some parents withdraw from their children in a number of ways. They may say, clearly or subtly, "Don't bother me now," when a teenager tries to talk with them. Some listen half-heartedly—not making eye contact, reading or watching TV—with minimal response while the young person is talking. Still others communicate the essence of the song from *The Wiz*, "Don't Bring Me No Bad News," to their kids. In these homes it is not O.K. to have problems and to talk about them openly. This lack of availability seriously impairs communication.

If you truly can't be available because the boss has come for dinner, you have a raging migraine headache, you're walking out the door and are late for work or the issue being raised is very troubling to you and you need time to think it over, it is more constructive to make this clear to your child and set definite plans to discuss it later. You might say how much you want to hear the teenager out and arrange a block of time together as soon as possible—as soon as the boss leaves, the headache subsides, when you get home from work or have had a reasonable amount of thinking time. If you find yourself avoiding an issue your teen is trying to raise, telling him or her how you feel may smooth the way to communication. Saying "I have a lot of trouble hearing about that. I have so many feelings that seem to get in the way, but I *do* want to listen and to understand your point of view" is more likely to elicit favorable results than "Don't talk to me about that."

Words and Phrases That Block Communication

There are many words and certain tones of voice that quite effectively block communication with your teenager. The following examples are only some of the most common.

"The trouble with you is . . ."
"In *my* day . . ."
"What you have to understand and can't seem to grasp . . ."
"You're wrong."
"Why would you feel like *that?*"
"That's a dumb thing to say!"
"Don't you dare talk back to me!"
"You're a real disappointment to me."
"You're . . . stupid . . . bad . . . incompetent . . . lazy . . . (etc.) . . ."
"Are you trying to drive me crazy or what?"
"How could you do this to me?"
"You're kidding!"
"Is *that* all? I thought it was something important?"

"Well, what did you expect? You're just a kid, after all."

"Don't bother me now."

What a teenager needs to tell you will not always be what you want most to hear, but, in building good communication and growing past blocking habits, listening and being there for your child—no matter what—is crucial.

CHAPTER 9

Where Does One Begin?

Why Pick on Parents?

TEENAGERS, LIKE PARENTS, block communication with their own array of habits, attitudes and phrases. They, too, can be uncommunicative and foil our best attempts at tolerance, compassion and getting back in touch. But to focus on teenagers would be self-defeating. You can only change your own feelings, habits and behavior. As you begin to relate to your teenager in a new way, your son or daughter may become more responsive to you.

Taking the first steps toward open communication may seem to be an overwhelming task. But improving communication—taken step by step and day by day—*is* possible and manageable. There are three major steps toward better parent-teen communication: 1) Developing empathy for your teenager, acquiring a new understanding of his or her point of view. 2) Creating an environment of respect and trust and helping your teenager improve self-esteem via honest praise and encouragement. 3) Acquiring new communication skills so that you can listen, give clear messages and share your thoughts and feelings, both positive and negative, in a new way.

Empathize with Your Teen

To develop empathy for your teenagers you must understand their point of view, see the world for a moment as they see it. Despite the fact that times and circumstances of family life have changed in many ways since your own adolescence, many of the major conflicts and concerns of the teen years have remained constant. It should be helpful, then, to take a trip back in time and re-experience your own adolescence.

"Remember those times as they *really* were, not as you may have romanticized them over the years," suggests Dr. Marilyn Mehr. "You can do this a number of ways. Maybe you could start a journal where you write down memories and relive them in that way. Or perhaps you can share memories with your spouse or with a group of friends who are also parents (although your kids probably won't be too interested in sharing these memories with you right now). Ask yourselves questions about all kinds of adolescent experiences and concerns, from skin problems to romances to fears. Immerse yourself in what it was like to be an adolescent."

Some questions to ask yourself include:

- What were three of the most terrible things that happened to me when I was a teenager?
- What things embarrassed me most?
- What things did I enjoy most during those years?
- What physical problems did I worry about most?
- What is the worst thing anyone ever said to me when I was a teen?
- Who was my best friend? How much time did we spend together? What did we enjoy doing most? What special secrets did we share?
- What did it feel like to lose a friend? Change schools? Get yelled at by a teacher?
- What were my grades *really* like?
- What dreams did I have for myself? What did I want most for the future?
- What was my idea of an absolutely perfect day back then?
- Was I *really* good about helping around the house or did I ever have to be coaxed, cajoled or nagged to pitch in and do my share of chores?
- What issues sparked arguments between my parents and me?

- How well did we resolve those conflicts?
- What did my parents criticize about me or my behavior?
- What qualities in me did they praise?
- What were my honest, deep-down feelings about my mother and my father when I was fourteen? (You might try writing a paragraph describing your parents from your fourteen-year-old perspective or hunting up an old diary if you had one.)
- What qualities in me did my parents particularly value or praise?
- How much time, from day to day or week to week, did I spend with my parents?
- How did I feel about participating in family activities versus being with my friends?
- How much did I *really* confide in my parents?

Recalling your own teenage pains, pleasures and experiences will help you to understand better what life is like today for your teen-age son or daughter.

"Remembering what it was really like to get a bad grade or a reprimand from a teacher or to lose a friend, remembering your feelings, your fears and your upsets will help you understand your teenager," says Dr. Merilee Oaks. "However, it is very counter-productive to go on and on to your teenager about what a hard time you had or, worse still, to compare your adolescence with his or hers by saying something like 'I had to live through much rougher times.' It is much better to say, 'I *know* it's hard for you right now.' "

Remembering your own adolescence will also help when you're feeling shut out and rejected by your teenager.

"If your teenager is trying to separate from you and you're re-acting with hurt, anger and fear and wondering, 'How is she going to cope without me telling her what to do?' just remember your own teens," says Dr. Mehr. "And ask yourself, 'How much did I *really* listen to my parents?' "

Create an Environment for Good Communication: Questions and Exercises

Communication grows and flourishes in an environment of mutual trust and respect, which is possible only when family members feel good about themselves and each other. Begin to evaluate and make changes in your home environment by considering the following questions:

How Do You Feel About Yourself?

Would you say that your own self-esteem is high, normally healthy or quite low? Do you accent the negative in your own life? If so, you may be passing this habit on by example to your child.

EXERCISE: Take a piece of paper and make a list of your good qualities and other things you like about yourself. Don't let any qualifications or negative comments creep into your list. Keep it positive. Include examples of situations you handled admirably—ways you coped socially, at work, at home, with others or alone—in ways that were constructive and helped you to feel good about yourself—even if these occurred years ago.

For example, Penny Riordan, the mother of three teenagers, likes the fact that she is "well-organized most of the time, a hard worker, a person who cares very much about my husband and children and who tries to tell them so both directly and indirectly. I'm also good at my job (computer programming) and I am conscientious and good at keeping confidences. I also like the fact that I can be diplomatic yet honest. I've had to work on developing my assertiveness and I've improved a lot in that regard. I can disagree and stand up for myself without being witchy. I can and do admit when I've made a mistake, too, which I like a *lot* in myself. I try to be sensitive to others' feelings. Sometimes I do well at this and sometimes I don't, but I'm pleased that I try to be considerate."

Take time to think about and list your strong points—it will help you get out of the habit of accentuating your negative qualities to the point that these take over your image of yourself.

When you begin to feel better about yourself, you will have more energy and confidence to improve your relationships with others. You will also be more likely to have and to express positive feelings about your teenager.

How Do You Feel About Your Teenager?

Do you see him or her as a trial, a burden, a mixed blessing, a difficult person, a stranger, brimming with promise or a hopeless case? How did you see this child as a baby? As a small child? Has your opinion of him or her changed drastically as he or she has grown? Some parents love and enjoy infants and small children but find little joy in sharing their lives with a teenager.

"The child in this instance can become very depressed and feel that he or she has let the parents down by growing up and becoming more independent," says Dr. Donald McKnew. "In our clinic, we also see a lot of kids who feel bad about not being able to live up to parental expectations and standards."

Do you have a need for your teenager to be a certain way—for example, clean-cut, industrious, an achiever, an "A" student, compliant or artistically inclined—to be acceptable to you? Or are you able to accept your child as he or she basically is? Do you have a long list of complaints about your teen? Can you find anything at all to admire and enjoy about him or her?

EXERCISE: List the complaints you have about your teenager. List the qualities you don't like about him or her and the areas of life that, in your opinion, need improvement. How many times have you gone through this list verbally with your teenager? How often do you tell him or her what you don't like?

Now list the qualities you like most in your teenager. If you're feeling very angry, battered by conflicts or confused and frustrated by your teen's depression, it will be difficult to come up with much at first. Keep at it. Make a vow to make the list of strong points and assets at least as long as your complaint list. Try to think of ways your teenager has been kind, thoughtful, helpful, resourceful, brave or honest.

"When I started on my list about my daughter Lisa, I felt it was pretty hopeless," says Dan Wiley. "All I could think about was how she was driving me crazy, how insolent she could be, how hard to reach and the like. Well, the first thing that occurred to me is that she seems to be a good friend to her friends. She's loyal and giving and listens for hours to their problems, stories about boys and school and whatever else they discuss. I've noticed that she listens well when her friends visit and when she's on the phone and that's a quality I admire. She is also very health-conscious and takes good care of herself, which is a good habit to get into at her age. She's very kind to the old woman next door who recently lost her husband —taking her cookies, helping her with shopping from time to time and always making a point of saying a friendly hello and stopping to talk a little when she sees her. I know she is also trying to get along with her pesky little brother lately. He goads her a lot, but she is getting much better at not rising to the bait. She's great at games—chess, backgammon, you name it. I enjoy playing those games with her because she gives me a real challenge. She comes up with some interesting ideas and I like her original turn of mind."

It's important to balance criticism with praise and to see a variety of qualities to praise in your teen, whether your child is a bona fide achiever or not. Some parents keep from praising an achiever because they don't want to favor him or her or because they begin to take the competence for granted. They may fail to praise a non-achiever because they can't find anything about this child to praise.

"All children need praise—the achiever and the less gifted child," says Dr. Richard Gardner, associate clinical professor of child psychiatry at Columbia University's College of Physicians and Surgeons and author of the book *Understanding Children: A Parent's Guide to Child Rearing.* "A gifted child should not be deprived of praise and a parent should also encourage a less academically gifted child to find gratification through other channels. It is important to be open-minded about this. If you are open to the value of each child's individual strengths, whatever they may be, you will do all your children a great service."

It's also vital to make sure that your expectations for your son or daughter are realistic. "Realistic expectations are *so* important," says educational psychologist Sarah Napier. "For example, normally a teenager can't go from a 'C' to an 'A' in a class in only six weeks no matter how hard he or she works. Also, if a child is gifted some parents expect the child to be gifted in all areas. This, again, is not realistic. In the same way, a learning disabled child is *not* disabled in all areas."

Some parents also miss the importance of positive reinforcement. They are quick with criticism and stingy with praise, perhaps echoing the words of one father who said, "When my kid messes up, he needs to be told. When I criticize him it's to help him do better. When he does well he knows it. I don't need to tell him. He *should* act that way. Why should I praise him for doing something he should do?"

Praising your child when he does something right makes such behavior rewarding to the child as well as to you. This positive reinforcement makes it more comfortable for your teen to choose these positive behaviors.

And praise from a parent who knows the child so well has a very special meaning to the teenager, even though he or she may not let on.

How Do You Criticize Your Teenager?

Do you label him or her as a person, or focus on behavior? Labeling, belittling and criticizing your child's personality instead of making it clear that you love him but disapprove of his behavior can be a factor in a teen's low self-esteem, depression and noncommunication. When you criticize, do you tend to get sarcastic? Do you ever ridicule or laugh at your child's mistakes? How do you react when he makes a mistake? When you make a mistake? Do you put yourself down as a person for your own shortcomings? Or do you see these—in yourself and in your child—as opportunities to grow, as challenges to be met? Do you see mistakes as disasters or as indications of poor character—or do you see them as potential learning experiences? How you regard mistakes in yourself and in your child can have a big impact on your child's self-esteem.

Also, can you admit it when you make a mistake, especially when you're wrong and your child is right? Or do you need to seem perfect, need to be right, need to win all the time? If you take the risk of being human and imperfect with your teenager, it goes a long way in building self-esteem, helping to ease the teen's worries about his own imperfections and bridging any of the communications gaps you have between you.

EXERCISE: Think of the last time you made a mistake. How did you react? How did you resolve or rectify the matter? Next, consider your reaction when your teenager makes a mistake or falls short of a goal. What is your reaction then? Are you as hard or as gentle as you are with yourself? Did you label, criticize and scold or did you encourage him or her to meet the challenge of growing from the experience? How could you make it better the next time?

How Do You Praise Your Teenager? And When Was the Last Time You Praised Your Teen?

Do you go for days, weeks or months without offering him some encouragement? When you praise, what is his or her reaction? If the reaction is negative, take a look at the way you praise. Are you being honest in your praise?

Some teenagers quickly pick up on phony or manipulative compliments and are quick to discount any praise that doesn't ring true. It is counter-productive to praise your youngster only when you want him to do something for you, or to be unrealistic in what you say. If, for example, you tell your teenager who is doing well in art class that he is the greatest artist you've seen, you both know that this probably isn't true and the teen will feel patronized and put down. It is more productive to focus on progress—for example, "I really like that new watercolor you just finished. You seem to be enjoying the class and making a lot of progress, too. I'm so happy for you."

It's important to express praise the same way you express criticism —focusing on a specific quality of behavior, not the entire person. Focusing on the person and making a value judgment about his or her worth may lead the teen to believe that his goodness or personal worth is contingent on achievements or that your love is conditional on these.

For example, it is better to say, "I appreciate the way that you cleaned up the kitchen and washed the dishes tonight. That really helped a lot," instead of "I love you for cleaning the kitchen. You're a great kid."

Or, when a teen has done something that took personal courage, it is more constructive to quietly say "I'm *so* pleased that you were able to get up in front of everyone and give such a good speech. It wasn't an easy thing to do. You really showed courage" instead of, "I was bursting with pride! You're always so brave!"

The teen, who knows that he isn't always brave or thoughtful, will be pleased that you've noticed the progress and growth but at the same time will realize that your love does not hinge on peak performances.

If you think that what you say doesn't matter, think again. No matter how tied teenagers are to their peers and how seemingly disinterested they are in you, your opinion matters a lot.

EXERCISE: Make an effort to give praise and positive feedback to your teenager is some way every day. It may be praise over some small matter ("I appreciate the way you started getting dinner ready on your own" or "It meant a lot to me when you asked me how things went at work today. It made me feel good to know that you're interested"). It takes time to listen to your teen—whether he or she is trying to tell you about a problem, a new friend at school, a hot news item or a very old joke. Making an effort to listen is a form of praise since it is a way of saying to your child, "You're important to me."

Letting your child take more responsibility is also a form of praise because it implies trust and faith in his or her ability to take more control over life.

"Giving your teenager responsibilities, acting as if the teen can handle more, can help his self-esteen grow and give the teenager a sense of security, a wonderful feeling of being valued and trusted," says family therapist Doris Lion.

It isn't always easy to trust or to praise at first. If this isn't done openly in your family, you will feel a bit awkward and self-conscious at first.

Bob Conway, a program coordinator at The Bridge, a runaway shelter and youth/family counseling service in San Diego, remarks that "All too often it's easier for parents and teens to hear and say negative things rather than positive things to and about each other. In one recent session, I asked a mother to tell her daughter directly what she liked about her. When the mother was praising her daughter, she wasn't able to look at the girl. And there have been some family sessions where people started crying, either when giving or receiving praise, but in most instances communication improved a lot after this."

When Was the Last Time You Told Your Teenager That You Loved Him or Her?

Have you ever been able to do this? Some families are quite reticent about such feelings, and even spouses go for months or years without actually saying "I love you" to each other. But in families where communication tends to be open, the various family members are able to say and to hear that they are loved and valued. When you're locked into conflicts with your teenager or when he or she is acting in a distinctly unlovable way, it is very difficult to summon up these feelings and words. But such times are when your teenager may need those words the most. There are times when your expressed love and commitment are what keeps communication going between you.

EXERCISE: Tell your teenager that you love him or her some time today. Or, if that is too difficult right now, you might write a note and leave it in his or her room telling the teen how much you love

him—in good times and bad and for himself or herself, not for
what he does or doesn't do. If a teenager knows this, he or she will
feel a renewed sense of self-worth and, perhaps, a new bond with
you as well. If your teenager knows that your love is unconditional,
trust, respect and better communication are more likely to grow.

Does Your Teenager Feel That He or She Belongs to the Family?

This sense of belonging is important to self-esteem. Even though
your teen chooses to spend a lot of time away from home and
seems uninterested in family activities, make an effort to include
him or her whenever feasible, giving the teen the option of participating or not.

It is also helpful to communication and your teenager's sense of
self-worth to include him or her in your feelings. If you try to hide
your pain and sadness, you're communicating several things: that
you don't trust the teen's growing ability to cope, that you see him
or her as a child in need of protection and that feelings of pain and
sadness are, somehow, wrong and should be hidden. Including your
adolescent in some of your feelings helps your teen feel closer to
you-the-person versus you-the-parent and also helps him or her
feel more comfortable and able to cope with his own pain.

"In being open, you make the teen an ally, not an enemy," says
Dr. Richard MacKenzie. "It's important to admit it to your child
when times are tough and when you are feeling sad."

Giving your teenager a voice in family decisions or asking for his
opinion, even in small matters, will help give him or her a sense of
belonging and importance so necessary for self-esteem.

"You might do this on an informal basis or utilize one mealtime
a week to raise issues about what's happening in your lives," Dr.
MacKenzie suggests.

It is also helpful to express your need to stay in touch with your
teenager.

"You might say something like, 'I see you growing up and living
more and more outside our home,'" says Dr. MacKenzie. "'John, I
really enjoy seeing you grow up and experience the world, but I
miss you. I would like to spend some time with you. Let's do something together—go for a hamburger, go sailing, something like that.'
Make it clear that this is *your* need."

Feeling needed and valued is vital to an adolescent's self-esteem.

EXERCISE: Make an effort to include your teenager in some special way today. Ask his opinion about something important to you or to the family and listen carefully to his reply without rejecting or discrediting it. Ask his opinion on a small matter or two that are of immediate concern (e.g., what dessert to fix for the big family dinner coming up next weekend). Ask him or her to participate in a family activity or something with just the two of you. Or share a special thought or feeling—maybe your need to stay in touch.

Remember that a teenager with high self-esteem will be more willing to communicate and compromise and less vulnerable to destructive peer pressure as well as to severe bouts of depression. Helping your child build a positive self-image is an excellent preventive measure. And even if your communication has broken down, even if your home is one of ongoing crises and confrontations, even if your teenager is already depressed, your attempts to empathize and to change the environment to one that encourages communication will help you and your teenager reach out and start to get back in touch with each other.

CHAPTER 10

The Most Important Step: Learn Good Communication Skills

E FFECTIVE COMMUNICATION IS an art, and there are some essential skills you should develop in order to get past communication barriers and start getting through to each other. This chapter describes these skills in detail.

Listening

Too often, what passes for conversation is really a long-winded monologue or two simultaneous monologues with neither speaker being heard by the other. This can be particularly true of "conversations" between parents and teenagers—with arguing, interrupting, making excuses, lecturing and leveling accusations all short-circuiting any real communication.

Listening is the first step away from this frustrating, no-win cycle. If you learn to listen, you will learn a great deal about your teenager and probably yourself as well. Your listening will also make your teenager aware of how much you care and will facilitate communication.

Many parents have a difficult time listening to their kids. One father's reaction to a counselor's comments about the importance of listening is typical: "Why should I have to listen to all that garbage?

I don't agree with any of it and I feel that my kid is screwing up his life. I want to talk some sense into his head before it's too late!" If you really want to get through to your teenager, listening is the best first step. It does *not* mean agreeing. "It doesn't mean that you're giving in to your kids," says Dr. Gabrielle Carlson. "What it means is that you're giving credence to their right to express themselves openly. It can be hard to hear what they're saying, but it's important to make an effort to listen."

Listening without interrupting can be difficult, but crucial. "No matter how strongly you dislike or disagree with what's being said, it's important to listen anyway," says Judith Davenport. "Keep back the 'but's,' the excuses, the attacks and the judgments. If you're serious about expressing the sentiment 'I love you no matter what' to your teenager, listening in this way is a good chance to prove it."

It's also vital not only to hear what's being said but also to understand the message and let your teen know that you understand. Many counselors and parenting skills instructors call this "active listening."

The value of active listening is that it clarifies the speaker's feelings and cuts down on misunderstandings and misinterpretations. Since teenagers are not always able to articulate exactly how they feel, active listening on your part will help them identify and express their thoughts and feelings more clearly. And you will find yourself becoming better able to understand the feelings behind their words.

The techniques of active listening may seem awkward at first, as you feed back to your teenager your understanding of what he or she says. This does not mean parroting back the teen's words, however. That can short-circuit communication in record time. The following dialogue is an example of unsuccessful communication due to faulty (parroting) active listening.

Teen: I'm never going back to that school again! I can't stand it any more! I'm so mad at my English teacher I could scream!
Parent: You're never going back to that school because you can't stand it anymore. You're so mad at your English teacher, you could scream.
Teen: That's what I *said!* Stop repeating everything I say. What are you trying to do anyway?

A more successful attempt at active listening might go something like this:

Teen: I'm never going back to that school again! I can't stand it any more. I'm so mad at my English teacher, I could scream!

Parent: Wow! You sound really angry and frustrated.

Teen: Yeah, I sure am! You know what she did? She marked me way down on that essay I worked on so hard and felt so good about only because she thought my handwriting was messy. She said the essay itself was excellent, but she gave me a "C minus" anyway because of my handwriting. I tried to be neat. I just have bad handwriting, that's all.

Parent: You feel that she was very unfair in doing this.

Teen: Yeah, I do. It isn't fair! There's got to be a way I can talk with her about this so she'll listen and start to give me a chance. I'm working so hard in that class.

Parent: You think that there might be a way to let her see things from your point of view.

Teen: I was thinking of asking her if I could type my essays. That way she could read them and wouldn't get mad and mark them down. And I wouldn't get marked down and all upset. What do you think, Dad? I think that might be a good solution for both of us.

Contrast this with the way the conversation might have gone with a couple of communication blocks thrown in:

Teen: I'm never going back to that school again! I can't stand it any more! I'm so mad at my English teacher I could scream!

Parent: Lower your voice! Stop overreacting! Now what happened *this* time?

Teen: Oh, forget it!

Parent: Come on, tell me.

Teen: You know that essay I worked so hard on? The one that was *good?* Well, she marked it way down! I got a "C minus" on it and only . . .

Parent: I'm sure she must have had a good reason for doing it. She's the teacher and a better judge of what's good than you are.

Teen: But I don't think she was fair! She as much as admitted that the essay was excellent but gave it a low mark only because of my handwriting. I can't help it if my handwriting is bad. I tried to be neat! I don't think the whole essay should have been marked down because of my handwriting!

Parent: Well, your handwriting *is* terrible. Your teacher is just trying to help you. How many times have I told you to work on it more? The problem with you is that you're just too stubborn and lazy to do anything about it. If you tried harder and learned to write better you wouldn't have problems like this. It's as simple as that.

Teen: (crying) I *knew* you wouldn't understand! I hate everybody!

In the last example, the conversation served no constructive purpose and simply reinforced the parent's and teen's negative views of each other. In the earlier, workable, active listening example, the teen ventilated his anger, confided in his father and drew closer to him while working out his own possible solution to his problem.

Sometimes, active listening means noticing your child's body language to pick up cues about feelings, then making an observation about this with a leading question and offer of support.

For example, when Sandra Lowell discovered her thirteen-year-old daughter Lisa coming quietly home from school and slipping into the family room to sulk (quiet homecoming + sulk = trouble at school; sulking in family room versus her own room = "Maybe I'd like to talk about it"), she could have reacted in a variety of ways.

If Sandra had used her old communication-blocking pattern of coming on strong with questions, she might have started a conversation that went like this:

Sandra: What's the matter with you, Gloomy Gus? Something happen at school?

Lisa: (sulking, no answer)

Sandra: Did you have a bad day? Come on, tell me! What's the matter? Did Paula get on your case again? Didn't you get to see Rick after study hall? Did that math teacher give you trouble again? Talk to me!

Lisa: I don't feel like it!

Sandra: But I'm you're mother. I care. Tell me what's wrong. It's good to get those feelings out into the open.

Lisa: Not now.

Sandra: Why not now? I have time. I'm here, ready and willing to listen. Is it so terrible you can't discuss it? Are you in trouble in any way? What could be so awful you can't tell me?

Lisa: I didn't say it was something earth-shattering, I just said . . .

Sandra: Is it because you think I wouldn't understand? I was a teenager once myself, you know.

Lisa: Oh, *Mother*, please! Just leave me alone!

But, on this particular occasion, Sandra *didn't* revert to her old ways. With an action plan involving active listening Sandra chose to gently let Lisa know that her depression was noticed and that she was there to listen and care if Lisa wanted to talk about her feelings:

Sandra: Oh, hi, honey. You slipped in so quietly I didn't even hear you.

Lisa (sulking, no response)

Sandra: It looks like you had a rough day.

Lisa: (sighs deeply, looks away)

Sandra: Feel like talking about it?

Lisa: (no answer, still sulking)

Sandra: I get the feeling that something is the matter, but you don't feel like talking about it just now.

Lisa: (staring ahead, nods slowly)

Sandra: That's O.K., Lisa. But if you change your mind and want to talk with me, I'll be glad to listen. (With a warm touch on Lisa's shoulder, Sandra turns to go.)

Lisa: (starts crying) Mommy . . . wait. I'm just feeling so down because . . .

If you're in a situation where you're listening to your teen complain about you or your rules, nonjudgmental active listening helps clarify feelings and keeps the confrontation from getting out of hand and becoming nonconstructive.

"Listen and make it clear that you're hearing the teen's message," says Judith Davenport. "If you need more information, ask for it. Put some responsibility for the relationship onto the teenager. You might, for example, reply to a teenager's charge that you're an unreasonable perfectionist who expects too much of him with, 'I hear you saying that I expect too much of you. I need more information about what makes you feel that way.' Then it's important to hear him or her out. If the teen says, 'You want me to go to Stanford, which I probably can't get into anyway. You want it because your friends will be impressed. What *I* want doesn't even count,' look and see if there is any truth in that. If you find a grain of truth, you can decide how you want to change or manage your own behavior."

Sometimes, too, brief, nonjudgmental comments (e.g., "I see") give your teen a sense of being heard and understood.

When you listen in this way, your teenager will be more inclined to grant you the same courtesy. Active listening seems strange at first, but if you keep at it it often brings communicative rewards.

"I was afraid to try it the first time after I learned the technique at a Parent Effectiveness Training class," says Susan Shelley, the divorced mother of two teenage daughters. "I thought at least one of my daughters would look me in the eye and say, 'Just what are you doing? What are you trying to pull anyway?' But when my older daughter raged in the door and started yelling about something and my response was, 'You really sound angry and upset,' Kerry paused—mid-scream—and said, in a normal tone of voice, 'Yeah, Ma, I really am,' and proceeded to tell me why in a calmer, more reasonable way than usual. I couldn't believe how delightfully different our conversation was from that point. I'm not always good at active listening and it doesn't always work so smoothly because we're all only human after all, but Kerry, Randi and I are able to communicate better now. They've started doing the same type of listening with me, entirely on their own. It really tickles me and pleases me to hear it!"

As Susan explains, active listening—a skill that can be developed on your own or learned in a parenting skills class (see Appendix) or in family counseling—is not a panacea for all communication ills. There will be times when your child refuses to talk with you. In such instances, it helps to realize that sharing can't be forced. Ask the adolescent if he or she wants to talk, gently express your willingness to listen and then back off. If your teen knows you respect his or her feelings and privacy needs, yet are willing to listen and help if you can, he or she is more likely to come around eventually.

"A little space and time for reflection helps a lot," says Shirley Lackey. "I've found that *most* people in families would really like to talk with each other. They're just scared to take the first step."

Through active listening to each other, you and your teenager may be able to get past that first step. This is of particular importance to the family of a depressed teenager who presents an especially tough communication challenge. "But a parent who can listen and validate the child's anger instead of immediately counter-attacking will be able to help alleviate the child's depression," says Dr. Richard Brown.

Recognizing the reality and validity of a teen's feelings through active listening helps trust, communication and the teen's self-esteem grow even when he or she is depressed. Dr. Richard MacKenzie suggests, "Instead of the old line, 'What do *you* have to be depressed about?' you might choose to respond in a more positive way. You might say, for instance, 'I admire the fact that you can admit that you're depressed. A lot of us try to run away from depression.' And then go on to help the teenager sort out his feelings and alternatives."

Give Clear Messages

It is important to express your feelings and needs directly rather than in a manner that might be interpreted as a personal attack triggering an immediate defensive reaction (a great communication blocker) from your teenager.

Say exactly what you mean in a constructive way. This means taking time to sort out and understand your feelings, perhaps by discussing them with your spouse, a friend or a counselor. "See what's going on in your own life," suggests family therapist Doris Lion. "Maybe you're seeing your child's problem as larger than it is because you are trying to work out your own problems through the child. Or maybe not. But it's a good idea to think about your part of the family problem and to realize what is yours and what is separate so you can express your feelings clearly to your child."

Giving clear messages means saying, "I feel hurt when you are not honest with me" instead of "You're a liar!"; or, "I feel worried and sad when I see you drinking and skipping school. I'm worried for your safety and for your future. I'm afraid you are going through a lot of pain alone and I feel frustrated because I don't know how to help you right now" instead of "You make me so mad! You're just too bone lazy to get up and go to school and you shouldn't be drinking either. If you keep this up, you'll never graduate and will end up digging ditches or on welfare all your life. *I'm* not going to support you the rest of your life, that's for sure! Why do you do this anyway? Why can't you pull yourself together?"; or, "I feel worried when you're late coming home. I get very upset when you're two hours late and I don't hear from you because I sit here wondering what might have happened to you" instead of "Late again! Do you know what time it is?" You're going to be the death of me! Don't you have any consideration for us? You're so selfish and inconsiderate! Why didn't you at least call and tell us you'd be late?"

What the "I" message does is to state clearly the *parent's* problem with the adolescent's behavior (letting him or her know that such behavior has an impact on the parent) while focusing on the behavior without attacking the person.

The basic form of the "I" message ("I feel _____ when _____.") works well in a variety of situations. This does not mean, of course, that you will always be heard, that your teenager will not attack you as a person or refuse to listen. But consistent use of clearly worded "I" messages helps improve communication by making your teenager feel less threatened and thus more amenable to reasonable discussions on important family issues.

It's important to give positive "I" messages as well, telling your teenager what behavior you enjoy and appreciate. For example, you might say, "I feel good when you stop to talk with me after you get home from school," or "I appreciated it when you were so patient with Grandma Lee today. I know it's hard to listen to her sometimes and I'm so pleased to see you treat her with such thoughtfulness and gentleness," or "I feel so happy when I come home from work and find that you've started dinner already. That helps a lot. Thank you."

By focusing on both positive and negative behavior you give your teen a clear and nonthreatening view of which behaviors you feel are O.K. and which ones you consider to be problems. It is an excellent way to set limits and communicate a clear sense that you and your teen are separate people who nevertheless have great impact on each other's lives and so must learn to communicate and cooperate with each other.

Respect Each Other's Separateness

Giving clear "I" messages and determining ownership of specific problems is only the beginning, more important is recognition of and respect for each other's separateness. This is a necessity. It means sharing opinions, not dictums from on high. It means not lecturing or assuming that your children will naturally share all of your values. While we always hope that our children will share the values most important to us, there is no law that says they must. And even though you seem incredibly at odds now, remember that questioning your values and acting or speaking in opposition to them is part of the separation behavior of adolescence. Chances are that when your teenager grows up he or she will share more values in common with you than he or she seems to do now. Or perhaps not, but that still doesn't mean that you can't love and respect each other.

You may find that your concept of what is best for your child will never match his or hers and that after making your own feelings and values clear you must accept what can't be changed, giving your son or daughter the space to make many choices, decisions and mistakes.

"It's important to nurture your child and allow him to develop in the best way he can, allowing him to feel good about what he can do," says Dr. Gabrielle Carlson. "It's critical to determine what you really want for your child. Do you want him to be the best he can be? Or the best way *you* want? There is a big difference between the two and some difficulty is in store for you if you feel that when your child disagrees with you he is rejecting you. You must both allow each other some freedom of choice."

"Your teenager may value qualities in himself that elude you, and it's important to respect them," says Ms. Lion. "And, in turn, you may value things that matter little to the child."

Tolerance for differing points of view cuts down a great deal on the nit-picking that erodes communication. By concentrating on crucial issues and accepting the less important differences as evidence of your child's separateness, you keep the lines of communication open, have a better chance of getting through to your teenager when it matters and help foster feelings of mutual respect in your home. The fact is, your children aren't likely to respect you and your feelings and values if you show no signs of respecting and accepting theirs.

Set Limits and Resolve Conflicts Together

Tolerating different points of view and giving your teenager the space to be his or her own person does not mean that you should not set limits. Teenagers need freedom, but they also need the security of knowing what is expected of them and what absolute limits exist in their homes.

"There are certain things you don't have to and shouldn't accept," says Doris Lion. "In fact, you need to set limits. In doing so, you are saying, 'I care about you. I can't control your behavior nonstop, but these are the things I *expect*.' Then invite your teen to share his negative or positive feelings about this. It's important to listen and be firm and consistent about what you expect from your son or daughter. Adolescents *want* limits. It's scary not to have them. In fact, some acting out behavior is a way of searching and asking for limits."

While your teenager complains and argues about your limits, he or she may also feel that you care enough to stand firm, nose-to-nose with him, and that you will *not* give up or give in and say, "Oh, do what you want. I don't care."

Special education teacher Mary Ann Dan has found limit setting to be a way of gaining new respect and closeness with her particularly difficult teenage pupils. "The whole reason I'm successful with these kids is that I care and I won't give up on them," she says. "They have been shuffled around with threats like, 'If you don't behave, you'll have to go to . . . ,' but my class is the end of the line. When a student gets defiant and says, 'So throw me out!' my reply is, 'No way are you getting out of here. You're going to stay here and things are going to change. You and I may end up wrestling each other to the mat. That's O.K. I'll roll on the floor with you if I have to.' When they get the picture and realize that I mean it, they say 'Oh . . . well . . . O.K.' This approach, which parents can utilize in especially tough situations, has worked even with my most difficult students."

The limits you set should be clear and reasonable. "Set limits on important matters and state these expectations clearly," Ms. Lion suggests. "On smaller, nonhurtful matters, you might choose to let things go. Don't pick over small things. Concentrate on major conflicts and concerns."

Reasonable limits are ones you can live with, ones you will stick to consistently, and ones that will help your teenager realize the necessity of cooperation and compromise as a member of a family and of society at large. However, if your limits fluctuate constantly or are unreasonable, they are no help to you *or* your teenager.

Dr. Gabrielle Carlson recalls the story of one particular family she is seeing in therapy whose limit setting leaves something to be desired. "This couple alternately infanticizes and jumps on their teenage daughter," she says. "A major conflict recently has been her irresponsible use of the family car and the fact that she never gets home on time. To 'solve' this, her parents recently bought their daughter a brand new car! That is *not* a good or reasonable way to set a limit. This couple is having a hard time seeing that they are rewarding bad behavior."

The key to effective communication about limits and conflict resolution is cooperation. If your family gets into the habit of working out conflicts together, it will do wonders for communication and harmony.

"Too many family conflicts are seen in terms of winning and losing rather than communicating and resolving problems," says Ms. Lion. "But the family is a system. What affects one affects all. If things are going to get any better around your home, you need family cooperation in resolving conflicts.

How can you begin to get this cooperation?

First, dispense with the old win-lose method of resolving differences. For example, maybe your teenage daughter screams loud enough and stomps around the house long enough to wear down your resolve, and thus "wins" her point. And you lose, feeling angry at her and at yourself for not standing your ground. Or, perhaps you see a problem and think up a solution you feel is best. Without listening to alternate ideas or plans for meeting the same goal that your teenager might have, you insist that he or she accept and follow your plan to the letter. You win the confrontation, but lose in the long run as your teen's resentment and rebellion against your solution build.

In place of the win-lose method of resolving family problems, try a "no-lose" way of working things out. This method of family co-operation is taught in a number of parenting classes—notably PET seminars and "How to Live With Your Teenager" classes (see Appendix).

Basically, the no-lose method involves the following steps.

1. Identify the problems between you. It is helpful to make a list of behaviors that you expect from your teen or that you can't live with. Invite your teenager to do the same with you.

For example, you expect your teenager to go to school regularly, keep his or her room reasonably clean, do specific household chores, speak to you in a civil tone of voice, observe curfew rules and not host drinking/drug parties at your home in your absence or otherwise. Your teenager's expectations might be that you quit nagging about exactly when chores are done, give him or her more space and privacy (e.g., not reading mail or diaries), speak in a civil tone of voice and get off his or her back about hair or style of dress.

Once these essential conflicts, wants and expectations are clear and out in the open, you can sort through your alternatives.

2. Brainstorm with your teenager about possible solutions to major conflicts. At this point, you could write down all suggestions without commenting one way or the other about them. When all suggestions have been made, go through the list together, each saying which alternatives might be acceptable. This way, it is usually possible to hit on at least one or two compromises to each problem that everyone can live with.

For example, you might both agree to speak civilly to each other. You might agree to relax your standards of cleanliness for your teen's room as long as dishes and food are not left in there to fester and the door is kept shut so you don't have to look at it. Your teenager may agree to do all expected household chores if you don't nag about it. You may agree to keep from constantly criticizing your teen's friends if your teenager will stop inviting them over when you're not home or so often that the family routine is upset.

This way, both parent and teen win a bit and compromise a bit. This exercise will help your teenager learn constructive ways of working out conflicts. He or she will also be more strongly motivated to follow through on the solutions and expectations because of having had a voice in making them.

3. Explore ways to implement your compromises and decisions. It's important to agree on how these rules and decisions will be enforced. In matters where solutions are readily agreed upon and quite easy to implement, verbal agreements (and gentle "I"-message reminders if someone slips up later on) are usually enough. In particularly serious or recurring conflicts, some families find a written contract useful.

Carol Calladine, a Cleveland-area social worker, mother of four sons ranging in age from eight to twenty-one and co-author (with her social worker husband Andrew) of the book *Raising Siblings*, says that contracts have worked well in her own family during continuing conflicts centering on use of the stereo, family car or television or on the assignment of chores. The Calladine family has developed a special contract for use of the stereo. Drawn up and signed by each member of the family, this contract allows hour-a-day use of the stereo for each family member with a weekly sign-up sheet to ensure each person a specific daily time slot. Those who violate the terms of the contract lose use of the stereo for a week.

"Contracting is the big discipline gun in our family," Carol Calladine says. "We don't dilute it with overuse, but save it for repetitive problems or cooperation issues."

4. Give the agreed-upon compromises a fair trial. Follow your agreements for a week or two, then get together to discuss how they are working. If a solution is *not* working, you and your teen should reevaluate it and explore other possibilities. If it is working well, share your good feelings about that fact—and each other—and agree to continue.

Working out problems in this way is not easy. Your teen may resist your efforts and refuse to compromise, reverting to old behavior patterns like tantrums, sulking or retreating. In such instances, it helps to hang in there. Give your teenager a clear, firm message that these tactics will no longer work with you, that you feel angry at such behavior and that you expect him or her to meet you halfway. Given the choice between compromise or continuing conflict, a teenager will often come around.

5. Make time for each other. Working out conflicts, giving each other clear messages and getting to know each other as unique individuals takes time. Give high priority to making time to communicate with your teenager, not only about conflicts and expectations, but also about happy, positive feelings and observations. Choose communication time wisely. Trying to snag your teenager for a talk when he or she is dashing out the door to school or a date is counter-productive. You both need time to express feelings—to listen, share and really connect with each other—without one eye on the clock or the TV screen or one foot out the door. If your lives are very busy and heavily scheduled, make a date with one another, giving yourselves time without distractions or pressure to communicate.

Making time for each on a regular basis gives you a chance to share all kinds of feelings and a myriad of experiences. Sharing vulnerabilities—laughing together, crying together, enjoying good times and hanging in through the rough times—does a lot to strengthen your relationship. Seeing each other as people rather than constant adversaries aids your communication tremendously, but this takes time and many shared feelings to accomplish.

Making time to have fun together and to enjoy each other between all the pain and conflict that adolescence may bring to your family keeps your bonds strong and the lines of communication open even in the midst of a serious crisis. The memories of your good times together and your love for each other will sustain you and your teen through a lot of storms.

6. Seek help if you can't get through to each other. Cultivating good communication is often a considerable challenge and may be impossible to do without professional help, especially if your family is in a serious crisis or your teenager is extremely depressed.

"I always stress the importance of a parent establishing an open line of communication with a depressed teenager, but I do this with some hesitation," says Dr. MacKenzie. "The problem is that depressed kids usually don't like to talk much, and it may be that they will find it easier to talk with a nonparental adult: a nurse, teacher, physician, minister or counselor. You should look for outside help in order to get through to each other."

Professional help (from a phychiatrist, psychologist, social worker, family or youth counselor or clergyman) may be necessary, especially if your teen *is* severely depressed or acting out in destructive ways—with alcohol or drug abuse, for example.

"Unfortunately, there are no set rules for helping a teenager through a crisis, no seven-rule strategy for constructive coping," says Dr. Alan Berman. "It may be helpful to get therapy, to get both your teenager and yourself involved, making it clear that you're doing this because you care. It's important to realize that instant results are unlikely. It took some time for the current problems to develop and it's likely to take some time to sort things out. A professional therapist will help you explore the dynamics of your problems with each other, how these came to be and how you might begin to help and change the situation."

Whether or not you need outside help in breaking down the communication barriers you and your teenager have built up over the years, getting back in touch with each other takes time. It will be a struggle. But effective, loving communication helps *prevent* depression from becoming a major problem for your teenager and your family. Most of all, breaking down communication barriers can help you get to know, have compassion for and enjoy each other better and more often. Growing in communication skills will give you both a lifetime of rewards.

PART IV

What to Do When Your Teen Is Having School Problems

CHAPTER 11

Your Teen and School Problems

JENNIFER SIEGAL, THIRTEEN, was an excellent student in elementary school. But the picture is changing now that she is an eighth-grader at a large suburban junior high school. Her parents have noticed a major change in her attitude and in her grades this year. "She doesn't seem to care," says Myra Siegal. "She procrastinates, sleeps a lot and then frantically rushes to get assignments done at the last minute—if she does them at all. She used to be an 'A' student. Now she's just getting by. We got a notice the other day that she's close to failing two classes. I've tried to find out what problems she's having but she just says she doesn't know what's the matter. It's so frustrating because my husband and I *want* to help, but we don't know how or what to do!"

Nancy and Don McElroy are similarly frustrated and alarmed over their fourteen-year-old daughter's school phobia. "We never had any problems with Kerry before this," says Don. "But now, every morning is a crisis. Kerry has been missing school a lot this semester due to a number of things. She has a stomach-ache one morning or cramps or feels feverish or can't wake up and get herself going in time. Or she cries and screams and simply refuses to go to school. Sometimes it seems like she's terrified of going to school, but can't give any real reason for it. Nancy and I both work and this morning battle, added to our tight schedules, is truly wearing us down. If we leave before Kerry does in the morning, we *know* she won't go to school. She seems unable to cope with school, and we're less and less able to cope with her inability to cope. Frankly, we're stumped at the moment."

Carl Watson, seventeen, has also had a sudden change of attitude and behavior. A senior in high school who, until recently, was an honor student, Carl has become a habitual truant. At first, he stayed home while his divorced mother was at work and watched TV most of the day. Lately he has been going to museums and libraries. Both parents, who had hopes that Carl would attend a prestigious university, are distraught. Not long ago, his mother took Carl to a counselor to find out the reasons behind his sudden behavior change. When the counselor gently asked Carl why he was not going to school, he shrugged, stared at the floor and said he didn't know.

All three teenagers in the preceding examples have subsequently been diagnosed as depressed. The causes are not clear. They demonstrated this depression largely through school problems, quite common among adolescents.

School is one area over which the teenager has a certain amount of control. While you may control finances, family life-style and domicile, curfews and the like, a teenager has a wide range of choices regarding his or her academic career. He often chooses whether or not to achieve to the best of his ability, to work hard or not, to get into trouble at school or not. Because of this, teenagers often use school achievement or nonachievement to assert their independence and to test limits.

School is also a handy and noticeable stage for acting out. While sulking around the house may be ignored, denied or relegated to the category of normal teenage behavior by the parent, a notice from school about behavior, academic or attendance problems is usually a sure-fire parental attention-getter and a way of telling adults there's definitely something the matter even if the teenager himself isn't quite sure what the trouble might be.

Finally, school is a considerable source of stress for kids and as such may be the breaking point for a depressed teenager. Attending a huge junior high or high school may be an alienating experience. Parents and teachers expect more and more. And the teenager may have escalating self-imposed standards and expectations. School is more important to many teens than adults imagine. In fact, in his studies of teenage priorities, Dr. Aaron Hess, a psychologist at the University of California Los Angeles School of Medicine, surveyed

625 fifteen- to eighteen-year-olds and discovered that doing well in school ranked number one among boys and number two among girls. If the teenager has a learning disability, low self-esteem or emotional or family problems that make it more difficult to cope successfully with the challenges that school brings, a self-perpetuating cycle of depression and school problems can result.

What kinds of school-related problems are depressed teenagers likely to have? There are many possibilities, of course, but most fall into four general categories:

Lack of motivation: Loss of interest and momentum in school, falling grades, loss of involvement in extracurricular activities or with teachers and peers.

School phobia: A tendency to avoid school via a myriad of symptoms, crises and excuses, ranging from a constant array of physical complaints, expressed fears of peers, teachers or the school setting, crying, temper tantrums, oversleeping, sullen withdrawal and stubborn refusal to attend classes on a regular basis.

Truancy: Failure to attend classes for days or weeks at a time or dropping out altogether. Unlike the phobic teen, the habitual truant isn't afraid of school or distraught at the idea of attending. He or she just isn't interested in what school has to offer and can think of many more appealing things to do than going to classes.

Serious problems with teachers, peers and school authorities: Some troubled teenagers get into angry confrontations and fights with teachers, school officials or classmates. Or they get into trouble because of other behavior such as drug or alcohol abuse. Or they may be so withdrawn and unable to relate to those around them that this becomes a problem in itself and is certainly a symptom of a very serious depression. It is the quiet, withdrawn teenager no one notices who is most likely to commit suicide. So *not* relating to others can be as serious a symptom as fighting.

Lack of Motivation

Jennifer Siegal's dwindling interest in school and her falling grades are fairly typical of the lack of motivation that can strike adolescents in junior and senior high school. This loss of academic motivation is often due to depression.

Some nondepressed teenagers lose motivation at this time because they are suddenly overwhelmed by developmental and social changes. With their rapidly changing bodies, growing interest in the opposite sex and in being one of the gang, some teenagers don't have the energy or inclination to devote as much time to school and studies. Then, too, the changes from elementary to junior high or high school can be unsettling and overwhelming.

"They go from a small and personal elementary school to a much larger school," says educational psychologist Sarah Napier. "Suddenly, everything is depersonalized. Teachers don't know them in quite the same way. Some kids feel like a number on a roll sheet and don't quite feel that they belong."

Most adolescents, however, eventually adjust to their many life changes and are able to get back to a consistent level of academic performance after a temporary fall-off in grades and interest.

For some teenagers, loss of motivation is culturally linked. For example, despite the growth of career opportunities for women, the proliferation of new role models and rapidly changing social roles, some adolescent girls lose interest in achievement when they hit puberty, sensing that competing successfully with male classmates might be a detriment to popularity or be regarded as unfeminine. They fantasize that, despite the growing necessity of two incomes for family survival, they will be cared for and supported by a future husband, and therefore learning and achieving on their own is not particularly important. Some come from traditional one-income families and others, despite economic realities at home such as divorce or two *necessary* family incomes, have trouble imagining themselves in anything but a passive, protected role.

Others may have role models for lack of motivation at home or among others close to them. Perhaps their closest friends don't assign much importance to academic pursuits and achievements. And maybe they lack models for hard work and persistence at home.

"Some unmotivated students have parents or other close relatives with work problems," Mrs. Napier observes. "For example, there is a boy in junior high here now whose father is currently unemployed and has never had a steady job. The family gets by—either on welfare or unemployment—and this boy doesn't see why he should stay in school and work to get a diploma when that doesn't guarantee job security and when lack of academic and work credentials doesn't mean starvation."

Still other teenagers have difficulty linking current efforts with future goals—goals that seem so far away. Many classes, from algebra to history, seem to have little to do with skills a teen wants to develop or distant goals he wants to meet. And so, for a time, the adolescent may coast.

The difference between lack of motivation due to these factors and that due to depression is that the former is often quite temporary, is not accompanied by any other serious symptoms or problems in most cases and is not as drastic a departure from the youngster's previous behavior. For example, a former "A" student may slip a bit in grades and academic interest during early adolescence, but he or she is unlikely to fail a class unless overwhelmed by depression or other emotional problems.

What are some of the factors linking depression and academic problems?

Many depressed teens, of course, suffer from low self-esteem, and this impinges on their school life in a number of ways.

For the teenager with a learning disability, there is a cyclical relationship between inability to keep up with peers in some academic areas and low self-esteem and depression.

For the teenager who feels that parental love hinges on his achievements or who feels unable to live up to high family expectations, depression and feelings of anger, frustration and hopelessness cause him to lose motivation. Carl Watson, the former honor student who was habitually skipping classes, is one of these.

"As we talked, it became clear that Carl was under a lot of pressure," says counselor Laurel Moore, a staff member of the Interface Community, a counseling service in Ventura County, California. "His parents expected him to go to a prestigious college, and a wealthy aunt had offered to pay the bills. He was on the brink of change and this led to his depression. He wanted to ease into the change by going to a local junior college with his friends and keeping a part-time job he had held for several years. The idea of starting all over in an entirely new environment triggered his depression. He ended up going back to school and graduating after asking his aunt if he could take her up on her offer after completing junior college."

Ms. Moore observes that Carl's reaction to his parents' expectations was not at all unusual. "We see this a lot in counseling," she says. "Parents want very much for their children to achieve what they couldn't. We hear a lot of 'She's everything I wasn't. She has the *potential* to be so much better than I was.' This adds to the pressures already present in the teenager's life. The teens, after all, are a time when everything—a driver's license, autonomy, a good job—all seem just a little out of reach. Many teens have the fantasy that things will get better as they get older, but every year brings different privileges and pressures. In the meantime, they watch shows like *Happy Days* and wonder if that's the way adolescence is supposed to be and feel bad because they're not star athletes, cheerleaders or extremely popular."

Self-imposed pressure to fit an idealized image, the inability to reach this ideal and a tendency to link self-worth with achievement can cause an adolescent to lose motivation, burn out and sink into depression. The teenager who feels pressure to succeed *all* the time, who has few friends or outside interests and who has trouble relaxing is in danger of experiencing burn-out—dwindling motivation and effectiveness, coupled with depression.

"This teenager doesn't realize that such expectations are just not realistic," says Dr. Bruce Bongar, a clinical psychologist who teaches a class in burn-out prevention to students at UCLA. "The American Dream is to be perfect, to succeed all the time. We aren't taught how to deal with failure in spite of the fact that nobody is good in everything and we all make mistakes. Also, the student who focuses all his energies on achievement—with balancing factors like hobbies, friends, physical exercise and goofing off time not present in his life—can burn out rather quickly. You can't go 200 mph all the time. One has to stop, relax and calm down at times to break the stress cycles."

Some depressed students with falling motivation have trouble separating who they are from what they do. Dr. Barry Schwartz, a psychiatrist in Bala Cynwyd, Pennsylvania, who, with Dr. Larry Snow, conducted a five-year study of academic burn-out among medical students at the Medical College of Pennsylvania, notes that this inability to separate self from academic endeavors was a major characteristic shared by the troubled students he saw during this time.

"Feeling that you *are* your work immobilizes you," says Dr. Schwartz. "The student feels, for example, that when a paper is being graded *he* is being judged and graded. This leads to procrastination and even complete immobilization. If a student's self-worth and self-image depend on what he does, he'll end up able to do nothing. Such a teenager must realize that what he produces is something he does, but it's not him and that there are many wonderful qualities he has that can't be measured academically."

In many instances, too, a teenager's depression over personal or family problems depletes his energy and interferes with his ability to concentrate. This causes a drop in grades, activities and other achievements.

How You Can Help

If your teenager is losing interest and motivation in his or her studies, there are a number of ways that you can help.

Talk with Your Teenager in a Nonjudgmental Way

Using "I" statements, express your concern and ask for more information from your son or daughter. You might say, for example, "I feel concerned when I see your grades and your interest in school falling. I wonder if there might be some problems you are having that could be causing this to happen and if there is some way I could help you." If your teenager is willing and able to share his feelings with you, you may get some valuable clues about what is happening in his life. It could be that he is simply struggling through physical and social changes or that he dislikes a certain class or teacher. Encouraging your teen to communicate his feelings may bring some problems out into the open and, by active listening, you may be able to help him or her explore constructive alternatives.

Communicate Unconditional Love to Your Teenager

Depressed teenagers feeling pressured by high parental expectations often feel that parental love and their own personal worth are contingent on fulfilling these expectations. Expressing your love for your child and making a verbal distinction between your love for him or her personally and your pride or concern over what he or she does can help your teenager make the essential separation between who he or she is and what he or she does and to feel more valued and cherished as a whole person. Help your teenager realize that while achievements give some satisfaction, these don't serve to justify his or her existence, which, in fact, needs no justification. Help your teenager understand that he or she would still be the same person and loved just as much without top grades, honors and prizes.

Help Your Teenager Reduce Stress

This means helping your son or daughter identify and value other areas of strength—from personal qualities, interesting hobbies, creative talents and the like—that cannot be measured academically. This is especially important if your child has a learning disability or low self-esteem stemming from an inability to live up to other unrealistically high expectations. Help your teenager explore reasonable goals. Encourage him or her to get regular physical exercise and to pursue some hobbies and activities just for fun. Make sure he or she has some amount of unstructured time and is not over-scheduled. Relaxing time, friends and hobbies can be important stress reducers.

It is also helpful to communicate to your child the importance of seeing setbacks and mistakes in a new way. "The young person must learn that even when he fails at something, it is *not* the end of the world," says Dr. Bongar. "We learn from our mistakes as well as our successes. A mistake can teach you something important and in many instances it can signal a new beginning."

Encouraging your teenager to talk about fears, feelings and experiences and listening actively as he or she talks also helps reduce his or her stress level and depression. When brought out into the open and discussed, many fears lose their impact, and seemingly impossible problems turn out to have a number of alternative solutions worth exploring. Just getting some feelings off his or her chest makes a difference for the teenager, and hearing these feelings gives you a chance to clarify any misunderstandings and misconceptions and to modify your own behavior if need be. For example, a young person may be feeling guilty about what part he or she played in a parental divorce, or may be resentful about your unrealistically high expectations or unsure of your love.

Help Your Teenager Take More Control over His or Her Life

If you communicate to your teen that you really want what's best for him or her and that ultimately he or she is responsible for each choice, you will help defuse nonachievement as a potent weapon. Many teenagers, too, can't see long-range consequences of present actions. Melissa, for example, is a fourteen-year-old who talks about wanting to go to medical school but who is unwilling to go to classes now because she's bored, hates her science teacher and has no real friends.

With a teen like Melissa, a helpful approach might be to suggest that together you explore ways to change these immediate concerns. This could mean finding interesting outside pursuits or doing extra credit work if schoolwork isn't sufficiently challenging, learning to cope constructively with her science teacher (developing the knack for getting along with difficult people is an important life skill) or, if the teacher is truly impossible, switching classes or simply toughing it out.

If a teenager is discouraged because some classes seem meaningless, it helps to explore ways that such things relate to future goals and effectiveness—whether by giving one a broader understanding of human nature or by enabling one to develop necessary survival skills such as discipline, flexibility and patience. Helping your teen find the opportunities for growth that exist in unpromising classes may ease some of his or her disenchantment.

It can be helpful, too, to show interest in your teenager's long-range goals and to encourage him or her to plan for the future.

Special education instructor Mary Ann Dan has a routine she does with particularly unmotivated students to point up the importance of life planning. "I ask, 'Do you mind your mother?' and the kid says, 'No!' " she reports. "Then I ask, 'Do you mind the people at school?' Again, the student says, 'No!' Then I say, 'Write your name on this manila folder.' The kid usually likes this. Then I tell him to open the folder and then I say, 'This is your life. What are you going to do with it?' That usually starts the teenager thinking."

Putting responsibility for life planning on your teenager while offering warm support and encouragement can help a great deal. If your teen has seemingly unrealistic goals—like being a movie star or a rock idol—it is important to listen to these without disparaging them. You could react with a comment like, "That's one thing you might do. Most of us have a number of things we can do well. Let's think of some other possibilities just for the fun of it."

If your teen has very limited aspirations, a tactful lead-in to further discussion may be in order. It would be a good idea to find out her special strengths and abilities and develop certain skills to help her cope with whatever comes her way. If you keep your comments nonjudgmental and gently suggest that she take primary responsibility for setting goals, your teen will be more receptive to your ideas and your help in exploring possibilities.

Encouraging your teen to begin taking control of his or her life and to explore strengths, talents, prospects and possibilities helps a depressed teenager realize that there *is* hope, that chances for change do exist and that he or she may actually have the power—and your loving support—to make some positive changes in his or her life. This is a crucial turning point in developing motivation to cope successfully with the challenges that come his way.

"All kids make a very serious internal decision about the time they're thirteen to sixteen years old," says Mary Ann Dan. "It is a decision that they are or aren't going to be able to take care of themselves in life. The ones who decide that they *are* going to cope go to school, look forward to holding a job and learn the skills of establishing and maintaining good relationships with others. The ones I see in my classroom have decided that they are not going to care for themselves. They have fantasies of living off the land, in the woods or on welfare, usually via getting pregnant or getting a girl pregnant. Motivating teenagers to take care of themselves at this crucial age makes a great difference in their life—now and in the future."

CHAPTER 12
School Phobia

KERRY McELROY'S SUDDEN aversion to school and her frequent absences due to a variety of physical ills and emotional upsets are bewildering and frustrating to her parents, but her behavior is not unusual. In fact, it is estimated that school phobia—an irrational, persistent fear of going to school—afflicts about 1 percent of all students at some point in their academic careers.

Why does school phobia happen?

School phobia can develop as the result of severe depression, which immobilizes the teenager and makes him or her feel that he or she can't possibly cope with the pressures and challenges that school brings. It can also develop as the result of an escalation of a number of fears and stressors. These combine to make school seem an impossible burden to a shy, sensitive, insecure adolescent.

Dr. Bettie B. Youngs, an associate professor in the department of educational administration at San Diego State University, recently completed a study in which she examined common student stress factors that contribute to depression, shyness, phobias, and hostility to authority. Among the stress factors she identified and cited: fear of undressing in a group; fear of coming to terms with one's sexuality; fear of being picked first (and having to lead) or last for a team or project (which can be interpreted as being unpopular), fear of confrontations with teachers, fear of getting poor grades, fear of participating in athletics and failing, fear of being 'not O.K.' or ridiculed in the classroom when asked to speak or demonstrate, fear of peers viewing one's physical self in a negative way—as fat, skinny or ugly.

A special problem with one stressor or with a combination of these can add up to a stubborn case of school phobia. Adolescent medicine specialist Dr. Charles Wibbelsman reports that he has seen teens who break into tears and say that they can't possibly go to school or participate in gym, for example, because they are too embarrassed to undress in front of classmates. "In junior high especially there is a wide range of normal physical development and a lot of noticeable differences," he says. "These differences are very significant to adolescents and if one feels he or she is less developed than classmates, it is very threatening to undress in the locker room and expose this fact to everyone."

Some teens become disinclined to go to school in order to avoid a certain class. Kim Fisher, for example, began developing headaches and missing several days of school a week soon after beginning her sophomore year of high school. The major factor behind her school phobia seemed to be a difficult and demanding geometry teacher.

"It just got worse and worse," says her mother Mary. "She was so afraid of this nun who yelled at students if they gave wrong answers or asked questions. She didn't dare ask questions. Her fear got in the way of her understanding the class material and she wasn't doing well. She was so afraid of getting yelled at for making a mistake that she avoided going to school whenever possible, which meant that she got farther and farther behind."

Some teenagers avoid school out of fear of their peers. Linda Jamison, fourteen, whose stomach-aches have kept her out of classes a large amount of the time lately, complains that a group of girls keep chasing her and threatening to beat her up. Her parents observe that these disabling stomach-aches never hit on weekends or school holidays.

And some young people are afraid to go to school because they feel responsible for holding things together at home. Sixteen-year-old Paul Smith confessed to a school counselor that he was afraid to go to school because his alcoholic father might physically harm his mother. Another teenager—thirteen-year-old Jana Colman—expressed her fears to a concerned teacher who called her at home that if she went to school her parents, who were having marital problems, might get into a major argument and decide to divorce. This fear and her feelings of heavy responsibility for holding her family together were the major factors in Jana's school phobia.

School phobia springs from a multitude of causes and too often parents unwittingly encourage it by making special demands or by allowing their teens to stay home day after day, thus reinforcing the phobia.

How You Can Help

Even though the situation seems to be at an impasse, with your teenager either passively or actively refusing to go to school due to fear, along with physical and emotional upsets, there are a number of things that you can do to help.

Examine the Reasons Behind Your Child's Phobia

Try to communicate your concern and encourage your teenager to talk about the feelings and the fears behind this sudden school phobia.

"Try to pinpoint the problem," suggests Mrs. Napier. "Kids will offer a lot of superficial reasons like 'Someone is going to get me' or 'I got beat up' or 'People tease me,' which may not be the entire problem. Some kids have trouble dealing with the total school situation."

Getting some of the teen's fears and feelings out into the open is an important step in resolving the phobia.

Listen Actively

Give your teenager the feeling that what he or she says is important. Don't disparage, ridicule, contradict or criticize any of the fears or feelings your child expresses. They may seem irrational, but they're real and painful. Allowing your adolescent child to talk freely will defuse some of this fear and help him or her problem-solve and discover possible solutions via this "thinking out loud" process.

Help Your Teen Explore New Alternatives

Some possible alternatives might be a change in the teen's own behavior and attitudes at school or toward him- or herself.

Carol Holmby, fourteen, was reluctant to go to school because she said that everyone picked on her, made fun of her because she was tall and slightly overweight and some classmates even followed her around, teasing her until she cried. With her parents' gentle help, Carol explored ways that she could change the situation. "Since you can't directly change someone else's behavior, can you think of some things you can do to keep people off your back?" her mother asked.

"Not give them the satisfaction of seeing me get upset?" Carol suggested. Then the family discussed the fact that perhaps refusal to accept the role of victim and failure to act in predictable ways would help Carol's situation. Her father suggested that she throw her tormenters off balance by agreeing with them: "Yes, you're right. I'm fat. And you wouldn't believe how clumsy I am!" Then he suggested she might ignore them. The point was to act in an unpredictable way that would confuse her attackers, make them feel silly and not give them the satisfaction of visibly upsetting her.

Carol and her parents also discussed the fact that no one can be liked by everyone despite the unrealistic expectations and desires for universal popularity we all occasionally have. Together they made a list of important people in their lives, people they loved and valued and who returned these feelings. They also made lists of people they would like to get to know better. Carol listed three possible new friends at school and decided that cultivating these few important relationships would be very high on her priority list, with the nasty and negative people at school relegated to a less important role in her life.

Carol didn't solve all her problems through this discussion, but it was a great help in giving her the confidence to try to make changes in her way of acting and reacting at school.

Through active listening and gentle support, Richard Lawrence helped his son Mark work through his fears about undressing in the locker room. Mark, who is small and relatively undeveloped for a thirteen-year-old, seemed reassured when his father told him that he, too, had gone through these fears and feelings as a late bloomer, that late development is often genetically linked and that his stage of development was normal for him. Mark, who had been worried that he was *not* normal and would never grow and develop, was relieved to hear this and said that he felt better about his body. Having made this step, Richard and his son discussed ways that Mark might feel more comfortable about undressing for gym. Together, they came to the conclusion that this was a threatening situation for most young teens and that maybe the people who were quick to ridicule were also feeling insecure and needed to build themselves up by tearing others down. While this realization didn't make everything 100 percent O.K., Mark says that the remarks don't hurt as much now and that he is able to dismiss them much of the time. Also, since he is not reacting to them in his old, predictable way, he is a less satisfying target for the locker-room bullies.

In exploring possibilities with your teenager, be sensitive to his or her reservations. If your teenager says, "Yes, but . . ." to a suggestion or observation, be supportive of this feeling with a response like "I get the feeling that you have reservations about that suggestion. That's fine. Let's talk about these reservations and some other ideas for changing the situation for the better."

If the teenager is mired in hopelessness or anxiety, another potentially helpful approach is to say, "All right, what's the very worst that could happen? Let's weave a story together about what that might be."

Dr. Howard Newburger, a psychologist in Rye, New York, uses this approach in an exercise he calls "Flooding," and he reports that it has good results in many instances. "If a teenager is afraid to go to class because he might be called on to speak and then get up and say something stupid or wrong, you can piece together a fantasy of the very worst that could happen," says Dr. Newburger. "Let's say that the teenager gives an obviously wrong answer in class. Everyone laughs and jeers. The teacher is so overcome that she rushes from the classroom to tell the principal about the teen's incredibly stupid remark. The principal makes an announcement over the PA system for an immediate all-school assembly where the unfortunate student is asked to repeat his remark for the entire student body and faculty to hear. They all jeer and laugh at him for the rest of the day. By late afternoon, a TV news film crew arrives on the scene and wire services are calling to get a direct quote. The next day, his dumb remark is a banner headline—with his most unflattering school picture underneath—in *The New York Times*.

Obviously this fantasy is ridiculous, but when carried to an extreme like this, it helps to put things in perspective. The teen will realize that this can't happen and that any embarrassing situation he experiences won't come close to this catastrophe."

It also helps to work on bolstering your child's self-esteem, making him or her feel good about himself as an intrinsically worthwhile human being. A number of teens with school phobia lack the self-esteem and confidence to tackle problems and challenges and, instead, feel overwhelmed by them.

Intervene with Care

There is a fine line between constructively intervening in a problem situation (e.g., a difficult teacher) as a necessary advocate for your child and undermining your child's self-esteem by taking over his problems and perhaps making them worse through your intervention. Before you make the decision to intervene, seek as much information as you can from your teenager and try active listening and problem solving together. If one teacher has a difficult, abrasive personality, it might be more useful if you listened with empathy to your teenager's complaints and then encouraged him or her to find ways to coexist with this difficult person. Learning to cope with someone who is demanding and perhaps a bit irrational can be a valuable life skill. On the other hand, if the teacher continues to be an overwhelming problem and is doing real harm—emotionally, academically or even physically—it may be best to step in and give your child a hand. Schedule a low-key, information-gathering conference with the teacher. If this proves unsatisfactory, talk with your child's counselor or with the principal.

In many cases you can help most by allowing your teen to fight his or her own battles—with your warm and constant support.

Encourage Your Teenager to Overcome the Phobia

Counseling and psychotherapy can be quite helpful to your teen in conquering the school phobia. Family therapy, which may uncover and resolve some of the underlying conflicts which contribute to your teen's school phobia, is also a good idea. Don't encourage such behavior by allowing the child to stay home regularly or for long periods of time. This only reinforces the phobia and makes it more difficult than ever for the teenager to return to school. Your patience, supportiveness and firm encouragement for the child to attend school at least part of every day will help a great deal.

When Cynthia Bachman's daughter Rachel sank into a deep depression that triggered an attack of school phobia, Cynthia discovered that a firm day-by-day, little-by-little approach worked best.

"During this time Rachel went to school only because I took her there," she recalls. "Every morning, I would go into her room, wake her up and, as if she were a five-year-old, pick out her clothes, feed her breakfast and drive her to school. I would drive her to school and back—some days as often as six times. She would call me, ask to be picked up and I would bring her home, talk with her and encourage her to go back and try just one more class. We wanted her to attend as many classes as she possibly could to have *some* normal functioning in her life. Gradually, she was able to stay longer and longer at school."

Some school districts handle school phobia in much the same way. "I've seen kids with school phobia who were deeply depressed, who would vomit at the thought of going to school and who might even run temperatures every school-day morning," says Sarah Napier. "We try to help them adjust by giving them shorter school days for awhile and by burdening them with fewer expectations. Some, who can't even leave their homes, qualify for home teaching for a time. Last year we had a few like this and now all are back at school. For most school phobics, however, we try to get them out of the house and into a special school setting for a while. Or we get them in school for only two periods a day with the idea that they will gradually increase the number of class periods in time or participate in work experience programs. Our main aim is to get the teenager out of the house and doing something—however minimal it may be."

Enlist the Aid of Your Child's Teachers

In many cases, school officials and teachers are valuable allies and advocates and may guide you toward special programs and support services as well as lending much-needed support during this trying time.

"When Rachel was having so much trouble with school phobia, I went to her guidance counselor and all her teachers and let them know about her problem," says Cynthia Bachman. "They were all wonderful to both Rachel and me. All said that this was not unusual, that they had seen the problem before in other students. That really surprised me. I had thought we were the only ones. Suddenly, I didn't feel that we were all alone—and that helped a lot."

CHAPTER 13

Truancy and Other Serious Problems in School

ALTHOUGH SCHOOL PHOBICS and truants both miss classes constantly, and suffer from depression and a myriad of other family and emotional problems, there is a significant difference between the school phobic and the habitual truant. The phobic is afraid to go to school. The truant doesn't want to go and will not go to school for any number of reasons.

Carl Watson's truant behavior—an attempt to escape the pressures of high parental expectations—is only one example of the many possible factors behind truancy.

A recent report from the California Assembly Office of Research revealed that California's truancy and dropout rate among twelve- to seventeen-year-olds is about three times the national average. While pregnancy and marriage were cited as significant factors in truancy and school dropouts, reasons most often given by students for truancy included dislike or boredom with school, family or personal problems, academic problems, difficulties with social adjustment and the influence of friends.

Those experienced with counseling truant teenagers agree that these are all significant factors.

"Some kids feel that school has nothing to offer and have friends who are also truant or who have dropped out," says Sarah Napier. "Some kids are overwhelmed by the pressures and expectations at school and simply can't cope."

141

And Corbett Phibbs, a Westlake, California, family therapist who directs a special "T-Program" to help truant students and their families, feels that there is frequently a link between problems at home and trouble at school. In fact, he notes, trouble at school can be an early clue to masked conflicts within the family. "The actual causes of pain within a family system are almost never observable by the family members themselves," he says. "These problems are also rarely the ones the family believes they have. Often, a child's destructive behavior has a very logical purpose, and in therapy I focus on teaching the family new ways to meet such purposes."

Control is a frequent source of family conflict, with school being the only area of life where the adolescent feels he or she has some measure of control. Parents are relatively helpless in keeping a teenager from flunking or skipping classes. "This is a very effective way to gain power, even if it is self-destructive in the long run," says Phibbs.

How You Can Help

What can you do if your teenager is truant or in continual trouble at school? There are a number of ways that you can help—and get help.

Be Open to All Alternatives

Although laws requiring school attendance up to a certain age vary by state, parents are usually notified and asked to cooperate in helping keep an underage child in school after attendance has become a problem.

If your teenager is truant or disruptive in classes, there are a number of alternatives for help. You may find special help via school-based programs, through outside agencies and through private counseling or therapy.

Some parents find it difficult to deal with the reality that their teenagers are having serious problems with school and require special services. "I was a highly motivated student all through high school, college and graduate school," says Sheila Hansen, the mother of a fourteen-year-old girl with a history of truancy. "My husband is a physician and also very goal oriented. It was very hard to accept the idea of our daughter attending any but traditional college prep classes. We've always wanted the best for her, educationally and every other way."

For a time, however, the best for your troubled teenager may be some form of alternative education. "With truant students, our object is to pinpoint their problems and keep them in school—or get them back to school," says Sarah Napier. "We try to get troubled kids involved in sports, special after-school activities or to develop special interests. This helps them a lot, even if there are tremendous problems at home."

Many school districts offer alternative or continuation programs that enable teens with attendance problems to stay in school and complete requirements for a high school diploma. Some of these special programs, which vary from state to state and district to district, include the following types of programs.

Work-Study Programs. Work-study programs combine shortened academic class days with work experience carrying academic credit. Often this means that the students spend half a day in the classroom and half a day on the job.

Special Classes. Alternative, night and special classes allow students to progress toward a diploma at an individualized pace. For the very depressed school-phobic teenager, this means temporary home teaching or a shortened school day, lighter class load and lowered stress and expectations. For a student who wants to work full time, night classes mean that he or she can work *and* get a high school diploma. For a student with special needs—for example, a pregnant teenage girl—many school districts have special classes or alternative schools for young mothers and mothers-to-be, combining academic work with training in practical concerns like nutrition and child care. Many offer on-the-premises day care so that these teens can finish high school. (Pregnancy is a major cause of teenage girls dropping out of junior high and high school.)

School Furlough. School furlough programs give students academic credit for working, with no class attendance required for a specified amount of time. In such a program in the Los Angeles school district, a student draws up a contract specifying what he or she plans to do during the furlough, which can last up to a year. If the plan is approved, he or she is allowed to take the furlough. The only academic demands during this time are regular meetings, about one a month, with a school counselor and a report at the end of the year. This report is evaluated by school personnel for graduation credit.

A new study of the Los Angeles program's early years of operation has revealed that after the first year of operation, 60 percent of the furloughed students returned to regular classes, and another 50 percent of the rest returned to regular school after the second year. Many educators in the program believe that it has been successful in getting dropouts or potential dropouts reinvolved with school.

Independent Study Programs. These are similar to furlough, work-study or alternative school programs. In 1976, for example, the California state legislature created an independent study program as an alternative to regular classroom study for students from kindergarten to twelfth grade. The major focus of the program was on high school dropouts or truants, but it has been utilized by students with psychological or medical problems and those with special career interests or talent in the arts or sports (e.g., competitive ice skating, ballet, music and the like). There has been some criticism of the program, which varies widely from district to district, primarily because some districts don't monitor students' progress adequately. More stringent guidelines are planned for the future with the hope that better, more uniform management will increase the program's effectiveness and its use throughout the state. (At present, some California school districts shy away from administering the program as prescribed by law because of the management problems.) In school districts using the program, participating students may attend school for a few hours each week or have special academic tutoring in a work setting. In one school district, teens studying for careers in ballet have short, intensive academic classes every day at the ballet school where they train. The school districts are trying to give talented, motivated teenagers—as well as disenchanted, depressed potential dropouts—a chance to finish high school *and* pursue their work and career goals.

Early Graduation. Early graduation opportunities offer students a chance to finish high school ahead of schedule and get out into the work force or into special vocational programs, or to go to college early.

While this concept, which involves taking a special proficiency exam to earn an early diploma, may appeal to many school-hating students or habitual truants, it is primarily aimed at the motivated, better-than-average student. Only a few states offer this option, and requirements vary. In Florida, the test is generally considered not too difficult, but the California test is another matter. The first year it was given, only 30 percent of those taking it passed. Now only students with better-than-average skills tend to try the test, and slightly over half of these manage to pass. A California state official explains that "the test was designed as a law-abiding way to freedom for motivated students." Students electing this alternative generally go on to work or to college. A number of other states are currently considering similar tests as an alternative for able, possibly bored, students desiring an early exit from high school.

If your teenager is bright but bored and is having problems staying in high school because of this, another alternative might be seeking more challenge by earning advanced college credit while still in high school or starting college early. A student can qualify for advanced placement (cutting the time and money he'll spend in college) by taking college-credit courses at high school or at a cooperating local college. Advanced Placement Examinations of the College Level Examination Program (CLEP) are other ways to get college credit in advance.

It is also possible for your academically talented but bored teenager to combine the last year of high school with the first year of college. In order to do this, during junior year he or she must apply for the program to one of the more than two thousand colleges across the nation that accept outstanding high school seniors as freshmen. Generally, your son or daughter will earn a high school diploma and one year of college credit at the end of that year.

To explore these and other alternatives further, you and your teenager might check with your child's school advisor or principal.

Other Programs and Options. In addition to school-based assistance programs for troubled students, there are a number of special services offered by community agencies and counseling organizations.

The "T-Program" in Westlake Village, California, is offered by the California Family Study Center and directed by Corbett Phibbs, a family therapist. It is specifically designed for truant teenagers and their families and is structured as a sequence of eighteen hours of family counseling, communication classes and student group counseling that helps provide information, experiences and skills to deal with truancy and related student problems. The first phase of the program offers four one-hour family counseling sessions, with all family members encouraged to participate. In these sessions, family communication barriers are explored and new communication skills practiced. Phase two is a continuation of communication skill building. In three two-hour classes for teens and their parents, assertiveness training and clear communication are the primary subjects. Finally, students participate in four peer group sessions, working with other teens to solve individual problems. Many of the graduates of this program (and similar ones) report that developing new communication skills has made an enormous difference in their lives—and in their teenagers' school attendance.

At The Bridge, a Burbank, California, center focused on helping teenagers who are in trouble at school or with the law, family and individual counseling is, once again, a key element. In addition, teens who are unwilling to attend school or who have been expelled attend a three-month "Survival Skills Training" course that meets five mornings or afternoons a week. This course combines counseling with teaching academic and social skills. The object of developing such skills is to increase self-confidence, motivation and the adolescent's ability to cope. Students are expected to return to school or go to work after completing the course.

In the course academic skills are given practical applications. For example, students practice math by totaling grocery prices, or hone writing skills by working on a job resume or application letter. This emphasis on positive, practical skills is very effective with truant or reluctant students, educators report.

"Our truancy officer builds a good rapport with the kids and gets them back to school by emphasizing their need for practical skills," says Sarah Napier. "He helps them see the need for learning how to fill out a job application and balance a checkbook. I remember one boy who returned to school recently *only* because he wanted to learn how to handle money and how to write a check. That desire to learn got him back. Now his interests have broadened and he is newly interested in school, seeing more of a practical purpose to many of his classes."

Besides school-sponsored alternatives or outside agency programs geared toward helping the truant or troubled student, it is helpful to keep other options in mind. For example, if your teenager is having difficulty dealing with authority and gets into constant trouble at school (fights with teachers or peers, or is detained or expelled for disrupting classes, being drunk or stoned in school, etc.), the hostility toward others may be symptomatic of emotional problems best helped by private psychotherapy as well as family therapy. (See chapter 29 for a discussion of the various types of professional help available and the Appendix for information about where to find these in your community.)

Jimmy Lyons, a fourteen-year-old ninth-grader, started having problems at school two years ago. He was belligerent and defiant to teachers and constantly disrupted classes with his clowning and joking around. Detentions and suspensions did little to discourage him. Finally, Jimmy's parents were convinced to seek psychotherapy for him. As a result, Jimmy's low self-esteem, rage and fright, as well as his depression over a myriad of family problems, came to light. The whole family became involved in the therapy, which is ongoing. The family's problems are severe, and there is no quick cure for these or for Jimmy's feelings and behavior. But his teachers report that the disruptive episodes have decreased considerably and that Jimmy is no longer hostile to school authority figures.

If your teenager has problems coping with school or relating to others due to extreme shyness and feelings of being lost in a huge school, psychotherapy or counseling with an emphasis on assertiveness training may be helpful. Another possibility: switch to a smaller, more personal school experience, such as a private school or a public alternative school program. While it is important for a teenager to learn to cope with stressful, competitive situations, being in a more personal setting for a time will help the extremely timid student build a stronger base of self-esteem and self-confidence.

Contracting

Regular attendance at school is probably one of the major expectations you have for your teenager. You should make your teen aware of your expectations and establish firm guidelines.

Donna and Sam Wilson, for example, developed a contract with their fifteen-year-old daughter Suzanne to put a stop to her pattern of truancy. During a family meeting, Suzanne told her parents that she felt she had no say about how she spent her time, and she was convinced that her parents' expectations that she make top grades were unrealistic. Instead of fighting a futile battle to meet these expectations, and in an effort to get free, unstructured time of her own, Suzanne had been skipping classes several days a week.

As a result of this discussion, the Wilsons drew up a contract stating that as long as Suzanne took the responsibility to attend school regularly and do the best she could, her parents would not pressure her to make the honor roll and would allow her to structure her time as she pleased if homework and household chores got done. The arrangement has worked very well for them over the past year. "We switched our expectations from requiring our daughter to be outstanding to expecting her to take responsibility for going to school and doing the required work," says Donna Wilson. "By lowering our expectations but stating what we *did* expect of her clearly, firmly and *on paper,* we ended up with more. Suzanne goes to school and is doing just fine. And as a family, we have far fewer conflicts now."

Deemphasize School Attendance As a Control Issue

As discussed earlier, school is often the stage for adolescent acting out because it is one of the few areas where teenagers feel they have a fair amount of control, and they use this control to fight back with parents who are overcontrolling them.

By making clear to your adolescent that school attendance is his or her responsibility and that he or she will have to face the consequences of not meeting this responsibility, you decrease the appeal of nonattendance at school as an acting out alternative.

It is important *not* to take on the task of lying for or covering up for your truant teenager. A number of parents do this against their better judgment because they hate to see their teens get into trouble with school authorities. However, such covering up simply reinforces the truant behavior and shelters the adolescent from its consequences. It is more constructive to let your teen get a taste of trouble and learn from this experience. This does not mean, of course, that you should not be supportive and concerned when your teenager is troubled and having difficulties at school. It simply means that you will help most if you avoid assuming the role of accomplice to his or her truancy—by writing notes excusing his absences or by otherwise covering up and reinforcing his behavior.

In some instances, it is best to let your teenager work out school attendance problems with a third party while you stay out of the discussion altogether, giving up the control for this area of your child's life and handing it over to your child and a counselor. This is a good alternative if control is a volatile issue between you and your child.

Melinda Robbins, for example, is a brilliant business executive with a forceful personality. She is divorced and the mother of Stephanie, fifteen, who suffers from low self-esteem and the inability to get up and go to school most mornings. Stephanie's school counselor suggested psychotherapy with a therapist who is particularly skilled in working with adolescents. One of the first suggestions he made after seeing Stephanie for the first time was that the issue of going to school become a matter that he and Stephanie would work with and that, for a specified period of time, Melinda would not raise the issue at all with her daughter.

"At first, I was quite dubious," Melinda says. "I thought she would stay home vegetating the rest of her life if I didn't nag her out of bed every morning. At first, that seemed to be the case. I think she was testing me to see if I would break my part of the bargain, which was to stay off her case about school. Gradually, though, things started to change. With the help of her counselor and some very supportive people at school, Stephanie started feeling better about herself, became more assertive and started going to school regularly. Strangely enough—or not so strangely, perhaps —we're experiencing some rough times. Before, the only way she could fight back with me (I'll admit that I'm a demanding, difficult person at times) was in a passive way, by not going to school and achieving in the way I expected her to. Now she is confronting me more directly on issues and we are arguing more. But nevertheless, we are communicating better and I admire her for standing up for herself. I feel proud of her, even when I secretly want to wring her neck for disagreeing with me or confronting me on an issue. And most of all I'm happy that she is no longer hurting herself by using truancy as a weapon. That progress came after I got off her back and let Steph and her counselor work things out. It wasn't easy for me to do, but I'm pleased with the results."

Take an Interest in Your Child's School

In these days of two-career families with many competing interests, parental involvement in school activities seems to be declining. However, your interest and involvement in your child's school may help rekindle your teen's own interest as well and give the feeling that you consider him or her—and this area of his or her life—important.

Make an effort to attend school plays, sports events, parent-teacher conferences and open houses, and become involved in parental activities related to the school. As an investment of your time, this can bring many rewards.

Know Your Rights and Be an Advocate for Your Child

By becoming involved, knowing your child's teachers and knowing your rights, you can help keep serious school problems from developing or you can help your child if there is trouble.

"By cultivating good relationships within the school setting and by knowing your teenager's friends' parents, you can get feedback from others about early symptoms of trouble so that you can help your teenager before his problems reach the crisis stage," says Mary Ann Dan. "Some schools will give you feedback and some won't. It depends a great deal on the teachers. Some are very helpful. Also, when it comes to dealing with school bureaucracies, a kid may need a parent to troubleshoot."

Troubleshooting may mean having a low-key information-gathering conference with an allegedly troublesome teacher if problems with that class seem to cause a great deal of pain, depression or school phobia in your child. It may mean gaining access to your child's school records to get an erroneous, potentially harmful notation removed. It may mean meeting with your child's counselor, teachers and other school officials to determine the best alternatives when trouble develops.

A number of parents have difficulty being effective and assertive within the school bureaucracy. You may be plagued by ghosts from your own academic past that caution you not to make waves. You may be stalled and frustrated by indifference, hostility or bureaucratic clichés like "that's not our policy" or "that's not the way we do things." Knowing the rules and your rights will make your advocacy easier and more effective.

"Find out how the school operates," suggests Ms. Dan. "Do they notify you after your child's third absence? Never? Would they be cooperative if you call in to check if your child is at school? Who might be a good in-school advocate for your child? Many parents assume that it is the child's guidance counselor, but this may not be the case. Counselors these days are overburdened. If your child's counselor is new and young, he or she may be a good ally. It's important to find the good guys within the school setting, such as an especially interested, involved teacher who can help your child. Also, encourage your child to tell you when he is in trouble. If there is a problem with one class and one teacher, your empathetic listening and gentle guidance—helping your child to see that some teachers do fall quite a bit short of the ideal but can be coped with—may be all your child needs. On the other hand, in serious matters you may be needed to troubleshoot. That's where knowing the school rules, who the good guys are and your rights as a parent come in handy."

Knowing your rights will help you get past bureaucratic clichés and red tape, Ms. Dan insists. "Know the law regarding class schedules, suspension and the like for your state," she says. "For example, in California a kid can legally take only four class periods a day and cannot be suspended for more than twenty days. The school may have its rules or offer you the standard 'But we don't do it that way here.' That's not a good reason. It's important for you to be knowledgeable and assertive enough to know what the *law* says."

Such knowledge has served a number of parents and students well. One mother, knowing that a 1974 federal law gives parents the right to examine their children's school records, was able to gain access to and correct an erroneous notation that her daughter had been arrested once for shoplifting, a rumor that had made its way onto her permanent school record. The mother, who had learned of the notation from a teacher, was initially refused access to the records. When she came back, armed with knowledge and proof of the federal law, she found that this law was news to the principal and she was allowed to see the records and correct the mistake.

Other important laws include a 1975 Supreme Court decision stating that minors cannot be expelled from school without due process and recognizing the right of parents in all states to take legal action against a school official if a child has been disciplined with 'excessive or unreasonable' physical force.

In many states a parent has a right to appeal an administrator's decision to place his or her child in a class for students labeled disruptive or troublesome.

There are a number of sources of information about your rights as a parent and the law regarding your child as a student. Two of the best sources are *You Can Improve Your Child's School,* by

William Rioux (Simon and Schuster, $12.95), and Rioux's National Committee for Citizens in Education. This organization will send you a free guide to Parent-Teacher Conferences and a Parent Rights Card (printed in either English or Spanish), listing twenty-one rights you have as the parent of a child in public school. These rights—granted by federal or state laws, court decisions and regulations prior to late 1980—cover four general areas: student discipline, student instruction, student records and other rights.

To get your free card and guide, send a self-addressed, stamped business-size (#10) envelope to:

National Committee For Citizens in Education
410 Wilde Lake Village Green
Columbia, Md. 21044

If your child is having problems at school, it's important to listen to feedback from teachers and school officials and consider their suggestions. "Some parents acknowledge that the child has a problem but want us to fix the child rather than seek help and work things out with the aid of a counselor," says Sarah Napier. "Others overreact to school problems or failures. I always try to reassure them by saying, 'Hey, your child is *not* bad. You just don't like some of his behavior.' If school personnel come to you with a problem, be willing to listen and talk about it and what can be done."

Some parents, beleaguered by teenagers with continuing school problems, can't imagine that any alternative will help matters. "This 'why bother?' attitude only reinforces the problem," says Mrs. Napier. "Some kids say, 'My parents have written me off, so why bother to change?' But I believe that in most instances there *is* a solution to a teenager's problem with school. The solutions and changes may not be instantaneous, but they can make a difference. I tell distressed parents, 'We *can* make a change. It may not be a great one. It may not be tomorrow. But, at this point, any change will help and it *can* happen.'"

Helping your troubled teenager overcome problems at school can be a slow, frustrating and frequently painful experience. You may need all the support—from school or family counselors, psychotherapists, teachers and other school officials—that you can get.

But trouble at school is a positive development when it functions as an early signal that all is not well with your teenager and you pick up this signal and act on it. If you are aware, informed, involved and open to all alternatives for help, school problems will provide you with an opportunity to assist your teenager early on and in a vital area of life. Offer your child your own special, caring help in coping with the stresses that school can bring, and you will enable your teenager to grow and develop resilience and independence—while ensuring a brighter future.

PART V

Medical Problems and Teenage Depression

CHAPTER 14

When Your Child Has Depression-Linked Symptoms or Medical Conditions

WHEN THE MACDONALDS moved from an urban to suburban setting their popular, active and outgoing fifteen-year-old Casey developed with a variety of symptoms: fatigue, stomach pains, loss of appetite and insomnia. At first her parents were alarmed and took her to the family doctor for a checkup. However, when medical tests failed to uncover any organic causes for Casey's physical complaints, her parents became baffled and annoyed by her continuing distress.

"They say I'm a hypochondriac," Casey says sadly. "Maybe I am, except I'm *not* faking this. I really *do* feel bad—honest. My stomach hurts real bad right now. So I know it isn't just all in my head like my Dad says it is."

At this time last year, Gina Lupi was slightly overweight and occasionally prone to cake, cookie and pretzel feasts. Then a gym teacher made a casual remark about the fact that, with a five- or ten-pound weight loss, Gina would look terrific and be in great shape. So Gina started a diet with an important difference: she stuck to it. At first her parents were pleased. Then Gina began to subsist on two lettuce leaves and a pickle a day, and to exercise frenetically every minute she wasn't studying or sleeping. Finally, when she shriveled down to seventy-eight pounds (while still insisting that she was a bit too heavy), her parents became genuinely alarmed. They finally convinced Gina to see a physician, who recognized her symptoms immediately as signs of anorexia nervosa, an eating disorder characterized by compulsive self-starvation. While the disorder may involve a number of factors, depression can play a major role in the development and progression of the disease. Frank Austin's diabetes was first diagnosed when he was ten. Once he and his parents adjusted to the dietary and life-style requirements that go along with successful management of the disease, things went smoothly—for a while. Now that Frank is fourteen, his diabetes and its management have become a central issue in family conflicts and in his growing depression. Frank accuses his parents of treating him like a kid when they try to help him manage his schedule of insulin injections, snacks and meals. And he fights back by refusing to keep on his schedule and by eating forbidden foods. His actions also show some evidence of denial—denial of the fact that his medical problem makes him a bit different in some respects. This fact is a very painful one for Frank. He wants to be one of the gang—to eat junk food, drink beer and eat when he feels like it instead of when he has to, to be free of urine testing, insulin injections, doctor visits and parental hassles. He fears that the difference diabetes makes in his life will keep him from living a full and normal life forever. Frank was particularly distressed when he read in a magazine article that diabetes can be a factor in impotence. He wonders if his disease will keep him from having a normal sex life— or *any* sex life. But this concern isn't something he feels he can bring up with his parents or even his physician, and so his depression and sense of isolation is deepening.

Casey, Gina and Frank are only three of thousands of teenagers suffering from a combination of physical and emotional ills. The mind-body link is a fascinating one and is receiving an increasing amount of attention in medical circles these days. Researchers are examining the link between stress or other emotional problems and physical illness, tracing susceptibility, disease progress and survival patterns in a variety of physical illnesses from the common cold to lupus to cancer.

One of the most famous studies on the correlation between stress and susceptibility to physical illness was conducted by Dr. Thomas H. Holmes III, professor of psychiatry at the University of Washington. The study resulted in the Holmes Scale, a stress-rating scale assigning points to both positive and negative life changes (from a death in the family to marriage, starting or leaving school, taking a vacation or enjoying outstanding personal achievement). Dr. Holmes has concluded that if a person scores 300 or more change points in a year, he or she has an 80 percent chance of experiencing a change of health. And since all change—both positive and negative—carries stress points, these points add up fast.

In an ongoing two-year study at Stanford University Medical Center, Dr. Gordon Pulford, a clinical professor of pediatrics, developed a stress scale especially for teenagers, assigning 78 stress points for marriage (at such a young age), 108 points for the death of a parent, 70 for a parental divorce and 39 for either a romantic breakup *or* for being accepted by the college of one's choice. Again, a total of 300 points or more is seen to be linked quite often with the development of physical problems.

In another study, this one by the Division of Adolescent Medicine at Montefiore Hospital and Medical Center in New York, physicians discovered that 30 percent of the teenagers coming in to the adolescent clinic for treatment of physical complaints were also suffering from underlying depression, which was detected through special testing.

The mind-body connection between emotions and physical ailments is particularly strong and troublesome in adolescence. There are a number of reasons why this is so.

First, faced with the dramatic and rapid body changes that puberty brings, teenagers are strongly focused on their bodies. "Being different or being in pain makes it particularly difficult for a teenager to cope," says Dr. Lonnie Zeltzer, a physician with the Division of Adolescent Medicine at the University of Texas Health Service Center at San Antonio. "Teenagers are so aware of their bodies and so worried about being normal. When they feel pain, they may panic and have a lot of anxiety about this being something serious, even fatal."

And defects, deviations, handicaps or physical illnesses can hit teenagers hard emotionally, often causing a poor body image and depression.

Second, adolescence is a time of strong and conflicting emotions: love and anger, a growing need for independence coupled with a yearning to cling and be protected by parents and strong new sexual urges countered by guilt—to name just a few. These conflicting feelings are stressful, often difficult to identify and impossible for some teens to express directly. So quite often the body does the speaking, signaling repressed feelings and conflicts through a variety of psychosomatic complaints.

These complaints are also a way of staying close and retaining a measure of dependence while growing toward adulthood and independence. "Being sick can be a binding thing that keeps the teenager tied to parents," says Dr. Marilyn Mehr. "And if illness is the only time the teenager receives attention and love from the parents, the body may signal what the mind is saying ('I need love!') via physical symptoms."

Third, the rapid growth that takes place in adolescence may cause physical and emotional depletion that can be a factor in depression.

The mind-body link shows itself in a number of ways. Depression or stress can trigger physical symptoms like headaches, stomach pains, fatigue and sleep disorders such as insomnia, with the body expressing feelings and conflicts that the teen is unable to verbalize. Depression can be a factor, too, in causing or intensifying certain physical problems like eating disorders (from anorexia nervosa to compulsive overeating) or asthma, lupus and other chronic disorders. It is also not uncommon for a physical condition such as diabetes, epilepsy, scoliosis or a physical handicap to be a major factor in a teenager's depression.

Symptoms and Conditions That May Be Triggered or Intensified by Depression

Physical Symptoms

The impact of depression and stress on your teenager's health may show in a number of ways. Have you noticed recently that your teenager has been

- Particularly susceptible to colds?
- Suffering from more headaches than usual?
- Listless, fatigued and sleeping a lot?
- Unable to sleep at night?
- Complaining about stomach pains?
- Suffering from frequent diarrhea or alternating bouts of constipation and diarrhea?
- Losing—or dramatically gaining—in appetite and weight?

If so, emotional conflicts may be a key factor. Some of the most frequently observed depression-linked physical symptoms include the following.

Fatigue. Maybe your previously alert and active teen has hit a slump and spends most of his or her time at home sleeping or lounging listlessly. Perhaps he or she complains of low energy, feelings of weakness and a sense of being tired all the time, no matter how much sleep he or she gets. And maybe your teen is completely immobilized by fatigue, unable to function in normal day-to-day ways. If so, depression is one of a number of possible causes to be considered.

"I've had a number of teenagers come in to see me complaining of fatigue and excessive sleeping," says Dr. Charles Wibbelsman. "They often come in saying, 'I think I have mono,' or 'I must be anemic or something.' That could be. But often, the teenager doesn't have any underlying medical problem. Yet he or she is tired all the time and sleeps twelve to fourteen hours a day. When a physical disease is not present, this fatigue could well be a sign of underlying depression."

Sleep Disorders. Depression can disturb sleep patterns in people of all ages, but it shows up in special ways among depressed teens. While a depressed adult may fall asleep at night with little difficulty, he or she may be plagued by early awakening in predawn hours, unable to get back to sleep. A depressed teenager, on the other hand, usually suffers from insomnia.

"A change of sleep patterns is a very common sign of depression in teenagers," says Dr. Richard MacKenzie. "Some teens (I've noticed this particularly in teenagers who are also suffering from anorexia nervosa) stay up all night and then sleep during the day."

Vague Aches and Pains. The depressed teenager may experience painful emotions through physical discomfort, complaining of annoying pain in a number of body areas. "Low back pain, in particular, may be tied to depression," Dr. MacKenzie observes.

Stomach Pains and Disorders. "The gastrointestinal tract, most notably the stomach and intestines, is quite easily affected by the emotions," says Dr. Wibbelsman. "It may take a stomach-ache, diarrhea or more alarming symptoms to point out to parents just how tense, depressed, frightened or angry the teenager is feeling."

Gastritis, the secretion of excess acid in the stomach, can occur as the result of tension and anxiety. This excess acid begins to digest the stomach lining, causing pain and heartburn and may lead to an ulcer.

Diarrhea can be another sign of emotional distress. "We see this quite often around exam times when teens are nervous about school performance," says Dr. Wibbelsman. "This condition can spring from anxiety or poor diet and frequently is due to a combination of the two."

Another condition with a possible link to emotions is colitis or spastic colon. It may be signaled by alternating bouts of diarrhea and constipation, pain, nausea, heartburn and a feeling of faintness. Ulcerative colitis, a potentially serious condition found primarily in young people, occurs when ulcers develop in the colon and the walls of the colon become inflamed and diseased. Symptoms of ulcerative colitis include cramps, bloody stools, diarrhea and painless rectal bleeding. A number of factors contribute to the development of this disease, but emotional stresses—depression and anxiety among them—play a major role in causing or aggravating this disease.

Headaches. Headaches are very common among depressed teenagers, especially teenage girls. "This may be because girls are particularly prone to internalize their feelings, to hold in their anger and depression," says Dr. Mehr.

Dr. Merilee Oaks observes that headaches are particularly common among a group of teenage girls she is encountering in her work at the Adolescent Clinic at Children's Hospital of Los Angeles. "I'm seeing a group of teenage girls of Latin origin and they have a lot of psychosomatic symptoms in connection with anger and depression," she says. "These girls are caught in a cultural conflict. They are growing up in the freedom of the American culture while living in families with repressive Old World parents and grandparents. These girls don't know how to fight back or express themselves because their families' cultural mores say that you must *not* argue with elders. So they have a lot of headaches. I've seen even *daily* migraine headaches among these girls. Underlying these headaches is a lot of anger and depression about being in a situation where the teen sees no way out until adulthood."

While headaches come from a number of physical causes including sinus infections, dental problems, allergies, high blood pressure, skipping a meal or smoking too much and, rarely, from a brain tumor, chronic headaches often result from a combination of physical and psychological factors. Feelings, including depression, can be involved in a number of different kinds of headaches—including tension, psychogenic or migraine headaches.

Tension headaches, stemming most often from anxiety and tense shoulder and neck muscles, are signaled by throbbing pain felt at the front or sides of the skull. A tension headache is often relieved by aspirin or other over-the-counter pain killers and rest.

Psychogenic headaches, which involve tense muscles in the face, head and neck, often stem from depression and feel like a tight band circling the head. These headaches tend to strike early in the morning and are usually seen in combination with other signs of depression such as sleep disorders. Pain relievers, emotional support and professional help may be needed in order to combat these headaches.

Migraine headaches (also called vascular headaches) are severe and may be triggered by:

- Hormonal changes—they usually occur for the first time in girls around the time of puberty and may occur more frequently around the time of the menstrual period.
- Environmental factors—smoke-filled rooms, bright sunlight, heavy traffic and gasoline fumes, etc.
- Life-style and eating habits—irregular sleep patterns, eating foods such as cheese, lima beans, pork, Chinese food with MSG and chocolate, or drinking alcohol which may stimulate the affected blood vessels.
- Emotional stress—especially when caused by repressed anger, frustration and depression.

There are a number of different kinds of migraine headaches. The two most common are classic and common migraines. In the classic variety, the victim experiences an aura—flashing lights or colors or spots before the eyes—or mood changes before the headache pain strikes. In common migraine, the aura may not be present, but the characteristic migraine symptoms are there: pain on one side of the head, throbbing initially and then becoming steady and unrelenting; sensitivity to light and noise; nausea and, in some instances, dizziness and loss of balance.

These headaches may be treated in a number of ways, often with a combination of prescription painkillers, dietary and life-style changes, biofeedback and stress management techniques and perhaps psychotherapy to enable the teen to express rather than repress feelings.

Why Do Teens Express Emotional Pain with Physical Symptoms?

Why do teens so often use their bodies to express the emotional pain and conflicts they feel? It may be because physical ills are often given more importance than emotional pain by parents, teachers or even by teens themselves.

"It's much easier for kids to ask for medical care than for psychological help," says Dr. Marilyn Mehr. "They often have a great fear of being crazy or of being *thought* to be crazy."

The reactions of significant adults like parents, teachers and physicians to these physical signals can be crucial in helping the teenager feel better or in making him or her feel worse. Some of the mistakes that parents make are typified by the reactions that Ed and Marilyn Hartman had to the recurring headaches and stomach pains their daughter Dana has suffered for the past six months.

At first they were concerned and took her to the family doctor for a checkup. When medical tests failed to detect any organic causes for Dana's distress, the physician, an older man with little interest in teenagers, told her parents, "It's psychological, part of being a teenager. I guess you'll all just have to bear with it until Dana grows up a little."

Now Ed and Marilyn discount Dana's symptoms when they occur —either ignoring her complaints or telling her to grow up, to stop whining and cease being such a hypochondriac. But Dana's body isn't listening. She still suffers real physical pain and deepening emotional pain, including depression, a growing sense of isolation and hopelessness.

This situation occurs, with less or more severe variations, in many families.

"Silence, lecturing or labeling doesn't make the pain go away," says Dr. Zeltzer. "I particularly dislike the term *hypochondriac* because it is so often misused as a label to mean 'faker.' I see many young people with stress-induced symptoms like chest and back pains, stomach-aches, headaches and fatigue stemming from depression. I don't think for a minute that they're faking anything. Their pain and problems are real!"

"I cringe when I hear someone say, 'It's *just* psychosomatic pain," adds Dr. Mehr. "The implication is that if it's psychosomatic, it isn't real. But of course the pain we see *is* real, both emotionally and physically."

Dr. Zeltzer points out that physical pain has many different causes. "When someone suffers pain, it may mean a disease like hepatitis, or depression over the loss of a love," she says. "Pain is a message. It is the body's way of signaling that something troubling is going on. The whole process of dealing with pain is to work with the person to help decode this message. Why is the pain there? What is going on? One person may have the flu, another may be depressed."

Some physicians are not always as sensitive as they might be to the psychological implications behind a teenager's pain. "Some, once they have ruled out physical disease, try to rule out the symptoms as well," says Dr. MacKenzie. "However, it's important to raise *both* possibilities of physical disease or a psychomatic cause at the same time so that both have equal status. For example, I might say to a patient, 'You've been having headaches, which signal many things. It could be a brain tumor, migraine, or low blood sugar —among many other possibilities. It could be muscular tension coming from an emotional problem.' I take psychosomatic complaints seriously and if the cause of a teen's pain is emotional, I give this equal validation. After all, a headache caused by emotional problems is just as uncomfortable as one caused by physical illness!"

How You Can Help

There are a number of ways that you can help if your teenager is having physical symptoms that are psychosomatic.

Watch for Changes in Your Teen's Health

Be aware of any changes in your teenager's health patterns or any troublesome physical symptoms. If these persist, mention your observations and your concern to your teenager. Encourage him or her to talk about how he or she is feeling, physically or emotionally.

Don't Automatically Reject the Reality of Symptoms

Don't dismiss symptoms with remarks like "It's probably just in your head" or "Don't be such a baby" or "If you don't watch out, you're going to turn into a hypochondriac" or "Just ignore it—tough it out—and it will go away." Pain is a valuable signal and should not be ignored or minimized. If a teenager needs to express emotional conflicts through physical distress, this is an important clue to a communication problem that exists within your family.

Seek Professional Help

Encourage your teenager to seek competent medical help and see that he or she gets it. Unless your teenager has a good and open relationship with the family doctor, consider asking for help from an adolescent medicine specialist (see Appendix) who has special training in communicating with and caring for teenagers. A doctor who knows how to listen and respond to a teenager's feelings and complaints and who will take the time to do so can be a great asset to your child's emotional and physical health.

"It's so important to spend time with a teenage patient and talk about feelings," says Dr. Zeltzer. "I'm dismayed when I hear of physicians who just give out pain pills or tranquilizers. They do this to relieve symptoms and to save time, but it doesn't work that way. If feelings aren't dealt with, the patient will be back again and again. So in the long run, talking can save time, decreasing the number of visits the teenager makes to the doctor. It also helps to decrease the patient's anxiety. If a doctor just gives a young patient a bunch of pills, the teen may become *more* anxious, thinking, 'Oh, my, I'm getting pills! Something is very wrong with me and my doctor isn't telling me what it is.' "

A physical examination is vital, too, to make sure that the symptoms actually are emotionally linked and not due to a physical disorder. When the probable cause of the teen's distress is pinpointed, he or she is in a better position to receive appropriate help.

Medical help may be the most acceptable alternative, maybe the only one your teen will go along with at this time. "Many teens are resistant to mental health care," says Dr. Richard Brown. "But they may go to a physician for a health checkup. If this physician is also sensitive to feelings and is good with adolescents, this kind of help is most valuable. The doctor checks the teen to eliminate the possibility of disease and makes an assessment of the teenager's complete health, including psychosocial development. If seeking professional help is approached from the standpoint of getting a health care checkup, this may be more acceptable to the teenager."

Be Gentle with Your Troubled Teen

If your teenager does have psychosomatic symptoms, be gentle with him or her. Don't label him or her as a hypochondriac, a baby or a troublemaker. It is much more constructive to validate the pain, saying, in effect, "I know you're hurting. And I want to help you in any way I can." Give special time, attention and expressions of love to your child not only when he or she is sick or in pain but at times when he or she is feeling well, too. Some parents unwittingly reward and reinforce sickly behavior by taking time to say, "I love you" or "I care about you" only when their children are ill.

Seek Family Counseling If Major Tensions Exist

If there are tensions within your family, try to get family counseling, finding ways to change your own behavior and taking the risk of communicating with each other. If you reduce some of these tensions and start to get feelings out into the open and learn to communicate more effectively, you will find that your child's symptoms may start to diminish. Some families are able to do this on their own, but many need extra help from a counseling professional. It's important to be open to this option if your family seems to be in trouble.

Preexisting Medical Conditions

Some medical conditions, while not caused by emotional conflicts, are adversely affected by such problems.

"We find that a lupus flare-up, for example, can be precipitated by emotional factors," says Dr. Oaks. "Also, asthma gets worse with emotional stress."

Because of the strong mind-body connection among many teens with severe asthma, some physicians treat these young people with a combination of drugs, psychotherapy and family counseling. In especially severe cases, the asthma victim may have to live away from home for a while.

Other medical conditions—colitis, ulcerative colitis, ulcers and migraine headaches—occur as the result of many factors, but are aggravated by emotional upsets.

How You Can Help

Consult Your Physician

Check with your child's physician for reassurance and supportive care. If the physician is not supportive of your child's emotional as well as physical needs, it is time to search for another doctor or for counseling to supplement your child's medical care and to ease the stressors in his or her life, teaching new ways of coping with the inevitable ups and downs.

Tell Your Teen That You Care

Communicate the fact that you care and that while the teen has primary responsibility for health maintenance, you're concerned and willing to help. Many parents assume that their teens know they care and will help. Never assume anything. Always try to make your loving, caring feelings clear to your child, but don't try to take over the problem.

Communicate with Your Teen About the Problem

Explore ways of dealing with stress and depression with your teenager. Approach this not as a lecture but as a dialogue, an idea-sharing session to help each other find more constructive ways to cope with tensions or troubling feelings. Share ideas with each other. Here are some possible stress reducers that you might bring up in the discussion.

- Take the risk of talking openly instead of repressing feelings.
- Reassure your teen that expressing anger, needs, frustrations and the like will not result in rejection. Then follow through on your word, making the resolution to listen even when you don't like what you're hearing.
- Revise your teen's own unrealistic expectations for himself and check out others' expectations (especially parental ones) to

make sure the teenager has an accurate sense of what these really are and whether they are realistic or not.

- Start a physical exercise regimen, with physician's approval. Carefully chosen physical exercise reduces both tension and depression and does wonderful things for the body. If your teenager is reluctant to exercise, especially if it means doing it alone, join the regimen, stressing companionship, not competition.

CHAPTER 15

Depression and Eating Disorders

E ATING DISORDERS BRING particular pain to a teenager. While a teen with mild temporary depression may lose his or her appetite for a few days, the problem can be much more severe in teenagers with serious depression and emotional problems.

"The eating disorders that are linked with depression cover quite a wide range," says Dr. Donald McKnew. "The teenager may have poor appetite and weight loss or engage in compulsive overeating and experience a considerable weight gain."

Dr. MacKenzie observes that, "an eating disorder represents a teenager's attempt to gain some control by engaging in a behavior which cannot be regulated by another person. But often this is carried to an extreme."

Extreme conditions, such as anorexia nervosa and bulimarexia on the one hand and compulsive overeating and obesity on the other, may occur in conjunction with depression. Even if your depressed teenager is not experiencing these extremes, the discussion of them, along with general tips for helping, may give you some ideas for coping constructively with mild *and* severe eating disorders.

The Starve-Purge Eating Disorders

Anorexia nervosa is an increasingly common psychosomatic gastro-intestinal disorder occurring primarily in teenage girls and young women. Only about 4 percent of its victims are male. If not helped, some victims (about 10 percent) actually starve themselves to death. Many more incur health problems due to their self-inflicted starvation diet and compulsive exercise routines.

The anorectic may drop 20 to 40 percent of her total body weight (often assuming skeletal proportions), lose her hair, stop menstruating, have low body temperature and low blood pressure as well as a distorted body image, seeing herself as fat even when painfully thin.

Who gets anorexia nervosa and why? The exact causes of the disorder are still controversial, but many medical experts agree that psychological problems and certain family configurations and conflicts play a major role.

"The personality of the typical girl with anorexia and her family relationships are like they came out of a cookie mold," says Dr. Gabrielle Carlson. "It's like the parents read a book on how to be the parent of an anorectic and the child studied up on how to be an anorectic. There is a very definite personality and family relationship pattern that we see."

Dr. MacKenzie, who treats a growing number of anorectics at the adolescent unit at Children's Hospital at Los Angeles, agrees with her. "There is a definite prototype of the anorexia victim," he says. "Most are female, middle to upper-middle class. They are usually excellent students and achievers, the jewels of their families. They have been problem-free children, the kids *other* kids consider to be goody-goody, the kids adult outsiders always praise and the kids of whom their parents have expected a great deal. The teenager has high expectations of herself, not wanting to let her parents down."

While the teen may have seemed problem-free up to this point, family troubles have been simmering under the surface. Maybe a sibling is troubled or disruptive. Maybe the parents have serious marital problems. And the developmental tasks of adolescence, which include growing away from parents, may be putting a special strain on the girl.

"Typically, the victim of anorexia is the child of protective parents and, as she enters her teens, she has a great deal of trouble separating from them," says Dr. MacKenzie. "There is a great deal of mutual dependency between mother and daughter, and the daughter finds it hard to express negative feelings toward the mother—which is a part of the natural process of separation. The father, typically, is of the absentee variety—there, but *not* there. He doles his affection out sparingly or conditionally, based on the child's achievements. It is not uncommon to find depression dominating the life of an anorectic adolescent because she has a tremendous sense of being a nonperson, of not being defined as a separate individual."

A teenager with anorexia often has a fixation on food—collecting recipes and preparing gourmet meals for family members, while not eating a bite herself. She exercises in pointless, frenetic patterns and binges occasionally, then vomits to keep from gaining weight.

A teenager with *bulimarexia* is not as easy to spot as the anorectic, since she is at a normal weight or even slightly overweight. She maintains this weight balance by binging then purging via use of laxatives and by vomiting at will. Again, most victims are female— with only 5 to 10 percent being male. It is estimated that 65 to 75 percent of all former anorectics develop bulimarexia.

Cindy Wayne, a nineteen-year-old who has suffered from both disorders, says, "It's really terrible, trying to keep control. I'm normal-looking and people are always complimenting me on my nice figure instead of saying I look terrible like they did when I weighed only 78 pounds. But if I didn't throw up after a binge, I'd be fat. I'm capable of eating a couple of days' worth of food when I'm on a binge. It makes me feel so ashamed. Until I read about this problem in a magazine recently, I thought I was all alone. I finally got the nerve to mention this to my doctor when I realized there were others like me."

Young women under great pressure to be thin—aspiring models, ballet dancers, gymnasts or the simply fashion-conscious—are especially prone to such eating disorders, their perfectionistic tendencies turning in the direction of diet and their yearning for control in at least one area of life combining to create a major health problem.

How You Can Help

See a Physician. Get help from a doctor, preferably one experienced in treating adolescents *and* anorexia nervosa and bulimarexia, immediately. The sooner your child gets treatment the better. Dr.

MacKenzie points out that there are several stages of anorexia, and those who get help in the earliest stage have the best prognosis. "First there is the onset phase, which may last from one month to one year," he says. "Symptoms are changed behavior and some weight loss. Then comes the stabilization phase where the person's pattern of eating or not eating to deal with emotions has become fully acceptable to her and she is more resistant to change. Next is the terminal stage where biological and physiological functions are giving way and death can occur. I remember two girls in that stage. One, who was being treated primarily by a psychiatrist, died. The other spent three months in intensive care and almost died three or four times, getting down to about 60 pounds. She recovered and recently graduated from college."

Dr. MacKenzie and a number of his colleagues believe that if caught early in the onset phase, anorexia may be cured. Those who have more advanced cases by the time they seek treatment may have anorexia for life and need help in dealing with their feelings and problems. Because early diagnosis and treatment are crucial, Dr. MacKenzie says, "We're always warning doctors, especially pediatricians and family physicians, to look for classic anorexia behavior patterns and not wait for extreme weight loss to occur."

At whatever stage treatment may begin, there is no fast and easy way to treat the starve-purge eating disorders. Treatment methods are diverse and controversial, with some authorities advocating psychotherapy, others behavior modification and still others drug or nutrition therapy. Some of the most successful treatment programs seem to combine a number of elements—most frequently, a period of hospitalization (to get the teenager into a controlled, therapeutic atmosphere and away from family tensions) with weight gain as a major goal and psychotherapy and family therapy in addition to behavior modification.

Dr. MacKenzie's treatment program uses this multifaceted approach. "We hospitalize the typical patient for about a month," he says. "During this time, while she's out of the family situation, we deal with her weight problem and try to establish a good rapport. In the first week especially, we restrict parental visits and emphasize a strict privilege system. All privileges—like making phone calls—are contingent on weight gain. We don't force-feed our patients. We don't even talk about eating. If you focus on it, you get a real battle going. The patient will play games, hiding food or throwing up after eating, just to keep control. We emphasize weight gain. If the patient wants certain privileges, she must gain weight and there's only one way to do that."

Along with ongoing hospital treatment comes the beginning of at least six months of family therapy, which usually includes parents and siblings as well as the patient. Therapists also advise separate marriage counseling for parents if marital problems are major and important in the family.

At first, it is hard to break long-established patterns of interaction.

"A chronic problem like an eating disorder is frustrating to treat because it threatens control and omnipotence in so many cases," says Dr. Carlson. "You tell someone what to do and he or she still won't do it. For example, I have an anorectic patient whose parents had been urging her to diet and be thin for years. I told them, 'So now she's thin. Don't mention food to her.' They *still* mention it."

There are times when family members sabotage a physician's attempt to help. Dr. MacKenzie recalls one mother who allowed her daughter to talk her into smuggling laxatives into the hospital. The girl ate twelve laxative sticks before being caught by nurses.

Generally, as therapy progresses all family members benefit.

"We emphasize the fact that we're here for everyone's purposes, that the child with anorexia is simply expressing problems shared by the family," says Dr. MacKenzie. "This takes a lot of pressure off the anorectic."

It's important, then, to be open to family therapy as well as medical treatment. If conflicts are not resolved, the problem will go on and on and may even become life-threatening.

Deemphasize the Whole Issue of Eating. If physicians like Dr. Mac-Kenzie deemphasize control issues and emphasize personal responsibility in their treatments, it is even *more* important for parents to do so. Let the physician and your teenager handle the problem. Compliment your teen on weight gains, emphasizing her new glow of health. And watch your own behavior carefully to identify ways you are contributing to the problem or sabotaging treatment. It is vital not to argue with, nag or lecture your teenager about eating or to attempt to take over and solve her problem for her. Control is a major issue in many eating disorders and the more you try to superimpose your views and convictions in this area, the more serious and stubborn the battle will become.

Realize That There Are No Quick Cures. Treatment of these eating disorders takes a great deal of time and patience. Habits are hard to break and depression may linger.

Leslie Pollack, seventeen, who now weighs eighty pounds (up from sixty-three), reports a lot of conflicting feelings as her treatment progresses. "When I had anorexia, I was a better student because I concentrated more," she says. "Everything had to be perfect. I was even a perfectionist in my sneaky ways of not eating. Now I've gained some weight, but I don't know, things aren't perfect. I never feel full. I always want more food and that scares me. Oh, there are a lot of things happening in my life, like family problems, but most of all I worry about getting fat. I still exercise a lot and try to keep real active. I don't want to gain any more weight than this."

And Gina Lupi—up to 128 from 78 pounds—reports that she feels better, is more assertive with kids at school who bug her and says that she and her mother don't always get along these days (something she couldn't deal with before). Still, this separation is undeniably painful. "I get scared to go to school and cry a lot in the mornings and my mom doesn't understand and gets mad at me," she says. As painful as her progress may be, it is progress. But it's important to be aware that, like Gina, your teen's recovery may be slow and painful emotionally for all concerned.

For more information about these eating disorders—and current treatments—you can contact information centers or clinics listed in the Appendix.

The Overeating/Obesity Disorders

Compulsive overeating and obesity can be a very painful problem for many teens and their families. Have you noticed that your teenager

- Eats a lot, even when not hungry?
- Eats quite normally at mealtimes or in front of others, but binges in secret (have you found cookie and candy stashes in strange places?)
- Seems to overeat when angry, upset or nervous, *or* when excited about an upcoming event or happy about something?

- Eats more—seemingly for spite—when you mention your concern about his or her dietary habits or weight?
- Has experienced a considerable weight gain (ten pounds or more) in a short period of time?
- Has always been heavy, but is getting obese?
- Is at least 20 percent over his or her ideal weight?

If you have answered "Yes" to any of these, your teen could have a problem with compulsive overeating.

Why do teenagers overeat? Some eat compulsively to anesthetize feelings of fear, anxiety and anger, as well as using food as a tranquilizer in times of positive or negative stress. So food becomes all-encompassing—used to comfort, calm or celebrate. The teenager may overeat after a family argument, while studying for exams, in the wake of a major disappointment *or* an important victory.

Dr. Neil Solomon of Johns Hopkins Medical School in Baltimore has found that 75 percent of the obese patients he has studied respond to stress by eating. He adds that very often the stress eater feels underlying hostility toward some person or situation but would rather eat than voice such hostilities.

Some teens take refuge in their fat in order to avoid romantic or sexual involvements and to postpone decisions about their sexuality. This is especially true for a teenager who has experienced some sort of sexual trauma at an early age. Dr. William Shipman of Michael Reese Hospital in Chicago did a study of obese women falling into this category and found that they were "affected for the rest of their lives—seeking solace in something safe like food rather than in something as dangerous as human contact, friendship, sex and love."

Some teenagers who are depressed, bored and losing interest in everything turn to food to fill the void in their lives. And some use food—and overweight—as a means of rebellion. In this instance, the compulsive eating disorder is much like anorexia, with the teenager struggling to seize control of her life in the only way she knows how. Teens whose parents put a high premium on good looks, physical fitness or popularity are especially prone to this sort of rebellion.

Dr. Johanna T. Dwyer studied a group of obese young women at Harvard University and discovered that many of them had mothers who pushed them to succeed at everything and who talked about thinness as some kind of moral virtue and being fat as the worst possible fate. These young women fought back by making their mothers' vision of the worst possible fate a reality.

"A power struggle is the basis of much adolescent obesity," says Dr. Oaks. "Obesity and sexuality are two areas where the teen can act out, saying in effect, 'I own my own body and there's nothing you can do about it!' "

Overeating may also be an expression of low self-esteem. "Overeating is a way of not caring about oneself," says Dr. MacKenzie. "The obese teenager is saying in effect, 'I'm not worthwhile. Why should I care about myself?' "

The price adolescents pay for expressing their feelings through overeating and obesity is high. Obesity reinforces poor body image and low self-esteem. It causes one to be socially ostracized. It sets the young person up for a lifetime of weight problems and health risks. All too often obesity is *not* a problem that a young person will simply outgrow. Medical researchers have found that fat children and teenagers often become fat adults because fat cells formed in the body during those early years of development and growth cannot be reduced in number (although they can be reduced in size). Thus, a young person who is obese and who has formed an excess of fat cells in childhood and early adolescence may always have to be careful of his or her weight.

Knowing the emotional pain and the health risks of obesity, a parent may become most anxious to help an overweight son or daughter slim down and shape up. But it isn't easy to help. Your teenager may be extremely resourceful in sneak-eating rituals and you can't be there twenty-four hours a day to monitor food intake. More to the point, the teen may actively resist all your attempts to help.

"It's so hard to know how to help," says the mother of an obese sixteen-year-old girl. "If I express concern, she says I'm nagging and to get off her back—and then she eats more just to show me. If I don't say anything, she keeps on stuffing herself with junk food and, I guess, convincing herself that it doesn't show all that much. But it does! Suzi is getting fat and I'm so worried about her. What can I do?"

How You Can Help

If your teenager has a problem with overeating and obesity, there are several ways you can help.

Communicate Your Concern in a Nonjudgmental Way. It is a temptation when you see your teen overeating and gaining weight to respond with anger, frustration and blunt observations like "If you don't stop eating like that, you'll weigh over 300 pounds!" or "You ought to cut out the junk food. You're getting fat!" or "Why can't you control yourself? Can't you see what you're doing to your body?"

Such comments set the stage for a real control battle. It is more constructive to express concern and ask for some feedback from your teen, confronting him or her gently with your own observations and then asking what his or her feelings are.

"If your child hasn't mentioned weight as a problem or doesn't seem disturbed by it, you might make the observation, 'It looks to me like you're gaining weight. Does this bother you?'" says Dr. Oaks. "If the teen says, 'Yes,' you might then ask, 'Would you like help?' and, with an affirmative answer, you might take the teen to a doctor and seek other resources as well. If the teenager says, 'No. It isn't a problem for me,' then express your own emotions—'I worry about you'—and encourage the teenager to check with a physician, letting the doctor and teen discuss and deal with the possible problem."

In talking with your teen, don't get negative, saying that he or she is bad, should be ashamed or is ugly. Accent the positive: the importance of being as healthy and attractive as possible now and learning healthy eating habits early in life to prevent more serious problems later.

If your teen gets angry and refuses to discuss the matter, don't push. He or she may not be ready to tackle the weight problem or may feel the need to reject any ideas you present. This doesn't mean that you haven't been heard or that the teenager will never be motivated to lose weight. It may help to say to your teen, "I understand that you don't want to talk about this right now. I won't say anything more about it. But if it does start to bother you and you *do* want to talk about it, I'd be happy to listen and to try to help in any way I can."

Then keep to your word, but at the same time keep the lines of communication open so that when your teen does want help, he or she will feel free to come to you.

Deemphasize Control and Emphasize Responsibility. To keep the issue of control from interfering with the teen's progress, don't nag your son or daughter to stay on a diet, monitor food intake or weight loss or play detective. If you see him or her eating some forbidden goodies, bite your tongue to keep from asking, "Is *that* on your diet?" or saying, "You *know* you shouldn't be eating that." The teen knows and may be experiencing a bout of self-sabotage or testing your resolve. If you don't get hooked into old reaction patterns, the power of overeating as a means of rebellion will be decreased. Communicate the concept, "It's your body and your choice what you feed it," to diffuse the power of such rebellion.

Encourage Your Teenager to Get Outside Help. To decrease the possibility of weight loss remaining an issue between you and your child, encourage him or her to look for primary help elsewhere in diet efforts. Encourage help from a physician or a special weight loss program. Organizations like Weight Watchers and TOPS—using a group concept, behavior modification and sensible, easy-to-live-with diet programs—have had a great deal of success with teenagers. If your teen is not inclined to groups, look into a program like the Diet Center (there are more than a thousand of these centers across the United States), which features daily weigh-ins before school, private counseling at weigh-in time plus a healthful, natural-food eating program and optional once-a-week nutrition/behavior modification classes. (To locate the Weight Watchers, TOPS or Diet Center nearest you, check the white pages of your telephone directory.)

If your teenager seems to prefer an entirely adolescent-oriented diet program, you may find help at a nearby adolescent clinic affiliated with a hospital (see Appendix).

At Children's Hospital of Los Angeles, for example, the Adolescent Unit offers a special program to young people from twelve to eighteen. Once a week, the teens come in for a two-and-a-half-hour program that provides medical and psychological evaluation, therapeutic activities, diet and physical education, hypnosis and relaxation techniques as well as sports therapy and psychodrama.

"In this group, I tell the participants that we're here to educate them and help them *if* they want to lose weight," says Dr. Oaks. "It's important to offer support while avoiding a control battle. To do this, one must realize and accept the fact that a teenager will *not* be forced to stay on a diet. He or she must make that decision and commitment independently."

Be Aware of Your Own Sabotaging Behavior. Even though on a con-
scious level you want very much for your teenager to lose weight,
you may have subconscious fears about the changes that significant
weight loss will bring. You may feel hidden feelings of jealousy or
competitiveness as your teenager begins to look more attractive. You
may fear change as your child becomes more assertive, more self-
confident and less dependent on you. Such feelings are not bad or
unusual, but it's crucial to be aware of them in order to modify your
own possibly diet-sabotaging behavior. You could be sabotaging
your teen's diet efforts by

- Trying to seize control and tell him or her what to eat and how
  much. You will help a lot by not saying anything and by letting
  your teen assume responsibility.
- Urging a favorite fattening food on your teen "just this once"
  as a reward or a gesture of love. For anyone with an overeating
  problem, a forbidden treat can be the beginning of a new
  round of binging behavior. Find other ways to reward your
  child and try to express your love verbally. If you tend to feed
  your child when you're feeling guilty over *unloving* feelings (no
  parent feels loving and giving to a child all the time), learn to
  express negative feelings in constructive ways (by talking the
  feelings out with someone, or working your anger and frustration out via physical exercise). Also, learn to compensate in
  nonfattening ways—for example, by making special efforts to
  listen and express positive feelings and appreciation, and by
  planning activities that get you and your teenager out of the
  house, active and away from food (e.g., a trip to the beach, a
  shopping expedition, a walk in the park).
- Regarding a diet as penance and punishment and making your
  dieting teen feel different. Those who have the best results in
  taking weight off and *keeping* it off are those who revise their
  eating habits on a long-term basis. If you make a major distinction between dieting and after-diet eating (e.g., "When you're
  slim, you can eat ice cream, cookies and candy like the rest of
  us"), you are setting your teen up either to quit the diet or to
  get caught up in the lose-gain, yo-yo pattern so many dieters
  face. For many, maintaining one's best weight is a lifelong effort
  —one made easier by healthful eating habits. Now is the time
  to modify your family's eating habits in general—eat more fish
  and chicken, more vegetables and fresh fruit and fewer starchy

casseroles, rich desserts and calorie-ladden snack foods. By serving more nutritious, low-calorie meals to the family, by stocking the pantry with healthful snacks like raisins, fresh fruit and plain, unsalted popcorn, you will do your whole family— especially your weight-conscious teen—a favor. It is very discouraging, after all, to munch carrot sticks when other family members are delving into chocolate cake. *Nobody* needs sugar-laden snacks. Removing these items from your home and your menus except for very special occasions will make your dieting teen feel less tempted and different and, at the same time, improve the eating habits and health of your entire family.

- Giving your teenager attention only when he or she fails. This can only reinforce dietary lapses.
- Complaining about the trouble of preparing diet meals. If you complain about preparing special meals, it will give your child a handy excuse to stop dieting. When you really don't have time, encourage your teen to take this responsibility—for example, "I think it would be great if you could learn to cook good, healthful meals. It will help you eat the right things for life *and* become more independent right now!"

Praise Your Teenager for Trying. If he or she has a great deal of weight to lose, it will be some time before the results are evident. Praise your teenager for strength and resolve in sticking to the diet, one day at a time. Tell him or her that you realize how difficult it is and how much you admire his or her efforts. Let him know that your love is not contingent on how much or how little he or she weighs.

Encourage More Physical Activity. If it would be helpful and appropriate, join him or her in some exercise or activity such as running, walking, bicycling or swimming as a way of giving time, attention and continuing encouragement.

Junk Food Junkies

Many teens have diets heavy on junk foods, snack items and fast food restaurant offerings.

"Teens of both sexes eat too many refined carbohydrates and convenience foods," says Dr. Emanuel Cheraskin, chairman of the department of oral medicine at the University of Alabama and co-author of a number of books on nutrition and preventive medicine. "Teenage girls have the worst diets of all because they combine eating junk food with attempts to diet. Teenage boys, on the other hand, eat constantly and may randomly bump into some nutrients."

Dr. Cheraskin contends that many emotional problems are actually rooted in improper diet and nutrition. "Medical investigators have known for many years that severe nutritional deficiencies can cause mental illness," he says. "Refined carbohydrates such as sugar and white flour are susceptibility agents—oversupply encourages disease. A vitamin-B$_3$ deficiency can be a real factor in depression."

A number of medical experts tend to agree. For example, Dr. Derrick Landsdale, a Cleveland pediatrician, has reported in a recent study that a steady diet of empty, junk food calories causes a thiamine deficiency and a beriberi-like disease as well as personality problems that began to disappear when the teens in the study were placed on a well-balanced diet. And some researchers have found that excessive intake of caffeine (which many teens ingest through cola drinks and chocolate as well as coffee) causes sleep disorders, restlessness, nervousness, anxiety and irritability.

How You Can Help

What can you do if your teenager shows signs of being a junk food addict? First, it's important to realize that eccentric eating habits are widespread among teens, who tend to do a lot of socializing over burgers, pizzas and the like and often spend lunch money on candy bars and soft drinks instead of hot lunches. Although your control over your teen's dietary habits is at this point probably quite minimal, there are ways you can help.

Make Home Meals Healthy. When your teen eats a meal at home, make sure it's a healthy one—with lean meat, fish or poultry and plenty of vegetables. If he or she has eaten out or brings home fast food, supplement the meal with a salad, milk, fruit juice or a serving or two of vegetables.

Keep Nutritious Snacks in the Home. Make sure the snack foods around your house are of the healthy variety: fresh, raw fruits and vegetables, fruit juice, plain popcorn. If your teen is like most, he or she will buy more than enough junk food outside and doesn't need an assist from you in supplying the empty calories of junk food snacks.

Learn About Nutrition in the House. Make a study of nutrition yourself and show your interest in this in a low-key way with your teen. You'll have little credibility in a battle against junk food if you adopt a "don't do as I do, do as I say" stance while munching snack cakes and potato chips. Let your own healthful habits be a quiet, positive example to your children.

Communicate Your Concern About Eating Habits. Express your concern in a neutral, information-sharing way. One mother, for example, told her daughter about an article she had read that had talked about how a balanced diet makes one's hair and skin more attractive. Many teens don't show much concern for nutrients per se but are quite concerned about appearance problems and grooming. If this is the case with your teen, a gentle suggestion that he or she might try a more balanced diet to see what impact this has on a particular problem might capture his or her interest and overcome the usual resistance to any of your ideas or suggestions.

CHAPTER 16

When Being Different Brings on Depression

S OME TEENAGERS ARE different from their peers for reasons beyond
their control.

- Bob Allen is fourteen but looks several years younger. He is
  mortified over his short stature and lack of physical development, especially when he compares himself to his peers in the
  locker room (and suffers from their jeers and taunts). He is
  wondering when, if ever, he'll finally grow up.
- Mary Lee Kane is depressed because she has to wear a correc-
  tive brace for her scoliosis for the next year. She has visions of
  becoming incredibly "out of it" and missing out on a normal
  life during that time.
- Jessica Dunning is embarrassed about her height: she's 5 feet
  8 inches tall at the age of thirteen and towers over most of
  the boys in her class.
- Mike Swanson has been depressed lately because he feels that
  his epilepsy will make him even more different from his friends
  as he grows older. He is already dreading next year when the
  other kids in his class will be getting their drivers' licenses and
  he won't.
- And Frank Austin, the young diabetic whose story appeared
  at the beginning of chapter 14, finds a lot of pain in following

or not following the strict regimen that his medical condition requires, a regimen he feels sets him apart from his friends and classmates.

Being different due to circumstances beyond one's control—because of late development, a chronic illness or temporary or permanent handicap—is especially painful for the body-conscious teenager. Being different or *feeling* intrinsically different due to a physical problem causes poor body image, low self-esteem and depression.

"We see a great deal of depression in chronically ill adolescents," says Dr. MacKenzie. "They feel different and bad about themselves because of this. They feel that their parents don't trust them. Also, the illness holds them back in the developmental process of emancipation from the family and this causes depression as their self-esteem plummets."

How You Can Help

While you may not be able to change your child's physical problems, you can help change his or her feelings and self-perceptions.

If Your Teenager Is a Late Developer

A medical checkup may reassure everyone that all is well or, if there is a problem, it may be a step toward getting help. In many instances, late development is genetic. If you or your spouse happened to be a late bloomer, share your feelings and experiences with your child—not minimizing the pain of being different right now, but reassuring your child that he or she *will* develop and that there is a wide range of normal development in the teen years.

If Your Teenager Is Unusually Tall or Short

Listen to your teen's feelings about height and explore ways to cope and compensate. If, for example, your twelve- or thirteen-year-old daughter is worried about being taller than many boys in her class, it's quite possible that most of them will catch up with her in a year or two and she will not always be so different.

If your son or daughter is past the age of puberty, is in the mid to late teens and is still significantly shorter or taller than peers, don't keep saying, "You'll grow!" or "They'll grow and catch up with you." It's important not to give your teen the idea that it's *not* normal or O.K. to be as he or she is. The concepts that men *must* be taller than women, or that women must physically look up to men are arbitrary, culturally imposed traditions—ones that are certainly worth questioning. In the past and even in the present, these traditions have prevented many loving, fulfilling relationships from happening and, more important, have caused many men and women to feel terrible about themselves. It is difficult to say, especially to a self-conscious teen, that cultural mores don't matter at all. But it helps to start exploring them with your teen, raising the question, "Why must we meet certain culturally imposed height standards if being a certain stature is physically normal for *you?*"

"I'm 5 foot ten and had a hard time when I was in junior high," says Sheila Culver, seventeen. "I got what I think you'd call 'mixed messages' from my mom. She said it was O.K. to be tall, but not *too* tall. She said it wasn't good to be over five eight. I felt just awful when I grew past that."

It is more constructive to help your tall or short teen accept and adjust to his or her body by pursuing special physical activities. Dance classes help a tall girl feel less gawky and more graceful. Sports like gymnastics or running are helpful to the small boy or girl. It has been reported that champion gymnast Kurt Thomas became interested in the sport initially because it helped him feel better about his slight build. Encouraging your smaller-than-average son or daughter to pursue some noncompetitive but body- and stamina-building sport like running, race walking, dancing of all kinds or weight training will build strength and enhance body image.

Find Ways to Help Physically Handicapped Teens Feel More Attractive

Good grooming habits, attractive hairstyles and flattering, well-designed clothes will help the disabled teenager acquire a more positive body image. Of course, personality and skill compensations are also crucial, but for the body-conscious teen, being as attractive as possible is an important step toward feeling more normal and less depressed and different. Encourage your teenager to take an interest in enhancing physical strong points instead of taking a "why bother?" attitude.

Put Responsibility for Management of a Chronic Disease on the Teenager

This is especially important in chronic conditions like diabetes and epilepsy where lifelong responsibility is an important factor in successful health maintenance. When possible, keep management issues between your teenager and the physician, so that the teen gets practice in taking responsibility and will not be as tempted to rebel against your authority by refusing to comply with disease treatment and management routines. If you ever comment on disease management, do it in a positive, neutral way, such as remarking that keeping the medical condition—whether it is asthma, diabetes, epilepsy or something else—stable and in control will free him to pursue a myriad of interests and possibilities.

Encourage Your Teenager to Build Life As a Whole Person

Help your teen realize that he or she is not defined by special medical needs or physical limitations, and help him or her discover what he or she *can* rather than cannot do. It may help to point out celebrities who are enjoying success and full lives despite their medical problems. For example, Mary Tyler Moore has diabetes, film director Martin Scorsese grew up with asthma, actor John Considine has epilepsy and the famous stunt woman Kitty O'Neill, totally deaf from birth, earned the title "fastest woman on earth" while racing a rocket-powered vehicle and was recently the subject of a biographical television movie. Also, a number of sports stars have had chronic illnesses.

There are many others—a number of them teenagers—occasionally spotlighted in the news who live normal lives with a variety of chronic diseases and handicaps. For example, Ted Kennedy, Jr., is an active sportsman despite the loss of a leg to cancer when he was twelve. Patty Wilson, a California teenager, has epilepsy, but has won fame as a long-distance runner.

And there are many more teenagers who don't make the news, but who lead happy, productive lives while coping with handicaps and chronic illnesses. One of these is Nancy Anderson, who has had diabetes since she was ten. "When I got into my teens, I got tired of my parents trying to take over my disease, and for a while I refused to cooperate or take any responsibility for myself," she says. "But when I realized that I was cutting down on my own freedom and endangering my future by not controlling my diabetes, I got scared and changed my attitude. I still have worries, fears and feelings of insecurity—like wondering if a man I would love would want to marry someone with a chronic condition. But now I've learned to share these feelings and doubts with those close to me and to cope with them. You have to learn to live with these feelings or you may destroy yourself."

As a parent, you will help your teen by listening to the negative feelings without trying to discount them or explain them away. You will also help by encouraging your teenager to live as full and normal a life as possible. Nancy Anderson, for example, is a talented singer, avid jogger and dreams of a career as an actress or in the medical profession. She has an active social life and recently took a rafting trip down the Colorado River with a group of friends.

"Having a chronic disease means taking extra responsibility," she says. "But then taking responsibility is what growing up is all about. Life isn't easy for anyone, but I believe you can do anything if you want to do it enough. Controlling my diabetes frees me to do *all* the things I love to do!"

By encouraging your teen to take responsibility for his life and expand his horizons, you will help improve his or her self-image.

"I don't feel that diabetes is the central focus of my life," says Nancy. "I'm a person who happens to have diabetes. But I am, first and foremost, a person. I want people to know me that way, as *me*, Nancy. Not Nancy-the-Diabetic. That's only a small part of who I am."

By encouraging your teenager's self-image as a person with a special medical need that is only part of who he or she is, you will help combat depression and develop confidence and a more positive body image.

The mind-body link, after all, can work in positive as well as negative ways. Teenagers at ease with their bodies and their special physical strengths, weaknesses, needs and abilities, will tend to have more hope for building a happy, productive life—now and in the future.

PART VI

Teenagers, Sexuality
and Depression

CHAPTER 17
Facts About Teenagers and Sexual Activity

D EE BARNETT IS still in shock over a discovery she made last week. "I went to put some clean underwear in my daughter's dresser and found a packet of birth control pills sitting there, right on top," she says. "I'm stunned and heartsick. Beth is only fifteen and I really had no idea. Well, I was afraid she was too involved with Rick. They've been seeing each other steadily for eight months and spend a lot of time together. But still, I can hardly believe it. Beth has always been a joy to me and now I'm hurt, disappointed and angry. I finally confronted her with the evidence the other day and she admitted to having sex. She says it's what people are doing and she feels it's O.K. if you love someone. I don't think it's O.K. for a a fifteen-year-old unmarried girl to have sex. I want her to stop and I've forbidden her to see Rick any more. Things are tense around the house these days—to say the least!"

John and Alice Peterson are trying to deal with another kind of shocking discovery. After several months of depression and withdrawal, their sixteen-year-old son Jason finally confided to them that he thinks he may be gay. Since this disclosure there has been a lot of confusion, much anguish and many tears around the Peterson house as all three members of the family try to cope with such a possibility in varying ways.

For the Scotts, crisis has escalated from possibility to reality since their fourteen-year-old daughter Suzanne told them she is three months pregnant. "We're devastated," says Faye Scott through her tears. "I had no idea she was having sex. Worse yet, she isn't sure who the father is. He could be one of three! This is the last straw on top of the marital and financial problems Ralph and I have been having. The worst thing is, Suzi has this romantic notion of having the baby and keeping it because several of her classmates have done this and the other kids look down on people who choose otherwise. But I'm worried about her physically—going through a pregnancy at such a young age. This probably sounds selfish and awful, but I can't help it—it would ruin our lives. There's no way Suzi could be a decent mother right now and we would end up parenting the baby. That's all we need. I went back to work a year ago. We need the money and I need my career back. I can't face giving it all up again to raise yet another child. Yet if Suzi cares for the child, she'll have trouble finishing school and will probably be on welfare or dependent on us the rest of her life. We saw a counselor who said it's *her* decision to make. Why is it hers—an immature kid's—when having the baby would ruin all our lives? As I see it, the only alternative is abortion. That's a very sad choice, but it's the only one I feel O.K. about right now. Suzi doesn't agree."

Joan and Fred Andrews aren't experiencing any crisis right now. As far as they know, their children, Clark, sixteen, and Polly, thirteen, are not sexually active. But every time they hear about other families, every time they read about teen sex and the problems surrounding it in newspapers or magazines, they feel anxious. "It happens to so many kids," says Fred Andrews. "We realize that we're not immune to trouble, that our son or daughter *could* become sexually active at an early age or have a problem related to sexual activity and it scares the hell out of us. They're so young, but there is so much pressure from friends and TV shows to flaunt it and use it. How can we counteract this and help them to keep their wits about them and wait to have sex until they're mature enough to handle it well?"

While all of these families feel quite alone right now, their concerns are not uncommon and are certainly understandable. The statistics related to teenage sex are shocking. A recent national study by the Alan Guttmacher Institute, a New York-based nonprofit research, policy analysis and public education corporation, revealed the following figures.

- An estimated twelve million teenagers—about half the total U.S. teen population—are sexually active. The average teenager begins sexual activity at age sixteen. By age nineteen, only 20 percent of males and 33 percent of females have not had sexual intercourse.

- Of these sexually active teens, two-thirds have never used birth control or use it only sporadically. And those who *do* use birth control regularly were, on the average, sexually active for almost a year before seeking birth control help from a physician or clinic.
- There are 1.1 million pregnancies among teenagers each year. Seventy-five percent of these are unintentional. Half of the pregnancies occur in the first six months of sexual activity—20 percent in the first month. And the sharpest increase in the rate of pregnancy is among girls fourteen and under!
- Some six hundred thousand of these pregnancies each year result in babies—and of those teenagers who do give birth, 96 percent choose to keep their babies. Often this is the beginning of a lifelong cycle of undereducation and poverty. Pregnancy is the most common reason for dropping out of high school among teenage girls. These teen mothers are often chronically unemployed, unskilled and on welfare.
- Teenage mothers have a considerably higher risk of health complications during pregnancy and delivery, and their babies are two to three times more likely to die in the first year of life than the child of a mother in her early twenties.
- Twenty-seven percent of pregnant teenagers marry and are at a much greater risk than older couples of getting divorced or living in poverty, since early marriage often means dropping out of school and job hunting with minimal skills. Other studies have revealed staggering divorce rates for teenage couples—an estimated 90 percent of marriages in which one or both partners are under eighteen end in divorce.
- Other statistics show that venereal disease is widespread among adolescents, with teenagers accounting for 25 percent of the one million gonorrhea cases reported every year.

Why Are So Many Teenagers Sexually Active?

These statistics show many possibilities for family crisis, personal pain and lifelong tragedy. Bombarded by such realities, parents are asking, "Why?" You may find yourself wondering, too. The reasons are incredibly varied. The following are a few of the more common causes cited by sex educators and adolescent behavior experts for the increase in sexual activity among teens today.

Teenagers Are Maturing Earlier

Teenagers are reaching puberty earlier, with an accompanying surge in sexual feelings, in a society that glorifies sex. A hundred years ago, the average girl didn't menstruate until she was sixteen or seventeen. Today the average age at menarche is twelve to thirteen. So the gap between physical maturity and emotional maturity has widened. Teenagers today have longer to wait between the attainment of sexual maturity and becoming true adults emotionally and economically. At the same time, sex is glorified and exploited in TV shows, movies and ads using precociously sexy teenage models. Thus, many teenagers have the physical ability to have sex, and the media encourage them to do so before their emotional growth catches up and enables them to make constructive choices about their sexuality.

Family Life Has Changed Drastically

The decreasing amount of intimacy and nurturing in many families causes teenagers to look elsewhere for such comfort and closeness. Many families today lead busy lives with little time for each other and for shared activities and confidences. Financial pressures due to inflation, the influence of television, demanding work schedules, a "do your own thing" philosophy and an increase in divorce all contribute to dwindling intimacy among family members. This has had a huge impact on very young adolescents who still need a great deal of nurturing. If the teen can't find love and caring at home, he or she will look for it from others and will see sexual activity as the ultimate step toward intimacy and the proof of being loved and valued.

Demographers John F. Kanter and Melvin Zelnik of Johns Hopkins University conducted a study of sexually active adolescents several years ago and found that among white teenage girls under the age of sixteen, those who had lost a father through death or divorce were 60 percent more likely to have had intercourse than those living in two-parent homes. And the sexually active teens who did come from two-parent families reported that their families were not close ones and that they were not able to communicate with their parents. For those over sixteen, family closeness did not loom as such a major factor. Among younger teenagers, the researchers found that these *is* a correlation between lack of closeness in the family and the young adolescent's inclination to have sex at an early age.

Peer Pressure to Have Sex Is Strong

Despite the flip side of the statistics showing that half of all American teenagers are *not* yet sexually active, the teenager who is still a virgin may feel like the last and only one in his or her school. In addition to real sexual activity, there is a lot of bragging, exaggerating and lying about sexual experience among teens these days.

"I felt sure I was the only virgin left in my crowd and it got to the point where I just wanted to get it over with and be able to say —like everyone else—that I had done it," says a sixteen-year-old named Jill. "Otherwise, it was like I was an outsider or a baby or something. I'm not sure it was worth it. I wasn't exactly thrilled by the experience. I felt guilty and bad about myself plus I was disappointed. I kept thinking, 'So what's the big deal?' But I did it mostly because everybody was doing it or *said* they were and I didn't want to be out of it."

This peer pressure can be powerful, particularly when parents are silent on the subject of sex. A teenager may see sexual activity as a way to fit in, to be normal, to have friends and to feel loved and desired. Those who have not yet discovered their own value as human beings are especially vulnerable to peer pressure to be sexually active. Teens who have plans for the future and who feel good about themselves, on the other hand, are less likely to see sexual acting out as the route to self-fulfillment and acceptance.

Sexual Activity Can Be a Form of Rebellion

If parents voice strict prohibitions against sexual activity of any kind and are very controlling in other areas of a teenager's life, he or she may see sexual acting out as a way to accomplish two goals. First, it is a means of rebelling against parental values, dictates and mores. Second, it is a way of proclaiming separateness, a way of saying, "I own my body and I can do whatever I want with it and you don't really have anything to say about it!"

Sexual Acting Out Can Be an
Attempted Antidote to Depression

The depressed teenager, in a desperate attempt to dispel the depression, may begin to act out sexually. A teen in this situation generally has very low self-esteem, a hunger for love and attention, a need for acceptance and caring. He or she may try to find the fulfillment of these various needs in sexual activities. Some teens hope that through sex they will become more valued, loved and accepted. They fantasize about sex filling gaps in their self-esteem and making them wise and adult. They dream that sex is the key to true intimacy and commitment.

Sex can be an antidote to depression, a vehicle for rebellion, a plea for acceptance or a search for closeness—but it usually creates problems for the teenager because, of course, it does not often meet these high expectations. It does not make one instantly wise and adult, bring acceptance, foster intimacy or guarantee a deep and lasting love. It is not even fun and doesn't feel good to some teens whose attempts at sexual sharing may be handicapped by lack of privacy, lack of time, lack of emotional maturity and lack of experience.

While you can't prescribe and mandate what your child's sex life will be like, you *can* have a major influence in this area of life if you approach the subject of sexuality in a new way.

Sexuality-related problems are particularly distressing to both parent and teenager, but these problems present opportunities for you to educate, communicate with and show your love and commitment to your child. You the parent are crucially important in helping your teenager get beyond this troubled passage, to grow in self-acceptance, responsibility and the capacity to love. This can't be taught in sex education classes, at the movies or in books. It can be taught by you: by what you say, what you do, how you live and how you share feelings and ideas with your teenager. You may not be able to make choices for your teenager. You may not agree with some of the choices he or she does make. But you *can* make a real difference in the way he or she feels and how he or she grows in the capacity for sharing love and joy and intimacy with others.

CHAPTER 18

Crisis Prevention: Raising a Sexually Responsible Teenager

S EXUALITY IS PART of all our lives, whatever our choices of expression. All people, from infants to the elderly, are sexual beings and are capable of responding to any number of sensual pleasures. Feeling good about one's sexuality is an important part of self-acceptance and the development of strong self-esteem. This, in turn, is a major factor in making responsible sexual choices. It's important to accept one's feelings, whatever these may be, without labeling them as bad or dirty. However, we *are* responsible for *actions*. With these actions come certain moral responsibilities to ourselves and to others. Acting in a caring, responsible way enhances self-esteem, improves relationships, minimizes pain and helps prevent sexuality-related crises.

How can you help your child not to deny sexuality or to abuse it, but to grow into a loving, responsible person sexually?

Take Responsibility for the Sex Education of Your Child

Schools can't and shouldn't do it all. Information from peers is often crude and inaccurate. And information from sex education

197

books, while often accurate and helpful, is purposely general and objective in order to reach a large cross-section of people. If you have good communication with your teenager, only you know exactly what he or she really wants and needs to know. Only you can discuss sexual choices in the context of your child's own upbringing and life experience. Since teenagers are bombarded with sex via TV, movies and advertising in all media as well as pressure from peers, it's up to you to help your teen make sense of all this and decide which choices are right for him or her.

It isn't an easy position to be in and many parents meet the challenge with confused or embarrassed silences. A 1978 study of fourteen hundred parents of children twelve and under in the Cleveland area revealed that 88 percent had never discussed sex with their children. Among parents of nine- to eleven-year-old girls, 40 percent had not yet explained menstruation—an alarming number since today many girls begin menstruating at ten or eleven.

Many parents who grew up in times when sex was not discussed openly find it difficult to change that pattern. Others are afraid that too much talking and too much information will put ideas into their kids' heads. Actually, the more information young people have, the better. A study of college students not long ago revealed that students who had the most accurate knowledge about sex (measured via a written exam) were less likely to be sexually active. Those who knew the least, on the other hand, tended to be the most sexually active. It is usually what teenagers *don't* know about sex—or what they assume to be true—that can hurt them.

Since silence and embarrassment about sex on your part teaches your child more than you realize, it makes sense to take the risk of communicating and educating your child in a more positive way. Examine your own feelings about sex—with an accent on the positive feelings you have. When you consider your negative views and your embarrassment about the subject, ask yourself where and how you got these attitudes and whether you really want to pass them on to yet another generation. Perhaps now is the time to break the chain of embarrassed and awkward silences.

Some parents try to compromise by offering their teenagers factual books about sex. This is a good beginning, especially if you review and discuss the information together. However, if it isn't used in this way, to facilitate communication and to provide solid facts for discussion, a book's ability to help is limited. A book cannot speak to your child in the personal way that you can. And "plumbing information"—straight facts about sex—is only part of what good sex education is all about. Your child also needs to know what sexually responsible behavior is, how to make choices that are right, how to grapple with mixed feelings and moral dilemmas. The teens who are most likely to act out and get in trouble sexually are those who have no concept of or plans for the future. Studies have shown, for example, that many teenage mothers have no sense of their abilities as individuals or of future possibilities. They tend to see motherhood as their only way to be special. Encouraging special hobbies and interests and helping to make planning for the future a pleasurable part of life can help your teen a great deal.

Explore Ideas and Issues in a Nonthreatening Way

Instead of asking, "Why do you want to know *that?*" when your teenager requests factual information, it is more helpful to give whatever information is requested, finding the answer together if you're not sure of the facts yourself, and to keep moral discussions on a nonthreatening level.

You can do this in everyday situations, using a book you are reading, a TV show or movie or the situation or crisis of someone you know as the springboard for an informal discussion. Instead of interrogating your teen about behavior, ask for and listen to his or her opinions and perceptions while being open about your own. For example, a TV show featuring an unmarried couple living together might be the springboard for a discussion.

A book about sexuality can open a conversation: "I've been reading this book and just discovered something interesting that I never realized before . . ." or "I was reading this book and am a little confused about this part. I'm not completely sure that I agree with it because . . . What do you think?" Or, if a family you know is experiencing a sexuality-related crisis, it will help to explore in a general way how such a crisis happened and how it might have been prevented. Discussing the general issue of premature parenthood in a realistic way is always helpful. Many teenagers romanticize parenthood.

"My daughter was feeling a little envious of a classmate who was expecting a baby because she was getting a lot of attention and was anticipating having a cute, cuddly baby to love," says Carolyn Mager, the mother of two teenagers. "One evening, I asked how Cece was doing and remarked that I feared Cece would be in for a shock once the baby came. I shared some of my own feelings about parenthood when I first became a mother at twenty-six: the moments of love and of desperation, the unrelenting demands as well as the joys of children, saying I was glad I was more mature and had had a lot of life experience before I took on the challenge of parenthood. I asked my daughter Lisa how she would feel if she were in Cece's place and if she would choose to be a parent at an early age. It started a really good conversation. I purposely didn't put on what Lisa calls my 'teaching voice.' I just shared ideas and listened to hers. We didn't agree on everything, but we did listen to each other and maybe some of what I said made an impression. That's certainly better than it used to be."

Faced with such an educational challenge, some parents feel intimidated. You may be among these, feeling that there is so much change today and so many things one should know that you aren't up to the task of giving accurate, up-to-the minute information to your teenager. Try to see sex education as sharing information rather than always giving it. "When my child asked me a question I couldn't answer easily or something came up about which I knew little, I felt threatened," reports one father. "Only when I gave myself the command not to be a know-it-all did we really start communicating. I began to say, 'I'm not sure about that. Let's find the answer together.' I find that when we explore sexual information and issues together, we talk quite easily and my children are better able to accept this information without embarrassment or rebellion."

Sharing information about sexuality as a natural part of life is a much more effective means of education than the one-time-only excruciatingly embarrassing Big-Talk-About-Life. Exchanging bits and pieces of ideas and concepts on a day-to-day basis puts sex where it belongs—as a part of life, as part of one's total identity, not as something mysterious, overwhelming, secret and totally forbidden (and possibly more attractive than ever to the curious teen). Growing up with a balanced view of sexuality and how it fits into one's life in general helps a child get a better perspective and begin to make responsible choices.

Build Your Child's Self-Esteem

If your teenager feels good about him- or herself in most areas of his life, he will not be as susceptible to peer pressure. If the issue of your child's sexual activity has come up, take a less judgmental approach that invites introspection and communication.

"It may help to raise a question," says Dr. Marilyn Mehr. "You might ask, 'Can you have sex in this situation and still feel good about yourself?' or 'Is what you're doing adding to or taking away from your feelings about yourself as a worthwhile person?' "

Instead of expressing strict prohibitions against teenage sex, state your reservations about such activity. You might suggest, for example, that many teenagers seem to rush into sex before they are emotionally ready and able to cope with the consequences of their actions. After expressing this opinion, ask your teenager what he or she thinks about this and explore ways that a person can tell if he or she is ready to become sexually active.

Here are some questions that you and your teen might explore together.

What Do Teenagers Expect and Want from Sex?

Some teenagers (and older people, too) seek personal validation through sex. Some look for intimacy. Some expect to find warmth and love through sexual sharing. These needs may or may not be met through sexual involvement. Exploring your teen's sexual expectations together is an opportunity for you to express the idea that when one comes to a sexual relationship with maturity, a strong and positive sense of self and a great deal of love and warmth to give and vulnerability to share, the chances of finding happiness in sexual activity are greater. It is also an opportunity to discuss the fact that self-esteem grows as a person grows emotionally and intellectually and that relationships grow as the result of many factors, including time, commitment, good communication and sharing in many ways—physical and otherwise.

How Can a Person Tell If He or She Is Ready for Sexual Involvement?

A person who may not be ready to share sex with another person tends to have a number of the following characteristics. He or she

- Wants to have sex because of peer pressure ("Everyone else is doing it!") or to rebel against parental values or because a boyfriend or girlfriend is applying considerable pressure to become sexually active. This teenager may feel guilty about having sex and may show this guilt by refusing to use birth control, thus pretending that sex is an accident instead of being preplanned.
- Has unrealistic expectations of sex, believing that it will make him or her instantly wise, mature, loved and valued and will be the binding factor in a love relationship that lasts forever.
- Sees the other person (or people) involved as objects, conquests or challenges, not as individuals with needs and feelings.
- Deliberately misleads a prospective sex partner to get what he or she wants.
- Is unable to communicate with the partner about sexual preferences, birth control or feelings.
- Has not weighed the pros and cons of being sexually active and is disinclined to consider possible consequences such as rejection, disappointment, painful feelings that come when violating one's own values, VD or pregnancy. Instead of acknowledging these negative consequences and taking responsibility for preventing them, the person who is emotionally immature says, "Oh, well, it can't happen to me."

What Is Responsible Sex?

Someone who is sexually responsible, on the other hand, has loyalty to his or her own values, sensitivity and consideration for others and a realistic attitude toward sexual activities and possible consequences. This person

- Has correct information about sex, not only about lovemaking techniques but also about birth control and VD.
- Chooses to have sex because the time, the person, the feelings and the circumstances are right, *not* out of fear of losing the partner or of being different and out of it. The sexually responsible person feels secure enough to be true to his or her own values, to make free choices about expressing sexuality right now. He or she feels as free to say no as yes. Choosing not to have sex when the person and the circumstances are not right, even at the risk of disappointing someone else, can be a positive

choice. He or she doesn't feel the need to prove himself via sexual activity.

- Does not use sex to exploit another person. This means seeing partners as people, not as objects to be used. It means putting an emphasis on sharing, not scoring, and on being a friend as well as a lover. A friend respects another's choices, privacy and feelings and will not try to force another to act against his or her own best interests. A friend will not abandon, ridicule or reject another in a crisis. A friend can enjoy the partner as a total person who has much to share besides sex.

- Usually has sex within the framework of a caring relationship in which the partners genuinely like and often love each other. They have realistic expectations about sex and each other and can communicate openly about feelings, fears, expectations and preferences. They are able to be vulnerable and real with each other.

- Is willing to take responsibility for his or her actions, not only in preventing unwanted pregnancy or the spread of VD, but also in taking the responsibility to be kind, honest, considerate and caring.

What Is the Difference Between Sex and Sexuality?

Sex is a description of gender and is often used to mean sexual intercourse. Sexuality is part of who we are, a fact of life from birth to death. As such, it is not bad or wrong, but simply a part of our lives. Sexuality is feeling and being in addition to acting.

Is Sex the Best Way to Express Love and Intimacy?

Sexual intercourse can be pleasurable in a number of circumstances and is a special joy when shared within the context of a loving, committed relationship. But it is not necessarily the ultimate proof of love, nor is it always necessary for the development and growth of love between two people. It may help if you and your teen could make a list of all the ways people show love for each other.

"There are many ways of sharing love," says noted sex educator Elizabeth Canfield. "Hearing a concert together is making love. Taking care of a loved one who is sick is making love. Working together on a project you really believe in is making love. Discovering a lovely flower together, having a good conversation, even sharing a disappointment or sorrow is making love. Love and intimacy mean a great variety of shared experiences, both good and bad. That's what real commitment is all about. It can be fun. It can also hurt. It means committing yourself to struggle and to share."

Making your teenager aware of the many ways of sharing love and the challenges and joys of true intimacy is a vital part of his or her sex education.

Don't Be Afraid to Express Your Own Values

It's important for your teenager to know where you stand. After a period of rebellion and testing, children often come to share parental values quite closely by early adulthood. It's important to express your values even if your teen disagrees. Disagreement and seeming indifference do not mean that you haven't been heard.

Avoid Either/Or Thinking

Realize that you and your teenager will probably have clashes of values and some differing ideas about sexual behavior and responsibility. When this happens it does not mean that your child, acting on his own convictions and feelings, does not respect you and your feelings. It's important to make clear to your child that mutual love and respect are not dependent on conformity to your values or your child's. At the same time, listening to your teenager's feelings and opinions and accepting them does not mean agreeing with or approving of them. It simply keeps communication open. A clash of values now does not mean that it will always be so. While you may never agree totally with your child's sexual choices, you may still wield some positive influence.

Although you can't usually mandate *no* sexual activity until a certain age or marital status or succeed in getting an already sexually active teenager to stop having sex just because you say so, you can encourage your child to be responsible, loving and non-exploitive of himself or herself and others. Such positive views of sexuality, whatever a person's life-style and choices, are essential to good self-esteem and rewarding relationships—sexual and otherwise. If, for example, you find that your daughter is taking birth control pills and this is the first clue you've had that she is sexually active, express your views on the matter but give her credit for responsibility, saying, "I feel a bit shocked about the fact that you are having sex. I feel that you may be too young to be so involved with someone else in this way. You also know my feelings about premarital sex. However, I'm pleased that you are taking the responsibility of preventing pregnancy. That shows a lot of maturity and good judgment on your part and that pleases me, even though I don't approve of some of your choices."

It is essential not to reject an adolescent on the basis of his or her sexual behavior. Threats or actual rejection reinforce hurtful patterns of behavior. Your teenager, convinced that he or she is not really loved at home, will look for such unconditional love in others, possibly in sexual relationships, and be vulnerable to a great deal of pain, low self-esteem and disappointment. It is far more constructive to let the child know that he or she is loved, even if you don't love a particular behavior.

Be Open to the Idea of Others Helping

Sometimes the whole area of sexuality is too difficult and overwhelming for a teenager and parent to discuss completely. This may be especially true with parents whose own upbringing and value systems do not include open discussions of sexuality or who find it so awkward and embarrassing that they fear doing more harm than good. It can also be true of a single parent raising a child (especially of the opposite sex) alone and feeling that he or she can't possibly tell the child everything that's necessary. That's when outside sources can help. Books (see Appendix), teen rap sessions (some sponsored by family counseling centers, Planned Parenthood, church groups and other organizations), school sex education classes and help from extended family members or friends are all valuable.

Contrary to the common fear, knowledge about sex does not equal action. It promotes responsibility. Ignorance, on the other hand, leads to experimentation out of curiosity, exploitation, unwanted pregnancies (teenagers are woefully ignorant of birth control and this doesn't seem to keep them from being sexually active) and the spread of venereal disease. It is what teens don't know about sex that can hurt them the most.

CHAPTER 19

Coping with Sexual Activity and Depression

SOMETIMES THE DEPRESSION comes first and the teenager uses sex in an attempt to anesthetize troubling feelings, seek comfort and love, capture parents' attention or act out in rebellion against parents' values. In other instances, the teenager has sex in response to peer pressure or his or her own curiosity and sexual feelings or as a means of proclaiming separateness from parents—and depression follows. This depression may come as the result of a number of feelings: guilt, rejection by a lover, fear of not being normal, disappointment over the experience and parental anger and rejection, real or anticipated. The young adolescent may have many mixed feelings about the experience.

You may know or suspect that there is a sexual link to your teenager's depression. Perhaps your child has left an obvious trail of clues. The fact that Beth Barnett left her birth control pills where she knew her mother would find them shows that, quite possibly, she wanted her mother to know that she was sexually active. Perhaps you simply have strong suspicions that sexual activity is going on. Or perhaps your teen has come out and told you that he or she is sexually active and troubled.

After the initial shock of the disclosure, how can you best cope and help your child? There are a number of possibilities.

How You Can Help

Don't Launch a Personal Attack or Take Personal Affront

Both these tactics are very common temptations, especially when you're feeling shocked, angry and confused. You may be tempted to say, "How could you *do* such a thing? I *knew* you couldn't be trusted!" or "You're a tramp! You're just like all the other kids today. You have no morals. I'm shocked and ashamed of you!" or, taking the behavior personally, your initial reaction might be, "How could you do this to *me?*"

Don't Label Your Teenager

It's also important not to label or exaggerate behavior. The word *promiscuous* is thrown around a lot and may apply to a boy or girl who has a lot of emotionally uninvolved sex with a number of different partners, perhaps in a compulsive manner. The term does not apply to a teenager involved in a caring, committed one-to-one sexual relationship. Applying labels, especially ones that don't fit, is hurtful and damaging to self-esteem and to your relationship with your teenager.

Communicate Your Concern in a Caring Way

Strong reactions, while common and understandable under the circumstances, are counterproductive, blocking communication, making the teenager feel worse, more isolated and depressed than ever and perhaps reinforcing the sexual behavior. It is more constructive to be gentle, open and empathetic. If your teen tells you about being sexually active, you might ask, "How does this make you feel? Does it add to or take away from your good feelings about yourself?" Or you might share some of your feelings: "I feel surprised and somewhat shocked to hear that. But most of all, I'm feeling concerned for you and wondering how this is affecting your feelings about yourself."

If your teenager hasn't told you that he or she is sexually active but has left obvious clues for you to find, you might say, "I get the feeling that you wanted me to know. Maybe you wanted to talk over some of your feelings. I would like for us to share some feelings about this."

When you simply suspect that your teenager is sexually active, it might be helpful to say, "I see you and _____ getting very involved with each other and I feel concerned. I feel the need to talk with you about what close involvements—including sexual involvements—can mean."

Other important areas of discussion: what such sexual involvement means to the teenager; what his or her expectations are about the relationship; and whether he or she has the knowledge and motivation to prevent pregnancy and the spread of venereal disease.

Since you can't actually change your teen's behavior, however much you might like to do so, it's important to make suggestions and ask gentle questions that encourage the teenager to examine behavior without feeling the need to act assertive by disagreeing with you. This way, your teen may come to the independent conclusion that some of his or her behavior needs to change.

If the teenager is upset and worried or depressed but can't pinpoint the negative feelings about a sexual experience, it will help if you make some observations in a very general, nonthreatening way. For example, "A lot of people wonder if they're normal, especially when a date doesn't call again," or, "Some people involved in a first sexual experience are disappointed. They have such high expectations and such little experience that it's quite understandable and very common to be disappointed at first."

If the teenager is sad about the loss of a lover or a date who didn't call again after a sexual encounter, it is more productive to acknowledge the sadness and disappointment: "You seem to be very sad and upset about this. I understand. You gave so much to this person and it can really hurt when that person doesn't call or want to be with you anymore."

Stifle the urge to say, "Well, what did you expect? He got what he wanted! You've been used. When will you ever learn?" Instead, show that you understand your teen's feelings, even if you disapprove of his or her actions. If you show your child that you care and can be trusted with feelings and confidences, you can discuss in a reasonable fashion the ways the teen might modify behavior to feel better about himself and to prevent such unhappy events in the future.

Help Your Teenager Feel Better About Himself

Tell him that he is a valuable, worthwhile person and in which ways. Help him or her to feel loved, valued and better about many aspects of his life. Teens who know they are valued as separate persons and who have good self-esteem are not as likely to get involved in hurtful, counterproductive sexual liaisons. Explore ways that the teenager can improve self-esteem and also discuss the ways one can express love and commitment, sex being only one of many ways that people say, "I care."

Keep Your Own Feelings Under Control

You may need to blow off steam to a spouse, a close friend or relative or to a professional counselor, but try to discharge your feelings in ways that will not damage your relationship with your teenager further. It's important to realize your limitations, that you probably can't stop sexual activity once it has started. You can, however, make your opinion and values clear in ways that will make your teenager listen.

When Betty Riley discovered that her fourteen-year-old daughter Heather was having sex with her boyfriend of one year, she expressed her opinion of the situation in a clear but low-key way. "I told my daughter, 'I feel very concerned about you because I feel that you are still very young to be involved in a sexual relationship.' I also said, 'I worry about the consequences for you both physically and emotionally. I love you and don't want to see you hurt. I realize that having sex is your choice. I disapprove of this choice, but I also realize that I can't be around twenty-four hours a day to stop you from having sex. I am saying that I wish you wouldn't have sex. I feel you aren't mature enough, but we seem to disagree on that point. If you make the choice to keep having sex, however, I *do* expect that you will take some mature responsibilities like using a reliable method of birth control.' Well, it turned out that Heather hadn't been using birth control. It was unbelievably difficult for me to do this, but I finally agreed to take her to our doctor and get her educated and started on a program of birth control. I agonized over whether this was condoning or encouraging her behavior. I came to the conclusion that it wasn't. She was having sex without birth control. What I had in mind was to prevent further problems, the real tragedy of a pregnancy at fourteen. As it turned out, she broke up with her boyfriend several months later and is not presently sexually involved with anyone. She even admitted that I was probably right about her being too young. We're closer now in many ways. At least we can discuss the difficult subjects and listen to each other. I think maybe she respects my opinions a little more now that she has seen I may have been right. I don't hit her over the head with that, though. I wish she hadn't had sex at fourteen, but she did and maybe she learned something from it, although I would have preferred she learn in other ways. But it was ultimately her choice, not mine. I just want to help her to make wiser choices in the future."

By empathy and open communication, you may get through to your teenager and help him or her make wiser choices in the future. You may help him or her realize that sex is not the best antidote to depression or a cure-all for low self-esteem. Most of all, you can offer your teenager the warmth, love and support he or she needs and wants so much.

Explore Other Sources of Help

There are Planned Parenthood rap groups, sexuality education programs and family counseling services that may help your teenager examine feelings and choices and enable you and your child to communicate more effectively with each other in this vital area.

CHAPTER 20

Pregnancy

IGNORANCE AND GUILT form part of a tragic equation that can result in a teenager becoming pregnant. Recent studies show that some 40 percent of all sexually active teenagers become pregnant each year and that thirteen thousand girls under the age of fifteen bore children in 1976.* The twelve- to seventeen-year-old maternal age group has been increasing annually and is the only age group registering such increases.

These young mothers and their babies face numerous health risks—complications of pregnancy, labor or delivery, congenital birth defects and infant mortality rates running 30 percent higher than for mothers over the age of twenty. The social risks are also high: undereducation, welfare dependency, early marriage and higher risk of divorce.

It is estimated that if current trends continue, four out of every ten teenage girls will have at least one pregnancy while in their teens. Studies have revealed that up to 80 percent of the nation's four million sexually active teenagers fail to use birth control, due largely to ignorance about methods or about the availability of contraceptive services.

Depression can also be a significant factor in teenage pregnancy, particularly when the pregnancy is at least partially intentional.

* Most recent figures available.

"A teenager may become pregnant as a way of feeling important and needed," observes Dr. Marilyn Mehr. "And this is a way of coping with her depression."

Some recent studies support this observation. In one group of unmarried teenagers who were pregnant for the first time, 36 percent revealed that the pregnancy was intentional. Adolescent behavior experts observe that the adolescent who gets pregnant on purpose is often depressed, has low self-esteem and poor relationships with others. She may see a baby as the antidote to her loneliness and lack of accomplishments. She may also use the pregnancy to keep a boyfriend, to retaliate against her parents or to soothe her feelings of grief over the loss of a loved one through death or a parental divorce. Teen boys with low self-esteem may encourage their girlfriends to get pregnant and see such pregnancies as proof of manhood.

Statistics and general facts about teenage pregnancy are alarming enough, but are nothing compared to the shock and desperation you may feel if you discover that your teenage son or daughter is involved in such a pregnancy. In the event of such a crisis, how can you best help?

How You Can Help

Take a Deep Breath and Think Before You Speak

You are shocked, angry, desperate and frightened. You feel like lashing out verbally at your teenager. You feel like saying "I told you so!" or "I've had it! You're on your own!" or "How could you *do* this to me?" You feel like punishing the teenager. However, the pain of telling you about the pregnancy, planned or not, is usually a punishment in itself for the frightened teen who needs your help, love and support now more than ever before. Try to take a deep breath, count to ten, twenty or beyond and then respond in a gentle and supportive way. Your first words will long be remembered so make sure that your response is memorable in a positive way! Concentrate on feelings before exploring action alternatives. Tell your teen that he or she is loved and that you will do everything possible to help in this moment of crisis. Not only will this help the teenager cope better with the crisis of pregnancy, but it will also greatly improve your relationship for years to come.

Jeannie Collins, now twenty-two, has never forgotten how supportive her parents were during her pregnancy crisis six years ago. "I thought my folks would kill me or throw me out. I thought they didn't love me," she says. "It took a crisis like that for me to realize how wrong I was. They were so supportive, it was beautiful. I could tell that they were disappointed and hurt, but they were really there for me and let me know they loved me and would stick by me. I made the decision to have an abortion. It wasn't an easy decision or experience but Mom and Dad were there for me and that's something I'll never forget."

Help Your Teenager Explore Alternatives in a Realistic Way

Sometimes this means helping your daughter or your son's girlfriend deal with a lot of peer pressure. The trend among young mothers—about 96 percent of those who do not abort—is to keep their babies. Classmates and friends can be cruel and judgmental toward their pregnant peers who choose otherwise, either placing the baby for adoption or having an abortion. However, many of these young mothers who choose to keep their babies are making a fantasy-based decision that could negatively influence their lives and the lives of their children for years to come.

It's important, then, to explore *all* alternatives thoroughly and to help the teenager to realize that no alternative is painless or trouble-free.

Marriage. The teenage couple choosing to marry faces a three times greater risk of divorce than couples who are over twenty. They also face a number of educational and financial hardships as well as isolation from friends whose interests and experiences are suddenly so different. With a lot of luck, maturity, emotional and financial help from their families, the young parents may have a chance to beat the odds and build a happy family life, but they would be exceptional.

If you and your teen are considering marriage as the alternative of choice, it would be wise to seek premarital counseling with a marriage-family counselor or member of the clergy. It is also a good idea for the teenage couple to participate in a support group for young parents sponsored by the National Association Concerned With School-Age Parents (NACSAP).

Adoption. The teenager who relinquishes a baby for adoption may be praised for a very unselfish act—giving the baby up for its own good to a couple who are much better equipped in many ways to raise it. There is undeniable pain, however, in putting one's own child up for adoption.

"I felt a mixture of grief and relief when I gave up my baby," says Sandi, seventeen. "I cried and cried. I'll always wonder about him, but I feel like I gave us *both* a chance at life by making the choice I did."

"It was really, really hard to give up my baby," says fifteen-year-old Deb. "But I didn't want her to grow up on welfare like I have. It's a bad way to live. Things aren't peachy, even though I did make the right choice for both of us. It isn't a happy ending like everything turning out for the best and nobody getting hurt. You *do* get hurt, no matter how sensible and right your choice is. It's just that maybe the right choice—for you—doesn't end up hurting as much."

If you and your teenager are seriously considering adoption as a primary choice, there are a number of excellent agencies offering counseling help and support. Crittenden Services and BirthRite, which operate nationwide, and the Children's Home Society in California are among the best-known services.

Abortion. Abortion is a controversial option, but one chosen by many teenagers. It is estimated that about one in three abortions in the United States today is performed on a teenager.

Most legal abortions, usually done in the first three months of pregnancy, are quite safe. While teenagers have a 60 percent higher death rate for pregnancy and childbirth than older mothers, they have the lowest abortion mortality rate.

Emotional aftereffects of abortion vary, depending on how the girl feels about her decision and how supportive her family and friends may be. According to a Harvard study, 91 percent of postabortion patients studied felt relieved and at peace with their choice. Other studies have shown that about 25 percent of patients have postabortion depression. Some feel that this is primarily an emotional reaction while others contend that it may be due, in part, to hormonal reactions much like those occurring after childbirth which trigger postpartum blues. Some women, however, feel guilty and emotionally upset if they have strong beliefs against abortion or feel that they did not make the choice freely. "If a girl feels forced into an abortion by her parents or boyfriend or if she has strong convictions against abortion, she may have emotional problems afterward," says the Reverend Hugh Anwyl of the Clergy Counseling Service in Los Angeles. "Some of these girls may become pregnant again right away to replace the fetus that was lost."

These comments point up the importance of not forcing alternatives on your teenager. Abortion may or may not be the right choice in your situation, but the teenager's pain will be less if she feels that she played an active role in making the decision.

If you and your teenager are considering abortion, Planned Parenthood-Clergy Counseling services affiliates across the nation offer you a wide range of services, from nonjudgmental counseling to abortion referrals.

Keeping the Baby. Having and keeping the baby is an increasingly popular option among teenagers, despite its obvious problems. Many, of course, don't anticipate the demands infants and children place on parents or the considerable expense of raising a child, and they also underestimate the difficulty of finding, holding and coping with a job as a single parent. Many expect that their own parents will raise their babies, then resent their help. Others begin a lifetime of welfare dependency.

There *are* success stories—like seventeen-year-old Johanna who recently graduated from high school and who is taking a nursing course at a local junior college while her mother cares for the baby. "But as soon as I get home from school, the baby is my responsibility totally," she says. "And once I finish school, I'm on my own with her. I have no free time and no social life, but if I want to raise my daughter and get an education, this is what I have to do." Most of the teen mothers who, like Johanna, seem to be coping well with a difficult life-style, are willing to work hard, to make drastic life-style adjustments and have help from their families. If any one of these elements is missing, the prospects for successful coping with early parenthood are not good.

If your teenager is thinking of having the baby and keeping it, it is essential to get counseling and advice from your physician or a family counselor. Participation in NACSAP rap groups before the birth will also help your teen realize the enormity of the responsibility she plans to take on. It is also helpful if you can find a cooperative friend or relative with a newborn baby you might borrow for a day or two (or, better still, for a weekend) and put your teenage daughter totally in charge.

Dr. Charles Wibbelsman suggested this idea to a fifteen-year-old pregnant patient recently. She took a friend's baby for the weekend and gained new insights into the demands of parenthood. "She came to the conclusion that she was not ready for such responsibility and decided not to keep her baby after all," says Dr. Wibbelsman. "If a girl can learn this *before* she has her baby, it can be most beneficial to mother and child."

State Firmly What Help You Can Give and What You Can't

While your emotional support is essential to your teen, it is also important that you make the limits of your ability and willingness to help very clear. This will help your teenager make realistic choices. For example, if you are unable and unwilling to take on the emotional, physical and financial responsibilities of raising yet another child, say so early on while she is considering alternatives. Don't let her assume that you will help raise her child if this will not be the case. It's vital to be realistic with yourself and each other. Explore your feelings about how much or how little you would choose to be involved in caring for the baby. Forget for the moment what you feel you *should* do or what you think *others* feel you should do. Consider what is right and acceptable for you—day by day for the next eighteen to twenty years. Express your feelings gently but clearly to your teen. While there may be some rough times, some disagreements and angry words, making wise and firm choices now will preclude tragedy later.

CHAPTER 21

Homosexuality

THERE IS A great deal of anguish and depression about homosexuality, either real or imagined, during adolescence. Many teens
worry about being homosexual, perhaps because they are not popular
with the opposite sex or because they are prone to have crushes on
older people of the same sex or because they have strong and loving
feelings toward a same-sex friend. Some, too, are worried about a
few homosexual experiences with friends, or group masturbation,
which are quite common in adolescence, especially among boys. A
Kinsey study over a decade ago revealed that at least 60 percent of
American men and 30 percent of American women have had at least
one overt, intentional homosexual experience by the age of fifteen.
Some teenagers, however, interpret an isolated experience as a sign
of set sexual preference and are distressed over the prospect of
being homosexual. And others discover during adolescence that
they do, indeed, prefer to relate sexually with same-sex friends. As
the parent of a teenager, it will be very difficult to cope constructively with a crisis in this area for a number of reasons.

First, there is little definitive information available about homosexuality and how people come to be that way. Many people are
confused over exactly who is or is not a homosexual.

"Many teens fear being homosexuals, yet don't really know what
a homosexual is," says Dr. Sol Gordon, sex educator and director of
the Institute for Family Research and Education at Syracuse Uni-

versity. "My definition of a homosexual—and I think a lot of people share this definition—is, 'Someone who, *as an adult,* has a constant, definite sexual preference for persons of the same sex.'"

Although most of us have definite sexual preferences one way or the other, very few people are 100 percent hetero- or homosexual, using strict definitions of the terms. The Kinsey Institute has designed a scale to rate sexual orientation, using numerical values ranging from "zero" to "six." A "zero" would be an extreme heterosexual who has never responded emotionally or physically to someone of the same sex. A "six" would be the other extreme: someone who has not and could not relate to someone of the opposite sex in any way. A high percentage of the American population falls in between these two extremes. This includes people who are almost exclusively heterosexual but who have had minor homosexual experience; people who have had experiences with both sexes but who prefer the opposite sex; people who have no special preferences; and people who prefer those of the same sex but who are not exclusively homosexual. Thus, black-and-white classifications and labels can be inaccurate, hurtful and confusing.

Those who do grow up to prefer same-sex sexual partners may recognize and come to terms with their feelings while quite young. Others may not know their true preferences for years. There is a great deal of debate about causes and contributing factors in shaping homosexual preferences. Theories range from biological to psychological causes, but to date there is very little hard data.

Dr. Evelyn Hooker of UCLA, one of the best-known researchers in the area of homosexuality, began her studies more than twenty years ago by challenging the prevailing idea that all homosexuals were sick. The American Psychiatric Association and the American Psychological Association echoed her contentions several years ago by removing homosexuality from the official list of mental illnesses.

Dr. Hooker contends that it is impossible to generalize about the family relationships of homosexuals, but she has said that in some instances early experiences influence sexual preference. Being approached or molested by a homosexual is *not* one of these experiences. Such occurrences are relatively rare, since most child molesters are heterosexual.

Instead, Dr. Hooker has written that unpleasant experiences with the opposite sex or puritanical parents who put too heavy an emphasis on the evils of heterosexual behavior may make a young person feel guilty and anxious about even thinking of the opposite sex. "The child sees homosexuality as the lesser of two evils," Dr. Hooker has said. There are, however, many other theories about the causes of homosexuality.

A second factor that makes homosexuality difficult to deal with is the social conditioning we all have. Homosexuality is seen as an illness, a perversion and a family catastrophe. Some parents say they would rather see their children dead than homosexual. Some are repulsed at the mere mention of the topic and are unable to discuss it at all. Still others, who are quite liberal in general, find that dealing with homosexuality in their own son or daughter is almost unbearable.

Charlotte Spitzer, a teacher and counselor, says that she was very comfortable with the subject of homosexuality and even socialized with some gay people. "I was very liberal and homosexuality never bothered me at all—in someone else's family," she says. "But when my twenty-two-year-old daughter told me that she was a Lesbian, I went to pieces. I went through the whole process: wondering where I went wrong, whose fault it was, wondering why this was happening to us, worrying about what the neighbors would think and then feeling very sad for my daughter. I finally came to the realization that she was still the wonderful girl I'd loved and been proud of for so many years. I asked myself, 'What do I really want for my kid?' I wanted her to be happy and if she's happy, I'm happy. But it took some time and a lot of tears to reach this point." Ms. Spitzer has since founded Parents and Friends of Gays, a self-help organization and hotline primarily for troubled parents of young people who are or may be homosexual.

What can you do if your child suspects or is convinced that he or she is homosexual? There are a number of ways you can help.

How You Can Help

Keep Your Feelings Under Control

As in other sexuality-related crises, watch what you say. If you're feeling too shocked, angry and heartsick to carry on a reasonable conversation, say so and call a time out. You might say something like, "I really want to listen and to talk about this, but right now I need a little time to sort out some of my feelings about all this. Can we continue our discussion a little later?"

This postponement, while certainly not preferable to an open, caring, on-the-spot conversation, *is* more beneficial than an impassioned showdown where you vent a variety of feelings, don't really hear each other and simply build more barriers to communication.

You may feel a lot of things—from fright to grief to shock and anger. If your child believes that he or she is gay and you're having trouble dealing with your feelings, seek help from a counselor, clergyperson or organization for parents. This will help you sort through your feelings and discover new, more constructive ways to cope and help your child.

Don't Be Too Quick to Apply Labels

A single or a few homosexual experiences do not a homosexual make. Warm feelings toward a same-sex friend or a crush on a teacher of the same sex are also more of an indication of the developmental process of adolescence than of homosexuality. Help your child see that everyone has had crushes. Admiring someone else helps one grow in self-discovery, and close same-sex friendships are vitally important, too. Responding in a positive way to a friend's kiss or embrace is natural. Most people enjoy being touched with warmth and love. It is important to realize, too, that sexual experimentation among same-sex teenagers, especially in early adolescence, is quite common and can be a means of exploring one's body and one's emerging sexual feelings in safe, nonthreatening ways. As a parent, do not overreact to these situations or allow your child to label himself on the basis of them.

Ask Your Child Why He or She Feels That He or She May Be a Homosexual

Some teenagers label themselves hastily on the basis of a few experiences or fantasies. With sufficient information from your teen, you may be able to reassure him or her that he or she is not homosexual. If your son or daughter reports that all sexual fantasies center on the same sex and that he or she feels a definite preference in fact as well as fantasy, there *may* be a primarily homosexual orientation. Before saying what *you* think about this or offering to find help, ask the teen what he or she thinks and feels about it. Is it a problem? Is it simply a part of who he or she is? Does he or she *want* any help or counseling? Is he or she asking for help from you or simply sharing feelings? It's important to know your teenager's feelings and needs before leaping into action. Maybe your teen doesn't want your help right now—just your love and support.

Reaffirm Your Love, Whatever Your Teen's Sexual Preference

The unconditional love of a parent is irreplaceable, and its loss is a terrible blow to a young person. In the midst of your shock and confusion, if you are able to express love for your child, it will do a great deal for him and for your relationship. It may even prevent tragedy.

Kara Ogilve first realized that she was a Lesbian when she was only fourteen. "I hated being different and tried to be what I considered normal in lots of ways," she says. "I started having sex with guys, but it didn't make any difference in my sexual feelings, and I felt even worse about myself. I tried to get rid of these feelings with alcohol and drugs and, by the time I was seventeen, I was on the verge of killing myself. I was so depressed I really didn't want to live any more. Then one day my mother came to my room where I was lying on the bed, crying as usual, put her arms around me and told me that she loved me, would always stand by me and would never put me down for being who I was. She had guessed my secret. I can't tell you what a difference it made. It was like I wasn't alone anymore. Eventually, my whole family came to know and accept my feelings, but it was Mom—a really beautiful lady—who reached out to me first and helped me to feel truly loved again."

Expressing love will keep you in touch with your teen and able to help if help is needed. It will also prevent the real tragedy of unnecessary estrangement when you and your child need to talk and be with each other most.

Express Your Reservations with Love

It is not easy to be different. As a parent, you feel sad that your child may lead a more difficult life than most because of sexual orientation. The fact that he or she could be the target of hatred, ridicule or discrimination is a very real concern. Express your fears and reservations in the spirit of, "This is what I fear . . . and why I feel so sad. I hate to see you unhappy and in pain." Reservations expressed in this way show your feelings, your love and your concern and are a basis for discussion—not arguments.

Learn About Homosexuality

Read books about the subject from all viewpoints. Consult other reliable sources of information, from your physician to a counselor experienced in crises of sexual orientation. If your teen is receptive to the idea, explore the subject together. It might also help to meet and talk with nonmilitant gay people (people you meet through friends or counseling services) who are living quite ordinary, productive, nonstereotypical lives. It will be reassuring to discover that many if not most gay people do not fit the popular stereotypes of homosexuals.

If Your Child Seems Troubled, Suggest Professional Help

You might consult your family doctor, a local adolescent medical facility or Family Service Association office to find a counselor or therapist who would be particularly sensitive to troubled feelings about sexual preferences. Don't urge your child into therapy on the premise that he or she should utilize it to change sexual orientation. This may not be possible. Some mental health experts feel that sexual preferences are learned behavior and can be changed. Other therapists believe that sexual preferences may only be changed in instances where the individual is highly motivated and wants the change very much. Even then, however, it is not certain that such therapy will alter one's actual sexual orientation or, simply, sexual behavior. That is, the person may learn to behave in a new way, but whether real feelings will change is still open to debate.

Today, a lot of therapy is aimed at helping gay people understand and accept their feelings. So it is important to approach therapy with flexible expectations, the primary one being that you would like to see your child feel better about himself or herself and live a happy, productive life, whatever his or her eventual sexual preference.

Therapy plus loving support from you will help your teenager grow in self-acceptance and in his or her capacity to give and receive love in a nonexploitive way.

"What's really important is not whether a person is gay or straight but how he or she manages relationships," says the Reverend Robert H. Iles, executive director of the Marcliffe Foundation, a counseling and education service in Pasadena, California. "The ability to give and receive love and the capacity to have a truly intimate relationship are so important. True intimacy is very rare and is the greatest challenge we face in life. Being heterosexual (or homosexual) won't guarantee this. It's who you are and how you feel about yourself that matters. Whether a person loves men or loves women is, in the final analysis, not as important as the fact that he or she is able to love."

PART VII

Substance Abuse and Other Risk-Taking Behavior

CHAPTER 22

When Your Teenager Has a Problem with Substance Abuse or Other Risk-Taking Behavior

PETER C. WAS twelve when he took his first drink from his parents' liquor supply. Now, six years later, that night still stands out in his memory. "That was the night I became an alcoholic," he says. "I remember I took little drinks from all the bottles in my parents' bar while they were out. I figured that they wouldn't notice any missing that way. I got very drunk and very sick and fell into bed before they got home. I don't think they knew for a long time that their model son was a drunk. That was just the beginning. It got so I kept whiskey in my locker at school and rushed to take a drink between every class. I needed it to get through the day. I also needed booze to get through a party or other social occasion because I was sort of shy and didn't like myself much. Drinking always made me feel better, for a while at least. But it eventually got me into lots of trouble at school, lost me some friends, caused countless hassles with my parents and finally got me in trouble with the police. I was arrested for drunk driving last year. That was when I decided to go to Alcoholics Anonymous. Things are better for me now. I've been sober for eleven months, but it's tough. I'm having to learn how to face my feelings and find new ways to cope with situations booze got me through before. I figure that emotionally and socially I'm about thirteen years old, so I have some catching up to do."

The past year has been one of continuing crises for Elisa Donnelly, fifteen. Her parents were divorced and her mother remarried. She doesn't get along with her new stepfather. There have been two moves, a change of schools and the loss of her best friend, whose family moved out of the state. Elisa has been coping with her depression by running away from home every time it all becomes too much for her. The first time, seven months ago, she stayed overnight with a friend. Two weeks ago Elisa ran to a special shelter and counseling facility for runaway teenagers in her community. She's still there, getting counseling and sorting through her options for coping with her difficult situation. Her mother is troubled about their future. "We've all had a lot of stress this year," she says. "But now every time anyone disagrees with or tries to discipline Elisa, she takes off or threatens to. This running away habit is very stressful and manipulative. We're getting counseling, but it's hard to know what to do. I'm scared that next time she runs it will be farther and that she'll end up like some kids you hear about, being the victim of an awful crime or becoming a prostitute or something like that. That really scares me. At the same time, her threats and actions are beginning to run my life—all our lives—and it makes me mad as hell!"

Pam Mariano's parents are also frightened and furious since their daughter was caught shoplifting at a local department store. Pam had the cash in her purse to pay for the earrings she was lifting, but did it, she says, "just to see if I could get away with it." Pam's mother suspects that her daughter had been able to shoplift undetected at least several times before. "She had some nice clothes that I knew she couldn't afford on her allowance and I asked her about them, but she always said she had borrowed them from friends," she says. "Now I wonder. I can't understand it. We've tried to teach her good moral standards and values and she's never gone without anything she really needed. I can't understand why she took such a stupid risk. It's humiliating, but even more, it's frightening because I don't think even Pam knows exactly why she did it."

Risk-taking behavior—from substance abuse to running away, shoplifting, having accidents or driving recklessly—can in many instances be linked with depression.

"Teenage boys, especially, may express their depression via alcohol use, power and speed," says Dr. Lee Robbins Gardner. "Being accident-prone is also a form of self-destructive behavior. If your teenager has a lot of accidents, see if he or she is upset. When one is upset, poor judgment and impulsivity are often present and make accidents more probable. And the results can be tragic: traffic accidents kill more than 18,000 young people a year."

Dr. Calvin Frederick observes that "risk-taking behavior—including a continuous pattern of accidents, other self-destructive behavior and substance abuse are frequently indicative of underlying depression. There is a definite correlation between depression and drug abuse and alcoholism and suicide."

And Dan Jones, a counselor for runaway teenagers at The Greenhouse, a shelter and counseling center in New Orleans, says that most runaways he sees these days are not in search of adventure, but are looking for help for a variety of emotional problems and family crises. "Many come from homes broken by divorce or death," he says. "A number have alcoholic parents and some are running away from abusive situations. I would say a fair number are quite depressed."

The statistics for risk-taking behavior are alarming. For example:

- The National Institute on Alcohol Abuse and Alcoholism reports, conservatively, that 1.3 million Americans between the ages of twelve and seventeen have serious drinking problems. A report from the Department of Health, Education and Welfare recently stated that more than 3 million youths nationwide have experienced problems at home, school or on the highways as the result of drinking.
- Former Surgeon General Julius B. Richmond reports that death rates for young adults and adolescents are worse today than twenty years ago—and mixing alcohol and drugs with driving is to blame for much of that toll.
- A study compiled for HEW in 1978 revealed that one in nine high school seniors was smoking marijuana daily—almost double the number of daily users in 1975.
- According to FBI statistics, a million teenagers run away from home each year.
- Over 50 percent of all shoplifters arrested in recent years have been teenagers. The FBI estimates that one out of three persons in the thirteen to nineteen age bracket shoplifts at least once.

Statistics aside, risk-taking behavior takes a dramatic toll on family life and the quality of life a teenager has now and in the future. Alcoholism, drug abuse and reckless driving are life-threatening.

Running away also exposes the teen to numerous physical and emotional risks as well as creating havoc for the family. Getting in trouble with the law has a huge impact on a young person's life for some time to come. And when depression is a component of the risk-taking behavior, as it often is, the result can be a troublesome, sometimes life-threatening cycle of ever deepening depression.

"A number of drugs that kids use and abuse, most notably alcohol, are depressants," says family therapist Shirley Lackey. "The teen is depressed and drinks. He may feel better for a while, but then he feels worse and even more depressed."

Statistics confirm this observation. The suicide rate among alcoholics is estimated to be fifty-eight times that of nonalcoholics, and young alcoholics are no exception to this rule.

Risk-taking behavior is not only a physical threat and a means of perpetuating depression, it also cripples a teenager's ability to cope with troublesome feelings and stress. Alcohol or drug abuse or running away are the methods a teenager uses to escape from the growing pains of adolescence, from the pressures of learning to get along in the adult world, from the necessity of establishing a strong and separate identity. The teenager chooses to run away from rather than face everyday pressures. And so quite apart from the physical risks, risk-taking behavior exacts a high emotional and social price when the adolescent does not pick up the essential life-coping skills usually learned during this time of life. The fact that teens may attempt to escape problems rather than face them, cope and grow as a result is not surprising to many counseling experts.

"Substance abuse—which is very common acting out behavior for depressed teenagers—is actually taught to our kids," contends Dr. Marilyn Mehr. "Drinking alcohol and use of prescription drugs such as tranquilizers are widespread habits among adults. Kids have a model in us. They get the message, 'If you feel bad, *take* something.' So they take something instead of *doing* something constructive and learning to cope with their feelings."

Parents can play a major role in helping their teenagers overcome risk-taking habits by identifying problem areas, serving as good models and encouraging their teens to get expert help in a crisis. Being alert to signs of substance abuse and knowing how to act in risk-taking crises are important steps in improving not only your teen's present life but his or her future one as well.

CHAPTER 23
Substance Abuse

MARILEE BAKER IS seventeen, a former cheerleader and above-average student. On first meeting her one would never guess that she has been battling a drinking problem. "I've been fighting it for three years," she says. "I've been winning the past year, but before then drinking was ruining my life. The problem really came as a surprise. After all, I drank only with friends and I stuck to beer. But I was in trouble. I couldn't stop drinking once I started. Every time I drank, I got drunk. I started not remembering things and had trouble getting up to go to school many, many mornings. Things really got bad before I realized alcohol was a problem for me. My parents took a while to catch on, too. I mean, they weren't crazy about the idea of me being fourteen and drinking beer, but they thought, 'Oh, well, it's only beer. Thank goodness she's not on drugs!' Of course, alcohol *is* a drug and for a long time, I couldn't live without it. When I was drunk, the fact that I'm not the most out-standingly pretty girl around or as smart as my dad would like me to be or as wildly popular with guys as I would like to be didn't hurt me as much. Sometimes I miss the escape, but I'm learning to live with each day as it comes."

Kevin MacDonald is still escaping the difficult realities of his life with a variety of drugs. He smokes marijuana daily and also is a frequent user of Quaaludes. He has tried cocaine and angel dust. His life and ways of coping revolve around drug use. In the meantime Kevin's parents are desperately trying to help their son become drug-free.

"We've done everything we know how to help Kevin," says Dwayne MacDonald. "We've talked with him. We've begged, pleaded, threatened. We've offered to get help for him. We've expressed our love and our concern. It's like talking to a brick wall. Kevin doesn't think he has a problem. He just wants us to get off his back. A couple of times he told us that he isn't taking drugs any more, but we always find out later that he's lying. Our son was never in the habit of lying to us before this. It's just throwing our family into an uproar. Jan and I fight more than usual and we're at the end of our rope with Kevin. We've tried to help and we're back to square one. He's still stoned all the time. His weird friends call in the middle of the night. He rarely goes to school and his grades are terrible. Our son is going down the tubes and nothing we do seems to make any difference."

Substance abuse is a very difficult problem to face and cope with effectively. Many parents are incredulous when they suspect that their teenagers may have a drinking or drug-abuse problem. They try to ignore it, hoping that their perceptions are wrong and the crisis will simply go away. Or they sit down with the drug-dependent teen for an earnest discussion about the dangers of drugs and alcohol abuse—and believe the lies they hear: that the teen was just keeping drug paraphernalia for a friend, that he or she has experimented but is not a habitual drug user. Then, when the lies become apparent, they feel confused and betrayed. Other desperate parents beg and plead with their teens to stop harmful habits, often to no avail. In fact, the teen may counter their expressions of caring with contempt.

Still other parents, afraid that their teenagers will develop substance-abuse habits, get desperate about preventive measures, giving their children impassioned lectures about the evils of alcohol and the dangers of drugs. All too often they lose credibility by taking an alarmist stance on both, by prohibiting any and all use of these substances and by adopting a "Don't do as I do, do as I say" attitude regarding certain substances.

Substance use and abuse is a very difficult issue to handle. A parent must learn and communicate the facts about drugs and alcohol to the teenager without being tuned out and discredited. Some of these facts are alarming and are not what the teenager wants to hear. Communicating them in a way that the teenager listens to is not easy. Dealing with a drug- or alcohol-dependent adolescent is an exhausting challenge. You must be tough yet loving, stress personal responsibility yet not abandon your child. You can help up to a point, but face the fact that when substance abuse is a problem for your teenager, your help alone may not suffice.

Preventive Measures

Before your child ever shows signs of substance abuse there are preventive measures you can take in order to insure that this will *not* become a problem for your child.

Set a Good Example

This can be very important!

- Do you constantly use cocktails or tranquilizers to calm down after a tough day or to fortify you for an ordeal ahead?
- Would you rather take a pill to alleviate physical or emotional pain than work on eliminating the source of the pain?
- Is your medicine chest crammed with prescription drugs to help you calm down, sleep or stay on a diet? In addition to providing a possibly negative example to your children, these drugs are a source of money if they choose to sell them to peers, and they are a means of experimenting if your child decides to try drugs.
- Do all your social gatherings with friends focus on drinking?
- Does someone in your family already have a drinking problem?

Having many drugs in the house or using alcohol habitually as an antidote to stress communicates the message to your teenager that one can always cure what ails one with a pill or a drink. Instead, promote the idea of coping without chemical crutches, without artificial highs, and practice this philosophy in your own life. When you or your teenager are feeling upset, depressed or angry, discuss what you can *do* to deal with these feelings—like finding constructive solutions to a problem, talking things over with someone else, diffusing angry energy or tensions through physical activity. Practice this yourself and encourage your children to do the same.

Educate Yourself About Frequently Abused Substances

It is important to know which substances are frequently abused and the problems that stem from such abuse. Use of heroin and LSD have declined among teenagers, and alcohol is the most abused drug today. Teenagers also abuse barbiturates (downers), amphetamines (uppers), marijuana, cocaine and PCP (also called angel dust). It is also helpful to know about the effects these substances have on the habitual user. Some excellent books, pamphlets and other sources of drug and alcohol information are listed in the Appendix.

There are a number of studies measuring the impact of various drugs on the health of the user and, in some instances, on the user's future offspring. While the long-range effects of marijuana are not yet known conclusively, recent studies tend to urge caution on its use. Knowing and reviewing these studies with your teen will be helpful to all concerned. These studies should be used in knowledge-sharing exercises, not as scare tactics, although some of the findings and observations are rather scary. In many instances, scientific facts about drugs have more preventive impact on a teenager than impassioned pleas and vague warnings from you.

Encourage Local Schools to Have Drug-Abuse Prevention Programs

"Many of these school programs will impress your teenagers more than talks from you," says family therapist Shirley Lackey. Why? Because they are more objective and therefore less threatening to a teenager. The message will be especially meaningful if a school program utilizes young ex-addicts and recovered alcoholics to warn their peers about substance abuse. If your school is reluctant to launch such a program, continued pressure from a group of parents may bring some needed changes.

Be Alert to Signs of Substance Abuse in Your Teenager

Some of these are the same as general symptoms of depression, and others are peculiar to substance abuse. "Yes" answers to even a few of the following questions could indicate a substance-abuse problem with your teenager.

- Has your teenager been neglecting appearance and personal hygiene recently?

- Has ability to concentrate faltered? Is this reflected in a drop in school performance, restlessness or loss of interest and vitality?
- Have you noticed liquor disappearing from your supply or prescription drugs missing from your medicine chest?
- Has your teen had red eyes or been using eye drops a lot lately?
- Has your child been getting more colds or illnesses lately? Has he or she complained of chest pains or had a cough? (Some substances seem to impair immunity, and physicians have noted that heavy marijuana users may experience chest pains.) Does he or she come home sick (i.e., vomiting) a lot lately?
- Has your youngster been drunk or stoned frequently?
- Does your teenager drink alone or feel the need to drink before and during social gatherings?
- Has your child lost time from school because of drinking or drug use?
- Have you noticed the smell of incense wafting from your teen's room lately? (Many pot smokers burn incense to mask the odor of the marijuana.)
- Does your teenager have blackouts, not remembering where he or she was or what he or she did last night or earlier today?
- Has your teen been getting strange phone calls, sometimes at late hours? Is he or she suddenly more secretive about friends and social activities? Has the circle of friends changed suddenly?
- Have you noticed drug paraphernalia such as pipes, cigarette rolling papers, a water pipe or bong, "roach clips," bags of marijuana or other unidentified substances around the house or in your child's room?
- Have you noticed a loss of weight or loss of appetite combined with occasional cravings for sweets in your teenager?
- Does your child seem suddenly hostile, vague, unreachable, unmotivated, secretive? Do you know or suspect that he or she is lying to you about social activities, friends, alcohol or drug use?
- Have you noticed money or other things of value missing from your home?

If you answered yes to any of these questions, it would be a good idea to keep a close and loving watch on your child. If you had several "yes" answers, take action immediately to help your child before a major crisis develops.

How to Cope If Your Teenager Is Abusing Drugs or Alcohol

Confront Your Teenager with Your Suspicions

Some parents avoid confrontations because they are afraid of upsetting their teens or of creating further distance between themselves and their children. Others simply don't know what to do. But parental noninvolvement is often interpreted as not caring, so having the courage and commitment to confront your teenager in a caring way is important.

"When you see your teenager in real trouble you really do need to confront him," says Dr. Mehr. "Make your expectations clear and offer to help in any way you can. It's vital to express yourself clearly. You might say, for example, 'I think that you're an alcoholic. I think you need help.'"

Your teenager may be less than thrilled with your observations and may act angry or resentful or deny that drugs are a problem. Denial is a frequent reaction to such a confrontation. Never try to confront your teenager while he or she is under the influence. Instead, choose a time when he or she is feeling a little down or sick as the result of the habit or when he or she is more open than usual to conversation. If the problem is not yet a crisis, approach the matter in a low-key manner by suggesting that the teenager has some "habits" that worry you and you're wondering if these might soon become a problem. Then throw out some questions regarding the habits to the teenager, either for discussion or for private reflection. Some questions you could ask your teen to consider:

- Does your habit influence your relationships with others? For example, is it causing problems at home? Causing you to lose friends? Keeping you from enjoying activities or hobbies you used to enjoy? Keeping you from being truly close to others?
- Does your habit require you to break a law in any way? Most abused substances are illegal for minors to buy under any circumstances and are illegally acquired. Also, if a drinking or drug habit is serious, it may be expensive enough to make a teenager steal to maintain it.
- Does your habit expose you to medical hazards? Here it is helpful to share some reputable and recent medical studies and

findings with your teen and ask him or her what he or she thinks about these.

- Is your habit creating personal problems for you? These problems may cover a variety of areas of a teenager's life. Maybe the teen is not feeling well physically or is troubled by deep depression after a drinking or drug-taking episode. Maybe he or she has had traffic tickets or an accident as a result of driving under the influence. And maybe the habit has caused an increase in hassles with family, friends and school officials.

Set Rules

You will have to set down very firm guidelines, particularly if your teenager is not receptive to reasonable discussion and self-examination. Some rules to spell out include:

- No drugs or drug use in the house.
- A strictly enforced curfew.
- Modified grounding for repeat offenses, allowing the teen to leave home only to go to school or to sources of help like counseling.
- No use of the family car until the substance-abuse problem is under control.
- No parties or gatherings at your home while you are out.
- No unexplained phone calls or secretive comings and goings.

You may not win any popularity contests, but you may get a handle on the situation and eventually earn your teenager's respect. You must be willing to say, "This is my house. I make the rules and this is what I will not tolerate."

Get Together with Other Parents

Ideally you should join with the parents of your teenager's friends to establish solidarity in rule setting, as well as to provide emotional support for each other. Some of these groups are very effective in counteracting peer pressure to engage in risk-taking behavior and can reinforce more positive choices within the peer group. It is possible, however, that some of the parents may not be ready or willing to face reality. For example, when Hollywood producer Joe Hamilton realized that his daughter Carrie and some of her friends were taking drugs, he called the parents of these friends, and none was willing to even discuss the matter. This may happen to you, but it's an idea worth trying. A supportive parents' group working to make changes among a group of problem teens is a great help. On the other hand, if you feel alone in your efforts, join a more structured parents' group such as Families Anonymous or Toughlove to give yourself some coping ideas and the emotional support you desperately need at this point.

Cut Off Your Teen's Cash Flow

This means careful monitoring of his or her allowance and keeping close tabs on goods that could be pawned or sold. You may want to keep expensive jewelry, collector's items, heirlooms, silver, gold and other possessions of value under lock and key, in safekeeping with a trusted friend or relative or in a safe deposit box.

Make It Uncomfortable for the Teenager to Continue the Habit

This means forcing your child to face the consequences of his or her choices instead of having you provide protection from them. For example, Gail Smith reluctantly decided to let her son Richard smoke marijuana in his room because she was afraid that he would be caught and penalized by the police if he were forced to smoke it elsewhere. When Richard eventually overcame his drug habit, he angrily blamed his mother for prolonging the problem by making it so easy for him to continue it. Gail feels caught in a no-win situation.

Letting your teenager face a confrontation with school authorities over unauthorized absences caused by substance abuse (instead of writing excuses for him or her), or even allowing him or her to spend a night in jail may be necessary steps toward the teen's realization that substance abuse is a problem, not an answer.

"If your child has an alcohol or drug problem, see how these substances are taking care of your child's needs and pain," says Dr. Alan Berman. "If the substances are working well, he may reject your help and think you're out of your mind to suggest other sources. But if he is experiencing secondary problems as a result of the habit, he will be more receptive to your suggestions."

Discover Your Best Sources of Help and Use Them

It is quite likely that you alone will not be able to help your teenager overcome a substance-abuse problem, so it's important to realize your limitations in this regard.

"With an addiction problem it may come to the point where you can't help any more," says Dr. Mehr. "You can't *make* someone stop drinking or taking drugs. In the final analysis, the individual must do this for himself."

And teacher Mary Ann Dan observes, "In most instances, parents really can't solve a drug problem. This is best dealt with by professionals because many times the issues precipitating drug-taking behavior are related to the parent-child relationship."

There are many sources of help that you can explore. (Specific information about sources of help is in chapter 29 and where to find such help is in the Appendix.) Your family physician, organizations like Alcoholics Anonymous (which has groups just for teens and young adult alcoholics), Al-Anon (for families of alcoholics), special parents' support groups, local drug or alcohol rehabilitation programs and your local Family Service organization are among these sources of help. Realizing that your ability to help may be limited and being open to outside help can be important to both you and your troubled teenager.

In interviews about their problems in helping their teenage daughter Carrie deal with her drug problem, Carol Burnett and her husband Joe Hamilton have repeatedly emphasized the importance of realizing one's limitations as a parent. "We want to reach out to other parents and say, 'Look, if your kid has a brain tumor, you're not going to operate!'" Ms. Burnett has said. "What makes you think just because you're mommy and daddy that you can deal with drug addiction? We thought we could; that we could reason with, threaten and otherwise get through to Carrie. It didn't dawn on us that we were dealing with a walking chemical. Then we got strong and forced her to get help. I would like to tell other parents not to be afraid of your children. Don't be afraid they will hate you. . . . Love them enough to let them hate you."

Overcoming a substance-abuse problem may take not only expert professional help but also time. Some backsliding is common. There are no easy solutions. But there is hope—if you have the courage and commitment to face the problem and reach out for help.

CHAPTER 24
Running Away

JENNIE-LYNN REESE IS fourteen and street-wise, having fended for herself for several months in the Los Angeles area before seeking help from a youth counseling service. "I'm an unlovable kid," she says. "Everyone back home in Fresno was down on me. My teachers were always criticizing me. I had no friends. My parents never wanted me. I figured I had two choices—to kill myself or to run away. So I ran away. What would *you* have done?"

Wendy Wilson, also fourteen, is huddled in a blanket watching television at a runaway shelter in St. Louis. Her voice rarely rises above a whisper as she tells her story: her parents' divorce and subsequent remarriages, family alcoholism, her feelings that there is no place for her in her parents' new lives, her growing pains and recent suicidal feelings. Running away seemed to be the most reasonable alternative. "I had to run away from home to save my mom's marriage," she says. "I caused too much trouble because of my suicidal tendencies and my depression and fussing and stuff. My leaving was better for all of us."

Unfortunately, tragedy trailed Wendy as she ran away. She was viciously assaulted on a St. Louis street by a man who tried to rape and then kill her. She matter-of-factly points out the bruises and cuts on her neck. Her eyes are distant, vacant. She pulls the blanket around her like a cocoon. "I need a lot of help and caring right now," she says. "I'm really scared and I don't know what will

240

happen to me. My folks don't want me back and I'm waiting for a
court date. I guess I'll be put in a foster home. I hope things work
out. I'm really trying to get myself together and be more confident
and trust people more."

Wendy's roommate at the shelter is Jane Harrell, sixteen, an
excellent student and aspiring journalist whose recent depression
led her to experimentation with drugs and caused her to run away
from her affluent Chicago-area home. "My parents didn't seem to
care," she says. "We couldn't communicate at all. All they showed
any interest in were my grades and the honors I won. They didn't
see me as a person. So I started taking drugs. They didn't say anything. I was hurting so much. I finally got on a bus and rode as far
as my money would take me, which turned out to be St. Louis.
Then I was scared. I picked up a phone at the bus terminal, dialed
the operator and asked for help. She told me to come here, which
was a lucky thing. I've been here two months getting counseling
and am feeling much better about myself. I'm learning how to say
honestly what I'm thinking. You know what I'm feeling great about
right now? My father came down to visit this past weekend and I
talked to him more than I ever have before in my whole life! I
feel much more ready to go home now and I want to get on with
my life. I want to go to college and study journalism. I have lots of
plans for the future now. I didn't before."

Jennie-Lynn, Wendy and Jane have many counterparts among
runaway teenagers. Counselors who work with young runaways
observe that teens often run away as the result of family problems
and depression. Some run after a disagreement with parents, others
to escape a crisis situation involving sexual abuse or family alcoholism. Some run in response to the stress of life changes.

Fourteen-year-old Patty Lund, for example, is bright and personable and until a year ago had never given her parents a hint of
trouble. She and her family enjoyed a comfortable life in their
Minnesota home. Then suddenly, everyone's fortunes seemed to
reverse. Her father's business failed, financial problems mounted and
Patty's mother went to work, becoming the family breadwinner.
Along with this dramatic change of family life-style, Patty's own
adolescent growing pains were adding even more stress to her life.
Finally one day she hitchhiked to a neighboring city and was picked
up by a man who took her to New York to work as a prostitute. Six
weeks later, the New York City Police Department's Runaway Unit
picked Patty up at 2 A.M. on a midtown Manhatten street where she

was stopping traffic and making offers to the drivers. For all its horrors, Patty's story has a hopeful ending. She was sent home, she and her family have been getting professional help and the family's financial situation has also improved.

"But it wasn't instant happily-ever-after," Patty says. "There were a lot of fear and tears and upset in between New York and now. I spent some time in a psychiatric hospital and then was in a group home. Eventually, I got back home and *now* things are very much happily-ever-after."

But Patty tends to be the exception among young runaways. "Most don't run thousands of miles away," says Cynthia Myers, executive director of the National Runaway Switchboard in Chicago. "They usually stay in their own immediate areas or states."

"The kids who go into prostitution are a definite minority," adds Bill Martin, the Switchboard's information director. "About half of the runaways who call us are staying with friends."

Whether a teenager runs across the street to a friend's home or across the country, running away is an indication of something seriously amiss. If your child has run away or is threatening to do so, there are several ways you can help.

How You Can Help

See Runaway Threats or Running Away As a Cry for Help

These are not simply manipulative gestures. You might say, "I feel very concerned when you talk about running away. Why do you feel like doing that?" If the teen expresses hopelessness about his current situation, give him hope by saying, "Let's talk and try to come up with ideas to change things in ways that will be okay for both of us." Also point out the fact that running away will only postpone or complicate a solution to the teen's problems.

If your child has run away, even overnight to a friend's house, this is an indication that he or she and, quite possibly, your family, needs counseling help. If possible it is crucial to get such help while the runaway behavior is still relatively mild.

Be Open to Help from a Runaway Shelter or Crisis Center

Today, many teens run to sources of help, and several years ago, Congress passed the Runaway Youth Act allocating $10 million in federal funds to establish and expand runaway shelters and counseling facilities nationwide, in addition to the toll-free National Runaway Switchboard in Chicago. To locate and make use of the special services in your area, call the National Runaway Switchboard or check the Appendix.

If your child runs away and calls you from a shelter asking for permission to stay, give it. Most shelters require that a minor get parental permission for an overnight or longer stay. Don't act out your anger and refuse permission, demanding that the teen stop this nonsense and come home immediately. You all need some cooling off time, and the shelter, which will keep your teen for several days or weeks under the supervision of trained counselors, will be able to give you this time *and* some valuable help.

"Kids don't always run to us," says Barb Henning of the Youth Emergency Service in St. Louis. "Some parents bring their kids in and say, 'Take him. We need a break!' "

"I think we also need places for parents to run away," says Bill Cormire, a staff supervisor at The Bridge, a shelter and counseling service in San Diego. "Both parents and teens need this time and space to sort out their feelings. We try to give them that while working to improve their communication with each other."

Most of the runaway shelters offer family counseling and crisis intervention. "We see the family as the real patient," says Harry Dawson, clinical coordinator at Project Oz, another San Diego-based youth shelter and counseling center. "A runaway teen is a symptom of family problems. We offer individual, group and family counseling while the kids are here and after they go back home. Those who can't go home are helped to find foster placement. We consider ourselves a delinquency-prevention program, a place where the pressure on both parents and teenagers is relieved so that the family as a unit gains some perspective on its problems."

"Most parents approve of our services and are delighted that it's all free," says Dan Jones of the Greenhouse in New Orleans. "They give their kids permission to stay quite willingly."

At Focus, a youth facility in Las Vegas, counseling, tutoring, life skills seminars and drop-in as well as live-in help is offered. These offerings are fairly typical of many similar shelters across the nation.

"Generally we try to work with the family to solve problems with a view toward getting the teenager back home," says director David

Williams. "We see ourselves not only as youth advocates, but also as family advocates."

Allowing such a service to help you and your teenager is a very wise decision.

Welcome Your Teen Back If He or She Wants to Come Home

If your teenager runs away, then calls and wants to come home, welcome him back. Don't use this time to express anger ("I told you so!"), deny permission or make bargains. Express your willingness for the teen to come home to talk and work out the problems. Once you are reunited, if you can't resolve your differences in a reasonable and satisfactory way, insist on getting some help—together.

CHAPTER 25

Other Risk-Taking Behavior

SHORTLY AFTER HIS older brother died of leukemia, Mark Salant, seventeen, began drag racing whenever he could get the family car for a night. In the course of his adventures, he has received two speeding tickets and been involved in a moderately serious accident that did expensive damage to the car and put Mark in the hospital overnight with a broken arm, cuts and bruises.

Pam Mariano's adventures in shoplifting, on the other hand, have had no clear-cut reason or starting point. She has always been something of a loner, shy and retiring with few friends and she looks considerably younger than her fifteen years. Although her mother noticed expensive clothing in Pam's closet several times before, her shoplifting did not become a family issue and a crisis until she was caught recently by a department store detective.

It is quite possible that both Mark and Pam engaged in various risk-taking behaviors in response to underlying depression. Shoplifting, reckless driving, vandalism and accidents occur as a result of many factors, of course, including peer pressure, alcohol or drug use or rebellion. But these acts can also be linked with depression.

Some mental health professionals believe that in many instances shoplifting is associated with depression and shoplifters take things to comfort and reward themselves. Because they feel essentially deprived (of love or material comforts), they believe they deserve to have what they steal. Others contend that the shoplifter has poor self-esteem and an underlying desire to be caught and punished.

Behavioral scientists at the University of Colorado and Baylor University in Texas have recently completed studies linking rash, impetuous behavior with depression. Such behavior may occur in conjunction with a series of "accidents" that are thinly disguised suicidal behavior.

"I remember a student last year who was identified by school authorities as a possible suicide due to his obvious depression and his many accidents," says Mary Ann Dan. "He got some supportive therapy and special classes, but is now back in regular classes, is active in football and competitive biking. He's doing well academically, but I still worry about him. He is still having a lot of accidents—several bike crashes in the last few months—more than one would normally have even in competitive situations. Right now, he's recovering from a broken leg. This continuing pattern of accidents may indicate that he is still feeling suicidal."

Accidents that aren't quite accidents are not uncommon among depressed teens. Some, such as one-car crashes, may be serious attempts at suicide.

Looking at her current roster of students requiring home tutoring due to physical illness or injury, Ms. Dan notes that half of these were injured in single-car crashes. "And all but one or two of these were marginal students with a variety of problems in their lives," she says. "Their accidents could well be indicative of suicidal feelings."

How You Can Help

Be Prevention-Minded

If your teenager is troubled but has not yet engaged in much risk-taking behavior, let him or her know that your attention and help are available without such activities. If your teen's friends show evidence of such behavior, discuss ways one can say no and the importance of putting one's own safety and welfare first. Make sure that your teenager understands that he or she can be implicated, even though innocent, if caught with people who are engaging in illegal activities.

At the same time, give your teenager a clear idea of what *your* rules, feelings and expectations are with regard to misuse of the family car, shoplifting and other risk-taking behavior. Be firm about what you will and will not tolerate. Some teens, especially if depressed, may act out in search of guidelines from you. Giving them firm direction and rules before trouble develops is an excellent preventive measure. It will also help your teen modify behavior if he or she has already been in trouble. For example, your teen may need to hear you say that shoplifting is not a lark, not a game, but *stealing*, and that you will not condone such activities.

Punish Risk-Taking Rule Infractions

If your teenager abuses a privilege by refusing to take the responsibilities that come with it, he or she should lose that privilege for a time. This means losing the use of the car, even if it is his or her own, or the right to shop alone until you are convinced that he or she will act in a more responsible way.

Don't Cover Up for Your Teenager

If he or she is in trouble because of risk-taking behavior, be as loving and supportive as you can, but do not protect him or her from the consequences of these actions and thus deprive your child of a much-needed lesson. For example, don't try to pay off the store if your teen is caught shoplifting; if your child comes home with stolen goods, don't simply let him or her off the hook with a stern lecture.

Marilyn Peters recently confronted her thirteen-year-old daughter when it became obvious that the loot she brought back from an afternoon of shopping was stolen. "It was difficult to know what to do, but I called the store and told the manager that we would be in to see him," she says. "We went in and I made Jill give back the merchandise she had taken. She was not prosecuted this time, but was given a very stern warning and told not to come back. She was badly frightened and I doubt that she'll try another stunt like that again. I think she learned a valuable lesson. It was tough for me, too. I felt I had to show her how to do the right thing and yet tried to be supportive. I tried to communicate the idea to her that I loved her enough and cared enough to get tough and expose her to some discomfort to change her behavior."

Until your teen feels discomfort as a result of risk-taking behavior, it's possible that he or she will see no reason to stop. So if you continually shield your teen from the consequences of such actions, you are perpetuating the problem and keeping your child from learning and growing.

Discuss the Feelings Behind Risk-Taking Behavior and Your Own Feelings As Well

Express your concern over the teen's behavior and point out that it indicates underlying depression or other uncomfortable feelings including low self-esteem (maybe your teen doesn't feel important enough to say no to friends who encourage him or her in risk-taking activities). Explore how the teen feels about himself or herself and the world. If he or she is troubled, talk about things that might be changed for the better. Work on building your teen's self-esteem and confidence in his or her ability to cope. This will help him or her to make safer choices.

If Your Child Is a Chronic Risk-Taker, Seek Professional Help

Such actions are quite likely to be symptoms of underlying problems and troubling feelings. Getting individual *and* family counseling can be a very constructive step toward a happier future. It may even save your child's life.

Risk-taking behavior, whether it is reckless driving, running away or drug abuse, can be a frightening and frustrating crisis for your family. But seeing it as a sign of trouble, a cry for help, a misguided way of coping with problems and stresses is a vital first step in helping your child change and grow.

It is important that your child does learn to grow past such behavior so he or she will not avoid learning essential life-coping skills and simply anesthetize his or her feelings with drugs, alcohol, sex, and fast cars. Risk-taking behavior only postpones growth and complicates life.

PART VIII

Teenagers and Suicide

CHAPTER 26
Suicide: No Idle Threat

S HAWN STEWART WAS seventeen, bright, handsome, talented and popular with his classmates. He was a model son in many ways, his parents agree. He had never given them a moment's worry except during those times when he became moody and withdrawn and locked himself in his room. Those moments, however, seemed insignificant in comparison to the good times—times when Shawn and his parents talked about his going to the best college, then on to medical school to prepare for a career as a surgeon. His life was full of promise and plans.

The depression that Shawn began to show last spring seemed incongruous with the realities of his life. His parents tried to cheer him up by pointing out how talented he was, how lucky he was, how proud he made them. But Shawn started withdrawing even more, spending more time alone in his room listening to Rolling Stones albums. He lost interest in hobbies and in school. His grades were beginning to suffer and his parents were worried. They were thinking about seeking help from a psychiatrist when, quite suddenly, Shawn seemed better. He was busy that Saturday, cleaning his room, writing letters and helping his Dad in the yard. Nancy Stewart remembers that he seemed almost cheerful at dinner that night and recalls how happy and relieved she felt to see her son looking so much better. She had no way of knowing that only a few hours later, Shawn would put a Rolling Stones album on his stereo, take his father's handgun and shoot himself in the head.

While Shawn Stewart seems to be an unlikely suicide statistic, he is not an unusual, isolated example. Indeed, teenage suicide statistics are alarming:

- Suicide is the third leading cause of death among teenagers in the fifteen to nineteen age range, with only accidents and homicides claiming more young lives. Experts believe that many accidents are, in fact, thinly disguised suicides.
- Some five thousand young Americans commit suicide each year. The suicide rate for young people tripled between 1955 and 1975 and *doubled* in the last decade. In 1977, the last year for which figures are available, there was a 20 percent increase in teenage suicides. In some areas, such as the affluent North Shore area of Chicago, the increases have been even higher. The incidence of teenage suicide in the North Shore suburbs has increased 250 percent in the past ten years!
- Each year, more than a million young people "move in and out of suicidal crises, thoughts and episodes," according to Dr. Michael Peck of the Institute for Studies of Destructive Behavior.
- An estimated four hundred thousand teenagers each year attempt suicide, an increase of 400 percent in the past ten years. Girls are more likely (a ten-to-one ratio) to attempt suicide, but more boys actually succeed in taking their own lives, largely because they use more violent means of self-destruction, such as guns, jumping from heights and hanging, with less opportunity for rescue. Girls are more likely to attempt suicide via a drug overdose.

Who are these young people behind the statistics who try to take their own lives before those lives have really begun?

All types of teenagers commit suicide: those from impoverished ghettos and those from affluent suburbs, achievers and nonachievers, kids whose problems have been obvious for some time and those whose lives seem ideal. Suicidal feelings occur in many young people. "One study of college freshmen revealed that 70 percent had thought of suicide in one given year," says Dr. Lee Robbins Gardner. "So the adolescent who has such thoughts and is convinced that he or she is all alone should be reassured that these feelings are *not* at all uncommon."

However, adolescents who *act* on these feelings, who actually attempt or manage to commit suicide tend to share certain characteristics, and they have been the subject of a number of studies.

At the Washington Psychological Center, Dr. Alan Berman and his colleagues recently completed a study of depressed teenagers with a history of suicide attempts, comparing them with a group of depressed teenagers who had not tried to kill themselves. "We found that the suicidal teenagers did share certain characteristics," says Dr. Berman. "Some had parents who were suicidal or who had committed suicide. Their example may have taught the child that 'if things get rough, this is one way you can handle the situation.' Also, if there is a history of suicide in the family, the child may be frightened about his own suicide being predestined. One patient of mine, for example, has had his mother and grandfather kill themselves and his father is feeling suicidal. This boy is very afraid that this will be his fate, too. Also, a suicidal parent may communicate the message, 'You should feel guilty for all the things you didn't do to make me feel better and the things you did to make me upset.' The kid loses both ways and comes to feel impotence and helplessness for not being able to help the parent."

The suicidal teens in his study shared a number of other characteristics. "Most had an inordinate amount of stress within the preceding twelve months and a home broken by divorce, remarriage or marital discord," Dr. Berman says. "They also tended to be firstborn children and had more third adults brought into their world to function in a parental role. Often this person was a grandparent, suggesting that the third parent was needed because the first two weren't doing too well. The child often becomes very attached to the grandparent and suffers a huge loss if that grandparent dies. We also found a great incidence of parental drug and alcohol abuse among suicidal teenagers and a great deal of anger in these young people."

Dr. Frank E. Crumley, a Dallas child psychiatrist who has treated a number of teenagers after suicide attempts, recently reported the results of his studies in the *Journal of the American Medical Association.* He found that the "typical" young suicide attempter is a girl who is severely depressed and impulsive, with a history of drug abuse. His patients have a tendency to react severely to loss and have poorly controlled rage. Most attempted to anesthetize their troubling feelings with alcohol or drugs, and some 40 percent had tried to take their lives before.

In his work with teenagers, Dr. Galvin Frederick has observed that poor communication within the family unit, a sense of isolation, feelings of rejection and lack of self-esteem are also factors in teen suicides. "No one of these factors individually brings about suicidal behavior," he says. "But it's when they occur in combination that they are dangerous."

Dr. Herbert Hendin, director of the Center for Psychosocial Studies at Franklin D. Roosevelt Medical Center in New York, agrees that lack of family communication and a growing sense of isolation are important factors in teenage suicide. "My own observation is that many of these young people have failed to win parental love," he says. "Often the parents of a suicidal child want him around, but without an empathetic connection. They want the child to fulfill their own expectations."

In a five-year study of college-age adolescents who were suicidal, Dr. Hendin noted that most were very concerned over academic achievement and had little emotional connection with their families. "They tended to be solitary and isolated," he says. "Often, they used schoolwork to withdraw from others. They were unable to give up sad, depressed ties with their parents and felt immobilized. Most were unhappy with their lives, but afraid of changes. However, in the high school age group, suicidal adolescents may be quite different—engaging in a lot of provocative behavior and showing little interest in school."

Dr. Frederick observes that with today's busy, mobile and often fragmented families, it is increasingly hard for a young person to fit into the family unit, and this adds to his or her sense of isolation. "The breakdown of the nuclear family, a lack of purpose, a loss of guideposts and a do-your-own-thing society that does not encourage connection with others are all factors in teenage suicide," he contends.

Some teens have a great need to be important to someone else, and, when such needs aren't met within the family, they try to find such validation in a romantic relationship. The loss of a love, added to an ongoing sense of isolation and rejection, may be the last straw. Dr. Frederick recalls Jeremy, seventeen, who was a talented musician and the member of a solid, church-going family. But Jeremy felt isolated and alone within his family and looked to his girlfriend Penny for most of his emotional support. One night, while talking with Penny on the phone, he asked, "Who is the most important person in your life?"

After giving the matter some thought, Penny replied, "I guess *I* am."

Jeremy suddenly exploded. "I can't take that!" he shouted into the receiver—then shot himself to death.

Unfortunately, Jeremy's story is not unusual. Some teenagers feel an ongoing sense of loss that becomes a crisis over a seemingly minor setback or a chance comment.

Eric, a thirteen-year-old, was brought to a hospital emergency room after an almost successful attempt to hang himself. His suicidal behavior was triggered by a chance remark from his eight-year-old brother. "This boy had a very sad and chaotic family history," says Dr. Charles Wibbelsman, who treated Eric in the emergency room and during his subsequent hospitalization. "He was the eldest of three brothers, and only the youngest child, the eight-year-old, had an identifiable father, who was trying to get custody of the child. Eric adored his little brother and was functioning as the father in the family. He had an incredible amount of responsibility and a huge emotional investment in his siblings, especially the little one. His mother was a nice woman, but her priorities did not include her children in a major way. She was more concerned about her social life, her job and her appearance and was not home much. Because of his many home responsibilities, Eric was isolated from his peers. His world was so limited and his focus so narrow that he was profoundly affected when his little brother told him, 'I don't love you any more! I'd rather live with my father!' His brother's rejection was the last straw for this already depressed teenager."

A suicidal crisis can also develop when a youngster who has had many successes in the past and who feels that parental love and his own self-worth are contingent on continuing achievement faces an obstacle or a failure. In such case, a setback can be devastating.

Dr. Michael Peck encountered a number of such teenagers in his work at the Los Angeles Suicide Prevention Center. "I remember Lucy, a high school senior, who studied ballet seriously for nine years," he says. "She wanted a scholarship to a prestigious dance school but didn't get it. She then lost interest in ballet and every-thing else that had been important to her. She felt hopeless and talked about suicide. She couldn't accept her failure—or herself—and experienced great emotional pain. With the help of a therapist, Lucy began to explore other goals and find ways to be less devastated by setbacks in the future."

Many teens, however, find themselves unable to break the cycle of isolation and hopelessness. "What many suicidal young people have in common is the inability or lack of opportunity to express their unhappiness," says Dr. Peck. "They find that their efforts to express their feelings of unhappiness, frustration and failure are totally unacceptable to their parents. Such feelings may be ignored or met by defensive hostility. This response often drives the child into further isolation, reinforced by the feeling that something is terribly wrong with him."

Suicide attempts reflect this feeling of helplessness and hopelessness in the face of stress that causes a young person to attempt suicide—whether the stress is brought on by a crisis, by ongoing parental pressure to measure up to impossibly high expectations or by the teenager's own inability to connect with anyone. Many think of suicide; some attempt it, and an alarming number of young people succeed in taking their own lives. Yet many of these sad, depressed, desperate youngsters don't really want to die. They simply want life to be different. What a suicidal adolescent may actually be saying is, "I want to escape my unhappiness."

It is crucial, then, to recognize the danger signs of possible suicidal behavior and to reach out to help before it's too late.

CHAPTER 27

How to Recognize the Warning Signs and Help a Suicidal Teen

Suicide Warning Signs

FOLLOWING ARE SOME of the most common danger signals to watch for in your teen.

Symptoms of Depression

These include sleep and eating disorders, mood changes, withdrawal, irritability, crying, a sudden weight loss or gain, a sudden drop in grades or interest in school, substance abuse, a combination of acting out behaviors, inability to concentrate, fatigue and loss of energy and interest in life.

Be aware of the fact that the prime danger point for suicide is not necessarily when the victim of depression is consumed and relatively immobilized by his feelings. A person is at the greatest risk of taking his life *after* the depression begins to lift and the victim regains some energy—the energy necessary to carry out suicide plans. Thus, some teenagers (like Shawn Stewart, whose story began the last chapter) commit or attempt suicide when they actually seem better. So if your teen is recovering from a major bout of depression, it would be wise to watch him or her carefully and not assume that the crisis is over.

257

Talking About Death or Suicide—Both Threats and Chance Remarks

One of the most dangerous myths about suicide is that people who talk about suicide don't do it. This is not true. Many suicidal teen-agers *do* give ample warning, and your ability to pick up on these signals can be life-saving. Some of these other signals are:

- *Previous suicide attempts.*
- *Sudden withdrawal*—especially withdrawal from friends and peers.
- *Making final arrangements*—such as writing wills or giving away prized possessions.

If you feel that your teenage son or daughter or some other young person you know has suicidal feelings or intentions, there are a number of ways that you can help.

How You Can Help

Take Your Teenager Seriously

Take *all* symptoms of depression, *all* comments about death, *all* suicide threats or attempts seriously. Don't dismiss such words or actions as attention-getting and manipulative. Don't assume that your child is bluffing about his or her suicidal intentions and urge him or her to go ahead. Don't lecture depressed adolescents, telling them how good they have it. That will only deepen guilt, depression and anger. See suicidal symptoms, threats and attempts as important messages from your child to you.

"You may feel that your teenager's suicide threats *are* manipulative, but that's not the real issue," says Dr. Alan Berman. "The real issue is that the kid is saying, 'Do something! I'm hurting!' If you don't attend to this, the fact that the behavior is manipulative may be academic."

"Suicide threats and attempts *can* be used as a weapon, as a way of saying, 'Look what you've done to me: I don't want to live!' " says Shirley Lackey. "But you can't dismiss such words and actions. Kids *do* kill themselves. If you ignore your teenager at this time, he or she may feel out on a limb, then go ahead and do it, opting for suicide as the ultimate dramatic gesture or as the only way out."

Show That You Care

This means taking the time and trouble to ask your child specifically about his or her feelings, even if this is a frightening prospect for you. Doing this will accomplish two important goals: It will demonstrate your commitment to help and at the same time give you some indication of your teenager's state of mind and the immediacy of the suicidal crisis. Some parents shy away, fearful that asking direct questions about depression and suicidal feelings will only encourage the teen to act on these feelings. Most experts contend, however, that this is not likely. Your teenager will be relieved that you notice how hopeless he or she is feeling, that you care and that you're willing to help.

How should you approach a young person who may be feeling suicidal?

"Try asking a number of gentle questions, each prompted by a 'yes' answer to the one preceding it," says Dr. Richard Brown. "For example, the progression of questions might be:

'It looks to me like you're feeling unhappy. Are you?'
'Do you ever get the feeling that maybe life isn't worthwhile?'
'Do you feel sometimes that you don't want to live anymore?'
'What have you thought about doing to end your life?' "

Specific plans for suicide are a sign that the teenager is in immediate danger. "If the young person has a method all thought out, he or she may require hospitalization," Dr. Brown says.

Unless you ask you will miss this vital signal and the opportunity to help your child. You will also miss the opportunity to show your child that you care about what he or she is feeling *and* what happens to him or her. Asking takes courage on your part, since your child's distress is frightening and disheartening. You may feel like a failure as a parent because your teenager is so unhappy.

"Your child's depression doesn't mean that you're a failure," says Dr. Gabrielle Carlson. "Listening to him and helping him learn to deal with painful feelings is an important and maybe life-saving first aid measure. After all, internal wounds are just as painful and in need of attention as external ones."

Help Your Child Recapture a Glimmer of Hope

You can communicate hope by saying something like, "I know you're hurting a lot right now and it probably seems that things will never get better. But depression, even serious depression, doesn't last forever and I feel that together we can come up with ideas to change things for the better."

"There is one important fact that you must emphasize whenever you can," says Dr. Calvin Frederick. "That is the concept that while life exists, there's a chance that problems can be resolved. But death is final." Dr. Frederick also suggests that offering something tangible —an immediate idea-and-feeling sharing session or an appointment with a mental health professional—will also give your teenager something to hang onto, a shred of hope that maybe life can change.

Life-Saving Changes for Your Child Mean Changes for You

This could mean spending more time with your child or listening more empathetically or modifying your life in some way to accommodate change in your teenager's life. Such changes may be difficult and inconvenient, but they are crucial to your child's recovery from depression and, perhaps, to his or her life as well. Failure to see the value of certain changes and unwillingness to compromise will perpetuate the crisis or even spell tragedy.

"I'm afraid that this is the case with Eric, the boy who tried to hang himself because he felt rejected by his little brother," says Dr. Wibbelsman. "Eric's prognosis is quite guarded at this time. When he was hospitalized, he started getting counseling from one of the psychotherapists here. However, the last time I talked with Eric, he told me that his mother had angrily put a stop to the counseling sessions. The therapist had been encouraging the boy to live more of his own life, to be himself and become more assertive about expressing his own needs—in other words, to make changes in his life that would be advantageous to him. Such changes would shift the load of household responsibilities from Eric to his mother, and she would not stand for this. She accused the therapist of fostering insubordination and withdrew her son from therapy. Now life is back in its old groove for Eric and he is dangerously depressed. His mother just can't or won't realize the role she plays in her son's problems and how vital it is that there be some change—and thus some hope—in his life."

Find Skilled Help

Professional help is vital when your teenager is feeling so depressed that he or she is suicidal. This help may include crisis intervention and long-term counseling.

"Don't try to help by sheltering your child when he has a serious problem," says Dr. Lee Robbins Gardner. "Part of taking the problem seriously is discussing it with your child *and* with a trained professional."

In a suicidal crisis, Suicide Prevention Centers, hot lines and other crisis intervention centers (see Appendix) are an extremely important and effective source of immediate help. "If your child hurts that much, it is better to take him to a professional specifically trained in dealing with suicidal crises instead of, say, starting with your family doctor," says Dr. Wibbelsman. "Your doctor is likely to refer you to someone better trained for such a crisis— which wastes time and adds to the teen's anguish. He or she may feel, 'Nobody can help me. Nobody wants to help me. They keep passing me on to someone else. I'm going to stop trying. No one cares.' On the other hand, if your child's first contact is with someone skilled in suicide crisis counseling, the immediate crisis will be dealt with sooner and more effectively and, if a referral for long-term counseling is needed later, it won't be seen in the same light— as a rejection in the midst of a crisis."

Learn to Cope Constructively with Your Own Feelings

As the parent of a suicidal or suicidally inclined teenager, you are likely to be in a great deal of pain yourself. You will feel tremendous guilt and anxiety. It may be helpful for you to get professional help in order to deal with these feelings instead of being immobilized by them.

The fact that your child is having a serious emotional crisis does *not* mean that you are a bad parent. The fact that you are aware and willing to admit that a problem exists and are concerned shows that you're a good and caring parent. You may need help in coping with your feelings or in learning to communicate more effectively with your teenager, but the fact that you care enough to hear your child's cry for help, to face difficult facts about your child's feelings and your family life, to seek professional help and be willing to make changes in your own life says a lot about you as a parent. None of this is easy or without considerable pain. So it's important during this difficult time to keep in mind that you have *not* failed your troubled teen. In fact, you may be playing a major part in saving his or her life by your listening, your love, your caring, your commitment to finding the best possible source of help and your continuing reassurances that as long as there is life, there is hope.

PART IX

Reaching Out
for Help

CHAPTER 28

How a Professional Can Help You

Help. Outside help. Professional help.

Help may be very much in your thoughts these days.

Maybe someone has said quite bluntly, "Your child needs professional help." Maybe you seek help in advice columns, magazine articles and books, including this one. Maybe you know another teenager or another family who is seeking help and you're wondering if that might be the answer for your teenager's problems, too.

Or maybe you've reached the end of your rope, the limits of your resources to help your teenager. You feel frightened, guilty, desperate, angry and very much alone. You want to seek help, but hesitate, unsure about what is available, affordable and best for you and your teenager. You wonder what professional help can do for you that you can't do for yourself.

Professional help, which means anything from psychoanalysis to family therapy to crisis counseling, is found in a variety of settings and with a number of different types of mental health professionals. While some people utilize such help to enhance already happy, viable relationships, hone communication skills and prevent major problems or crises from arising, many more seek it when a crisis occurs and they are not able to help themselves and their children. Whether professional help is utilized as a preventive measure or in a crisis situation, such therapy can help in a number of ways.

Therapy helps you understand and come to terms with your own past. Our early experiences are very much a part of who we are. Parental voices—in the form of long-ago labels, admonitions, criticisms, predictions or praise—stay with us throughout our lives, influencing not only how we see ourselves but also how we relate to others, including our children. "Counseling helps you understand your own growing up and what you may be projecting onto your children because of this," says family therapist Doris Lion. "Maybe you felt unloved because you didn't have rules in your home, for example, so now you have too many rules for your own child. Therapy can help you grow up at last and find your own way."

With the help of a therapist, it is possible to discover and silence some hurtful voices from the past, to learn new ways of seeing yourself and your alternatives, to develop new skills for loving both yourself and others and for living fully.

Therapy helps you and your family get feelings out into the open in a nonthreatening atmosphere with a skilled professional who will moderate the discussion and help you deal with all your feelings in a constructive way. It offers relief from cyclical patterns of fighting, depression and hopelessness. "Therapy helps people step back and give themselves a breathing spell," says Dr. Lee Robbins Gardner.

Therapy helps you improve your communication skills, express feelings clearly and listen with new understanding to those you love.

Therapy helps your child find his or her feelings, begin to build a more positive self-image and make changes that will bring more hope into his or her life, easing depression.

Therapy for your family helps to mend faulty, hurtful patterns of family interaction. It helps you to break old habits that block communication, cause misunderstandings and perpetuate unhappiness.

Therapy gives you hope and direction in the midst of crisis. But professional help is no miracle, no cure-all, no instant panacea for all that ails you and your family. The possibilities mentioned above are the ideal results of professional therapy, not the inevitable outcome you can expect if you seek such help. How valuable therapy will be for you and your family depends on a number of factors, including how soon you seek such help, how carefully this help is chosen, your attitude about it, how you utilize the help (how hard you're willing to work, to compromise and to risk change) and how willing your teenager and other family members may be to do the same.

Do I Need Help?

You and your family may need professional help if:

- You're caught in hurtful, nonproductive patterns of behavior that create and perpetuate problems and tensions.
- Your teenager shows signs of depression over an extended period of time.
- Your teenager's behavior worsens and shows sharp changes or dangerous turns such as drug abuse, withdrawal from peers or suicide threats or attempts.
- You feel depressed, angry, frightened or desperate about a situation or feelings you can't seem to change or have no energy left to try to change.
- Your teenager is troubled and you can't seem to help.
- Your family life is being seriously disrupted by your child's behavior.
- Your child's teachers, school counselor or nurse, your family doctor or someone else in a position to seriously evaluate your child's behavior or state of mind has suggested that you seek professional help.
- *You* think you or your child may need professional help.

CHAPTER 29

What Kind of Help
Is Available?

Different Types of Therapy

Psychotherapy is a catch-all phrase that can mean individual, family or group therapy with a psychiatrist, psychologist, licensed marriage, family or child counselor or therapist, psychiatric nurse or psychiatric social worker.

Psychoanalysis is an intensive form of individual psychotherapy with a psychiatrist or psychologist who has special training and experience in analysis. This analysis is useful for people with long-time personality disorders but may not be the immediate treatment of choice for a teenager with a pressing mental health crisis. Analysis takes place over an extended period of time—typically, one to five sessions a week for several years. Some analysts concentrate on exploring the patient's past in order to correct ways of thinking that are causing discomfort and continuing problems at the present time. Other analysts focus more on current situations and problem behaviors.

Individual counseling/therapy involves intensive work with current problems, past experiences, self-concept and other matters of importance to the individual. The therapist may be a psychiatrist, psychologist, marriage, family or child counselor or therapist, psychiatric social worker, psychiatric nurse or other mental health professional. This one-to-one therapy is typically more behavior- and present-oriented than psychoanalysis and isn't likely to last as long or to require as many visits per week.

Family therapy attempts to treat the family as a unit, focusing on the concept that most problems exist with the family system, not totally with any individual family member. Many therapists believe that a troubled teenager is often expressing symptoms of family conflicts through his or her depression or problem behavior. And so one person may be the *identified* patient, but the whole family or significant parts of it may actually be treated.

In *group therapy*, a trained mental health professional presides over a group of unrelated individuals who share feelings, experiences and observations in an effort to identify and resolve problems and conflicts.

Family and group therapy may be offered by a psychiatrist, psychologist, social worker, or marriage or family counselor.

Crisis counseling or *crisis intervention* is emotional first aid to help an individual or a family weather an immediate crisis, evaluate the situation and determine what additional long-term therapy may be needed. Such help is meant to be short term, but can be invaluable in a crisis. Hot lines and crisis intervention centers fall into this category. The helpers cover a variety of possibilities, from mental health professionals to trained volunteers who work under the supervision of a professional. These helpers have been trained to listen, to help you sort through your alternatives and determine your best sources of further help.

Other sources of help include *self-help groups*—sometimes supervised by a mental health professional, but often not—made up of people sharing similar problems who get together to offer support and coping guidelines and to air feelings. These groups are very helpful to people with certain types of problems. Alcoholics Anonymous is the best known. Others include Al-Anon (for families of alcoholics), Parents Anonymous (for parents who are having problems with their children) and Toughlove (for parents with troubled, acting out adolescents).

Often an individual or family utilizes a variety of outside help services—individual *and* family therapy plus a self-help group, for example.

Who Are the Therapists?

Who are the helpers you're likely to encounter as you explore the possibility of therapy?

A *psychiatrist* is a medical doctor (M.D.) who has special training beyond medical school in treating mental and emotional illnesses. He or she may be particularly well equipped to deal with severe mental disorders. Only a psychiatrist can prescribe drugs which may be needed to treat severe depression and other mental disorders. (However, patients going to a mental health clinic or a non-psychiatrist may get a prescription from the clinic's medical director or from a psychiatrist who works on a cooperative basis with other mental health professionals.)

If you are choosing a psychiatrist, check to see that he or she has special training in psychiatry. He or she should have three to four years of intensive training after medical school in psychiatry and, ideally, should be certified by the American Board of Psychiatry and Neurology, which means that he or she is a fully licensed doctor with special training in psychiatry and passing marks in a series of special examinations determining competence in the field. (However, since this credential is fairly new, some excellent older psychiatrists may not be board-certified.)

A *psychologist* who is a therapist is usually a clinical, counseling or school psychologist and has a Ph.D., Ed.D. or Psy.D. degree from an accredited university plus several years of supervised clinical experience and passing marks on a special licensing examination. A psychologist can be a good choice for treatment of emotional problems and disorders.

A *licensed marriage, family* or *child counselor* or *therapist* usually has at least a master's degree in marriage-family-child counseling or psychology. He or she will also have passed a state licensing exam and have three thousand hours of supervised clinical experience. These counselors are particularly focused on the family as a unit and on helping improve communication in important relationships.

A *psychiatric social worker* has a master's degree in social work (M.S.W.) along with supervised clinical experience. He or she is especially trained to evaluate and work with emotional problems in a social context, and may help a family with everything from marital problems or a troubled teenager to financial difficulties. Some psychiatric social workers have additional certification from the Academy of Certified Social Workers. This certification means that the degree is from an accredited social work program and that the social worker has completed the required supervised experience and passed a national qualifying examination. Social workers must also be licensed by the state.

A *psychiatric nurse* is a registered nurse who has at least a master's degree in mental health nursing and supervised experience in working with emotionally distressed individuals. Psychiatric nurses may also be certified by the American Nurses' Association. Such certification means that the nurse has met degree and clinical experience requirements and has passed a written exam.

Helpers in crisis centers and with hot lines may be volunteers with several weeks or months of training in listening empathetically and referring callers or clients to appropriate sources of further help. Some of these, especially well-trained peer counselors, may be particularly able to reach teenagers. Such help, of course, is meant as emotional first aid and is not a substitute for ongoing psychotherapy if a teenager is seriously troubled. Many centers and hot lines also have licensed mental health supervisors present who work in conjunction with the volunteers.

Help is available in a variety of settings. You might go to a therapist in private practice, to a private clinic or to a community clinic. If your teenager is in considerable distress or danger of suicide or your family is in too much turmoil to solve existing problems, residential care for your teenager may be necessary at a hospital, residential treatment center, group home, halfway house, runaway shelter or a temporary "cool home." Some of the latter are foster homes sponsored by community clinics to give parents and teens time out from each other in order to work through their problems in a calmer, more constructive way.

The setting you select will depend on a number of factors, including your financial resources (private therapists and clinics are generally more expensive than community mental health clinics), how immediate the crisis is (you may sometimes encounter a waiting list at a community clinic) and whether you and your teenager prefer individual therapy or family or group therapy.

Costs are a major consideration. Psychiatrists charge a median price of $60 per visit. The fee for marriage or family therapists or psychiatric social workers averages $40 per visit. Group counseling in a clinic setting is often about $20 per session. Private clinics charge highly variable set fees for their services, while community clinics often charge according to ability to pay, typically from $5 to $50 per session. Some therapists in private practice will also lower their fees and charge according to ability to pay for those in need of help whose financial resources are limited.

Insurance coverage for psychotherapy varies a great deal; if cost is a consideration for you, check with your insurance company to see what is covered before choosing a mental health professional. Generally, medical insurance covers psychiatrists' fees and, in some states, the fees for licensed psychologists. The services of a family therapist or psychiatric social worker may not be covered by insurance except when these professionals are part of a medical group or work under the direct or indirect supervision of a psychiatrist, psychologist or other physician who will sign insurance forms.

What Type of Help Is Best for Me and My Teenager?

The best therapist or therapeutic alternative for you or your teenager may not be the one with the most impressive degrees, sterling credentials and steep fees. What matters most is the therapist's empathy for you and your child, a comfortable fit of personalities, his or her ability to help in your specific situation and his or her availability to you. (For example, if your concerns have not reached a crisis, being on a waiting list for a few weeks may not be a problem, but this may be highly unsatisfactory in a crisis.)

If your teenager is in a suicidal crisis, call your local Suicide Prevention Center or crisis hot line for instant help and later referral for longer-term therapy.

If your teenager is not obviously suicidal, your best first step might be to check with your family doctor or, if your teen is resistant to seeing him or her, to a doctor or medical center specializing in adolescent health (see Appendix). A physician will eliminate the possibility of disease (some can have emotional as well as physical symptoms), evaluate your teenager's emotional and developmental condition and give you appropriate referrals to mental health professionals.

"In evaluating a patient, I not only do a thorough physical exam, but also take a careful psychosocial history," says Dr. Richard

Brown. "How the teenager is functioning at school, at home and with peers is very important. I consider all these relationships as well as attitudes about self, about drugs and alcohol, future plans, goals, hobbies and interests."

Dr. Brown points out that going to a physician initially helps ease a reluctant teenager into the health care system. "A number of teenagers are especially resistant to mental health care, but are less reluctant to get a physical health care checkup," he says. "This way, the possibility of disease is eliminated and psychosocial development evaluated."

The next step is to get referrals from your doctor, friends or professional organizations for possible therapists. In considering the referrals, make a list of what is important to you and your teenager, including cost, geographic preferences, your teenager's problems, preferences and prejudices (he or she may prefer a same-sex or opposite sex therapist or someone fairly young), whether you want more say in choosing your own or your child's therapist (in which case a therapist in private practice or in a private clinic is preferable to a community clinic where therapists are often assigned to new cases on a rotating basis).

It is also important to consider what works best with your teenager in resolving conflicts. "In adolescence, family therapy is the treatment of choice since most conflict centers in the family," says Dr. Donald McKnew. "If the teenager is extremely disturbed, he or she may also need a therapist for individual counseling." Other mental health professionals observe that teenagers also respond well to group therapy.

Methods of treatment are also a consideration. You may prefer seeking family-oriented as opposed to individual therapy or be reluctant to seek help from someone who uses drugs in conjunction with psychotherapy to treat depression. You should realize, however, that in cases of severe depression, drug treatment may be necessary for a time.

"There are times when it just isn't possible to reach and treat a severely depressed person with words," says Dr. McKnew. "I think it's malpractice to try talking alone with someone who is massively depressed. In such cases, the individual is so down and the world looks so hopeless that talking is an exercise in futility. Chemical treatment may get the person to the point where talking can be effective. It is true though that you cannot treat depressive illness with chemicals alone. Psychotherapy is also needed. A combination of drugs and therapy can have good results in the event of massive depression. If a teenager is manic-depressive, we usually start with lithium. If that doesn't help, we add a tricyclic antidepressant. And if that doesn't do it, we add an MAO inhibitor. Some need all three. If we're sure there is no biological component of depression, we start with a tricyclic antidepressant like Tofranil or Elavil, moving on to MAO inhibitors if need be. Adolescents get good results from these drugs."

Teenagers who take MAO-inhibitor drugs (which include Parnate, Eutonyl, Marplan and Nardil among others) must observe restricted diets, since combining these drugs and foods containing the substance Tyramine (e.g., bananas, aged cheeses, pepperoni, salami, sour cream and avocados) has serious, even lethal, side effects.

Also, whether your teenager receives outpatient care or is referred to a residential program depends a great deal on the seriousness of the problems and a mental health professional's evaluation of the teen's prognosis for recovery either in or outside the family environment.

It is vital to take time and a great deal of care in evaluating possible professional helpers. A mental health professional may have sterling credentials, but if he or she can't relate well to you or your child such things don't matter. On the other hand, checking the professional's credentials is an important safeguard for your family, since incompetent, untrained and unethical pseudo-therapists are found in most areas.

To check credentials, contact the state chapter of a related association such as the American Psychiatric Association (psychiatrists), the American Psychological Association (psychologists), the American Nurses' Association (psychiatric nurses), the Academy of Certified Social Workers (psychiatric social workers) or the American Association for Marriage and Family Therapy (marriage, family or child counselors or therapists—see Appendix for the central office of this organization) to see if the mental health professional you have in mind is a member. Referrals from your physician, a local teaching hospital or the psychology department of a local university also help you get a head start in finding someone who is well trained and respected professionally.

How the mental health professional relates to you or your adolescent, however, is equally important. After talking with the professional on the telephone or meeting with him or her, ask yourself the following questions:

- Can we relate to this person and work well with him or her? Does he or she show empathy and flexibility? Does he or she listen well? Encourage us to work at seeking our own solutions?
- Is this someone I feel I can trust? Does he or she seem to care?
- Does he or she make extravagant promises about results? Or have a hard-sell approach? (If a therapist tells you he or she can "cure" your teen in three sessions or is inflexible about life choices and philosophies, beware. The object of therapy, after all, is to find your own way of coping and dealing with life challenges. Such results are rarely easy or instantaneous.)
- Is he or she a therapist who will work *with* me, helping me learn new skills for personal growth, communication, self-acceptance and constructive coping with problems? Or will he or she tell me what to do in twenty-five words or less or try to change my life for me? Change is a personal matter, a personal responsibility requiring time, effort and commitment.

"The film *Ordinary People* shows an example of a good therapist," says Dr. Lee Robbins Gardner. "The psychiatrist in that film is excellent. He is professional, caring, nonintrusive, and nonjudgmental. He helps the child acknowledge parental flaws yet at the same time guides him toward respect for the parents. He helps him to enjoy the loving feelings that exist in the family."

CHAPTER 30

Making the Best Use of Professional Help

How to Get Your Teenager Involved

MAYBE YOU'VE FOUND an excellent source of help for your troubled teenager but just one problem remains: Your teenager angrily refuses to go, insisting that he or she doesn't need help, threatening that if forced to seek help he or she will run away. If this situation sounds familiar to you, you have company. Many teenagers are resistant to professional help. They fear that going to a mental health professional will brand them for life as "crazy" and that their friends will tease them. Other teenagers resist the idea because it's a parental suggestion, and still others feel unjustly accused of creating problems they believe are shared by the family. Hopelessness plays a major role in teen resistance, too. The young person feels hopeless about change and considers professional help a needless hassle and waste of time.

This development is immensely frustrating to a parent who is caught in a stressful cycle with a teenager in distress. The teen's behavior may be at a crisis stage and yet he or she refuses to take any steps that might lead to constructive changes.

What can you do in these circumstances?

276

Express Your Willingness to Participate

"A lot of teen resistance is broken down by parental involvement in therapy," says Dr. Merilee Oaks. "Once a parent gets over his or her *own* resistance to seeking professional help, once he or she is willing to invest time and energy in family therapy and is able to stop targeting the child as the sole patient or problem, the teenager's resistance may lessen. Go into therapy with the notion that 'I am worried because my child is depressed. We are concerned that something might be going on in the family to cause this and we want to help by changing the pattern.' Don't dump all blame on the child, but go in with the idea, '*All* of us could use some help.'"

Insist That Your Teenager At Least Try Therapy

This can be a risk, but it's one worth taking.

"You have to get tough and make it clear how much you're willing to allow," says Judith Davenport. Part of this tough approach is to say that things cannot and will not stay the same, that therapy is a must, not an option.

Your teenager may run away, throw a tantrum, dig in his or her heels and refuse to budge or barricade himself or herself in the bedroom. But it is *also* possible that your insistence will provide new hope and incentive to change.

"The teenager may hear your insistence on getting professional help as an 'I care about you!' message," says Dr. Alan Berman.

Present Therapy As an Opportunity, Not a Punishment

If you tell your child that he or she is bad, crazy and hopeless and so must go into therapy, it is likely that he or she will resist. If you see therapy as shameful and express this to your child, it is highly unlikely that the adolescent will go willingly to a mental health professional. Putting therapy in a punitive light, viewing it as punishment, will not only make your teenager feel angry, embarrassed and resentful about going, but if he or she does go, could also interfere with progress.

It is far more constructive to see and present therapy as an opportunity to get in touch with one's feelings, become a happier, more loving person and make changes that can bring a lifetime of rewards.

Go Yourself and Gradually Involve Your Teenager

You may seek therapy yourself and get a great deal of help in dealing with your situation. In the course of your therapy, you could involve your teenager in small, but important ways. For example, ask the teen to come in for one of your sessions in order to help *you* learn to cope or to communicate better. If the teen feels that you are the primary patient, he or she may be less threatened by therapy. You can work out some conflicts in your relationship and your adolescent may find, once there, that he or she doesn't mind therapy, that it isn't at all what he or she imagined. Your teen might even want to have more sessions or therapy of his own.

If the teenager refuses to go to a mental health professional even if this requirement is minimal, try to get him or her involved in an even less threatening way. Dr. Oaks, for example, is seeing the mother of a very depressed fifteen-year-old girl and has talked with the girl occasionally on the telephone.

"This girl has steadfastly refused to come in to talk with me," says Dr. Oaks. "But one day not long ago, I called to talk with her mother and the girl got on the phone and started asking me questions like, 'Why would kids go see a shrink anyway?' and 'You mean they talk to you about sex and dope?' I assured her that they did, adding, 'Why not?' She replied, 'If I did that, you'd think I was *crazy!*' She felt that all the kids at school would say she was crazy if she saw a shrink, but she was grateful for the chance to talk over the phone. I gave her the number of a local hot line especially for teenagers. Preserving her anonymity is very important to her, so for the time being telephone counseling is her best alternative."

Seek Help for Yourself Via Therapy and Involvement in Parents' Groups

What if your teenager refuses to get help under any circumstances and you've done all you can to lead him or her to sources of aid? Your best alternative is to concentrate on dealing with the stressful home situation and on learning how to improve your own communication skills and be tough and firm and loving all at once. By sharing your feelings with other parents you can pick up some good ideas for coping and get some reassurance that you are not alone, that your situation is not hopeless and that you can make a difference.

Getting the Most Out of Professional Help

Many people seek professional help halfheartedly and are not surprised when miracles fail to happen. Typically, they announce with an air of triumph that the therapy is not helpful at all and discontinue it after one or a few sessions. Others, in search of fast help and answers, become discouraged quickly when such instant aid is not forthcoming and quit before a therapist has the time and the opportunity to help them. Still others seek therapy yet sabotage all efforts to help them.

If you've reached the point of needing professional help, how can you and your teenager make the best use of it?

Approach Therapy with Realistic Expectations

Some people go into therapy expecting instant results. Others expect that in one or two sessions the therapist will fix everything and tell them exactly how to solve their problems. If you start out with such expectations, you could be in for a disappointment.

"Instant results are unlikely," says Dr. Berman. "It took several years to build up to the current problems and it will take time to sort things out. Unfortunately, there are no easy answers for helping a teenager and his family through a crisis, no seven-rule strategy for constructive coping."

"Ideally, professional help is *not* the ultimate word about what to do," says Dr. Lee Robbins Gardner. "It is only helpful in clarifying your feelings and your problems and finding the best ways for *you* to cope."

It's important to give your therapist time to help you, to give yourself time to resolve some of the problems and conflicts that caused you to seek help in the first place.

"Many times, parents go out in search of an answer," says school psychologist Sarah Napier. "They find some method of coping or communicating, try it for a week or two and, if it doesn't bring about change in that time, they say it's no good. Keep in mind that you've had these problems for some time and you're not going to change it all around in three weeks."

Don't Sabotage the Therapy

You can sabotage your own therapy in a number of ways—by dishonesty with the therapist, by focusing on details and anecdotes instead of dealing with the feelings behind them, or by refusing to consider suggestions that the therapist has.

You can sabotage your child's therapy, too, by refusing to become even minimally involved, by putting him or her down for needing help and by being too intrusive about the therapy or quick to act if he or she expresses negative feelings about it.

Mental health professionals report that they see examples of sabotage every day. "I'm seeing an extremely depressed sixteen-year-old girl now whose family is quite troubled," says Doris Lion. "If her parents would get therapy too her progress and prognosis would be much better. Instead they say, 'She has problems. We don't,' and so the girl feels stigmatized. Seeing a child's problems as isolated is a trap. Generally, the family can *all* benefit from therapy, either separately or together."

Social worker and psychotherapist Judith Davenport has some suggestions for parents whose teenagers are in therapy. "First, respect their privacy and don't insist on knowing all that goes on in the sessions," she says. "Let your child know that you're available to help, but learn to let go and let your teen be close to others. That is essential to growth. Don't put your kid down for needing help. I'm seeing a girl now whose mother tells her, 'If you were *really* mature, you'd be able to solve your own problems.' It takes a tremendous amount of strength and resolve for that girl to get on the bus and keep coming to see me. And many troubled depressed teenagers don't have that strength so they can't make the best of—or even get—therapy."

Don't be too quick to intervene on your child's behalf or to quit therapy if your child complains about it.

"When therapy gets tough—as it often does before things can change and improve—your teenager may try to pull you in to intervene for him or her," says Ms. Davenport. "Don't jump in to defend your teen or believe everything he or she tells you at face value. Give the therapy and the therapist a chance."

If your teenager complains about the therapy, listen empathetically but remind him or her that change is often difficult and even painful, that he may have to feel worse for a time before he feels better. Of course, if you have serious questions about the therapist's competence or ethics, it would be a good idea to change therapists. Often the best move is to offer your child encouragement and support while insisting that he or she give therapy a fair chance.

Keep an Open Mind and Risk Change Yourself

In order for your teenager's problems to change, *you* may have to make some changes, too. You may need to change your schedule or learn new communication skills or see your teenager's behavior from a new point of view. You may need to examine your own past, your attitudes, your relationship with your child. None of this is easy or without pain. But it's important to be open to the idea of making some constructive changes if necessary, instead of expecting another person to do all the changing. Taking the risk of change—trying new ways of being, of sharing your feelings and of relating to your teen—is a way to get back in touch and eventually grow in mutual respect and rediscover your love for each other.

Such goals may seem distant right now as you and your teen struggle through a myriad of feelings: depression, anger, desperation and a great deal of shared pain. You wonder if you'll ever again be close, if you'll ever again be happy, if you'll ever again have peace in your home. No one can give you any 100 percent guaranteed promises, then make them come true instantly. No one can give you easy answers or guaranteed-to-work-in-every-instance suggestions for coping. But you need not struggle alone. There is expert and compassionate help available to enable you and your teenager to find new ways of reaching out to each other and of sharing all that life has to offer—love and anger, tears and laughter, growing pains and triumphs, bittersweet memories and new dreams.

Appendix

Books

Ackerman, Paul, Ph.D., and Murray Kappelman, M.D. *Signals: What Your Child Is Really Telling You.* New York: Dial Press, 1979.

Brenton, Myron. *How to Survive Your Child's Rebellious Teens: New Solutions for Troubled Parents.* Philadelphia: Lippincott, 1979.

Buntman, Peter H., and Eleanor M. Saris. *How to Live with Your Teenager: A Survivors Handbook for Parents.* Pasadena, Calif.: Birch Tree Press, 1979.

Bush, Richard. *A Parent's Guide to Child Therapy.* New York: Delacorte, 1980.

Cross, Wilbur. *Kids and Booze: What You Must Know to Help Them.* New York: Dutton, 1980.

Eimers, Robert, and Robert Aitchison, Ph.D. *Effective Parents/Responsible Children.* New York: McGraw-Hill, 1977.

Fairchild, Betty, and Nancy Hayward. *Now That You Know What Every Parent Should Know About Homosexuality.* New York: Harcourt Brace Jovanovich, 1979.

Fine, Louis. *After All We've Done for Them: Understanding Adolescent Behavior.* Englewood Cliffs, N.J.: Prentice-Hall, 1977.

French, Alfred, M.D., and Irving Berlin, M.D. *Depression in Children and Adolescents.* New York: Human Sciences Press, 1979.

Gordon, Sol. *Let's Make Sex a Household Word: A Guide for Parents and Children.* New York: John Day, 1975.

Gould, Shirley. *Teenagers: The Continuing Challenge.* New York: Hawthorn, 1979.

Kappelman, Murray, M.D. *Sex and the American Teenager.* New York: Readers Digest Press, 1977.

Killinger, John. *The Loneliness of Children.* New York: Vanguard, 1980.

Linder, Robert L., Ed.D., Steven E. Lerner, Ph.D., and R. Stanley Burns, M.D. *PCP: The Devil's Dust.* Belmont, Calif.: Wadsworth, 1981.

Melton, David. *Survival Kit for Parents of Teenagers.* New York: St. Martins Press, 1980.

North, Robert, and Richard Orange, Jr. *Teenage Drinking: The #1 Drug Threat to Young People Today.* New York: Macmillan, 1979.

Oettinger, Katherine B., with Elizabeth C. Mooney. *Not My Daughter: Facing Up to Adolescent Pregnancy.* Englewood Cliffs, N.J.: Prentice-Hall, 1979.

Rosenbaum, Jean, M.D., and Veryl Rosenbaum. *Living with Teenagers.* New York: Stein and Day, 1980.

Individual and Family Counseling

The Family Service Association of America, with member agencies nationwide, offers low-cost individual and family counseling, family life education programs, special rap groups for teens and family advocacy activities. The following listings—used by permission of the Family Service Association of America in New York and with the cooperation of the Glendale, California, Family Service Association—include member agencies in the United States and Canada.

Alabama

Family and Child Services
3600 Eighth Ave. S.
Birmingham, AL 35222
(205) 324-3411

Family Services Center
930 Franklin St., Suite 107
Huntsville, AL 35801
(205) 539-5717

Family Counseling Center
6 South Florida St.
Mobile, AL 36606
(205) 471-3466

Family Guidance Center
925 Forest Ave.
Montgomery, AL 36106
(205) 262-6669

Alaska

SNA Youth Center Counseling
  Hotline
(907) 452-5085

Family Focus Youth Counseling
940 Cowles
Fairbanks, Alaska 99701
(907) 452-5802

Arizona

Jewish Family and Children's
  Service of Phoenix
2033 N. 7th St.
Phoenix, AZ 85006
(602) 257-1904

Family Counseling Agency
151 S. Tucson Blvd., #262
Tucson, AZ 85716
(602) 327-4583

Arkansas

Family Service Agency of
 Central Arkansas
North Little Rock Community
 Center Building
P.O. Box 500
North Little Rock, AR 72115
(501) 758-1516

California

Alameda Family Service Agency
746 Eagle Ave.
Alameda, CA 94501
(415) 521-4151

Family Service Agency of
 San Mateo County
1870 El Camino Real
Burlingame, CA 94010
(415) 692-0555

Family Service Agency,
 Pacifica Office
80 Eureka Square
Pacifica, CA 94044
(415) 692-0555

Family Service Agency,
 Sequoia Office
35 Renato Court
Redwood City, CA 94064
(415) 365-2284

Glendale Family Service Association
3436 N. Verdugo Blvd.
Glendale, CA 91208
(213) 248-2286

Family Service of Los Angeles
1521 Wilshire Blvd.
Los Angeles, CA 90017
(213) 484-2944

Family Service of Los Angeles,
 Harbor Area Office
605 South Pacific Ave.
San Pedro, CA 90731
(213) 547-1126

Family Service of Los Angeles,
 Metropolitan Area Office
2221 W. Olympic Blvd.
Los Anegles, CA 90053
(213) 738-5985

Family Service of Los Angeles,
 San Fernando Valley District
6851 Lennox Ave.
Van Nuys, CA 91408
(213) 908-5030

Family Service of Los Angeles,
 Santa Clarita Valley Office
Plaza Posada
23560-220 Lyons Ave.
Newhall, CA 91321
(805) 255-7553

Family Service of Los Angeles,
 Southeast District
11455 Paramount Blvd.
Downey, CA 90241
(213) 923-6548

Wesley Social Service Center
8317 S. Vermont Ave.
Los Angeles, CA, 90053
(213) 751-5128

Family Service of Los Angeles,
 Western District
La Brea Plaza
111 N. La Brea, Suite 506
Inglewood, CA 90306
(213) 641-0443

Family Service Association of the
 Mid-Peninsula
375 Cambridge Ave.
Palo Alto, CA 94306
(415) 326-6576

Family Service Association of
 Riverside
3903 Brockton Ave.
Riverside, CA 92501
(714) 686-3706

Family Service Association of
 Riverside, Corona Office
114 E. 10th St.
Corona, CA 91720
(714) 371-2641

Family Service Agency of the
  Greater Sacramento Area
709 21st St.
Sacramento, CA 95814
(916) 448-8284

Family Service Agency of
  Sacramento, Roseville Office
515 Sunrise Ave.
Roseville, CA 95678
(916) 782-3263

Family Service Agency of
  San Bernardino
1669 N. E St.
San Bernardino, CA 92405
(714) 886-6737

Family Service of San Bernardino,
  Suicide/Crisis Intervention
1657 N. E St.
San Bernardino, CA 92405
(714) 886-6730

Family Service Association of
  San Diego County
7645 Family Circle
San Diego, CA 92111
(714) 279-0400

Family Service Association of San
  Diego County, Carlsbad Office
756 Grand Ave.
Carlsbad, CA 92008
(714) 729-4981

Family Service Association of San
  Diego, Encinitas Office
454 N. Old Highway 101
Encinitas, CA 92024
(714) 753-1627

Family Service Association of San
  Diego, Escondido Office
503 E. Grand Ave.
Escondido, CA 92025
(714) 745-3811

Family Service Association of San
  Diego, Fallbrook Office
208 E. Mission Rd.
Fallbrook, CA 92028
(714) 723-8181

Family Service Association of San
  Diego County, Imperial Beach
  Office
1340 Imperial Beach Blvd.,
  Suite 204
Imperial Beach, CA 92032
(714) 424-5138

Family Service Association of San
  Diego County, La Mesa Office
7373 University Ave., Suite 222
La Mesa, CA 92041
(714) 698-1601

Family Service Association of San
  Diego County, Oceanside Office
509 E. Fifth St.
Oceanside, CA 92054
(714) 729-4982

Family Service Association of San
  Diego County, Poway Office
12759 Poway Rd., Suite 101
Poway, CA 92064
(714) 486-1190

Family Service Association of San
  Diego County, Vista Office
114 Hillside Terrace
Vista, CA 92083
(714) 726-0960

Family Service Agency of
  San Francisco
1010 Gough St.
San Francisco, CA 94108
(415) 474-7310

Family Service Agency of
  Santa Barbara
800 Santa Barbara St.
Santa Barbara, CA 93101
(805) 965-1001

Family Service Association of the
  Rio Hondo Area
10016 S. Pioneer Blvd.,
  Suites 109 and 110
Santa Fe Springs, CA 90670
(213) 949-9691

Family Service Association, Rio
Hondo, La Mirada Counseling
15901 E. Imperial Highway
La Mirada, CA 90638
(213) 943-3611

Family Service Association, Rio
Hondo, Whittier Office
7702 Washington Ave., Suite C
Whittier, CA 90607
(213) 698-7941

Family Service Association of
Orange County
17421 Irvine Blvd.
Tustin, CA 92680
(714) 838-7377

Assistance League of Fullerton
Branch
Family Service Association of
Orange County
224 W. Amerige
Fullerton, CA 92631
(714) 871-0075

Family Service Association of
Orange County, Central Coast
350 E. 17th St., Suite 112
Costa Mesa, CA 92626
(714) 645-8390

Family Service Association of
Orange County, South Coast
31882 Camino Capistrano
San Juan Capistrano, CA 92675
(714) 493-3190

Family Service Association of
Orange County, West County
12491 Beach Blvd.
Garden Grove, CA 92640
(714) 534-8862, 897-7671

Colorado
Human Services
1555 Xavier St.
Denver, CO 80204
(303) 825-3283

Human Services, Adams County
Office
2090 E. 104 Ave.
Thornton, CO 80229
(303) 451-5555

Human Services, Arapahoe County
Office
300 E. Hampden, Suite 401
Englewood, CO 80110
(303) 761-9971

Human Services, Aurora Office
11111 E. Mississippi, Suite 34
Aurora, CO 80010
(303) 344-5001

Human Services, Boulder Office
2825 Marine St.
Boulder, CO 80302
(303) 449-7488

Human Services, Jefferson County
Office
8790 W. Colfax Ave., Suite 100
Lakewood, CO 80216
(303) 234-1160

Human Services, N.E. Denver Office
2035 E. 18th Ave., Suite 6
Denver, CO 80201
(303) 321-2230

Human Services, Shelter Care
for Teenagers
Commerce City Facility
7191 Holly St.
Commerce City, CO 80022
(303) 289-3194

Human Services, Westminster
Facility
7640 Lowell Blvd.
Westminster, CO 80030
(303) 429-4440

Human Services, Westside Office
716 Knox Court
Denver, CO 80201
(303) 571-1679

Connecticut

Family Services—Woodfield
800 Clinton Ave.
Bridgeport, CT 06604
(203) 368-4291

Catholic Family Services—
Archdiocese of Hartford
896 Asylum Ave.
Hartford, CT 06105
(203) 522-8241

Child and Family Services
1680 Albany Ave.
Hartford, CT 06101
(203) 236-4511

Child and Family Services,
Northeast District Office
110 Main St.
Manchester, CT 06040
(203) 643-2761

Family Service Association of
Middlesex County
27 Washington St.
Middletown, CT 06457
(203) 347-3346

Family Service
32 Vine St.
New Britain, CT 06052
(203) 223-9291

Family Service, Bristol Office
285 Main St.
Bristol, CT 06010
(203) 583-9225

Family Counseling of Greater
New Haven
1 State St.
New Haven, CT 06511
(203) 865-1125

Family Counseling Service of
Guilford
Major Lathrop House
55 Park St.
Guilford, CT 06437
(203) 453-2925

Madison Family Counseling
Madison Green
Madison, CT 06443
(203) 245-4498

Orange Family Counseling
637 Orange Center Rd.
Orange, CT 06477
(203) 795-6662

Woodbridge-Bethany Office
Meeting House Lane
Woodbridge, CT 06525
(203) 387-6780

Jewish Family Service of
New Haven
152 Temple St.
New Haven, CT 06510
(203) 777-6641

Family Service Association of
Southern New London County
11 Granite St.
New London, CT 06320
(203) 442-4319

Family Service East
3 Fort Rachel Place
Mystic, CT 06355
(203) 536-4231

Family Service West
Grand St.
Niantic, CT 06357
(203) 739-0464

Family and Children's Services
60 Palmer's Hill Rd.
Stamford, CT 06902
(203) 324-3167

Family and Children's Services,
Darien Office
41 Corbin Dr.
Darien, CT 06820
(203) 655-0547

Family and Children's Services,
New Canaan Office
103 South Ave.
New Canaan, CT 06840
(203) 972-0556; if no answer,
call (203) 324-3167

Jewish Family Service of
Greater Hartford
740 N. Main St., Suite A
West Hartford, CT 06117
(203) 236-1927

Delaware
Family Service of Northern
Delaware
809 Washington St.
Wilmington, DE 19801
(302) 654-5303

Family Service of Northern
Delaware, Brandywine Hundred
Office
Webster Building, Concord Plaza,
Suite 108
3411 Silverside Rd.
Wilmington, DE 19899
(302) 478-8050

Florida
Family Counseling Center
2960 Roosevelt Blvd.
Clearwater, FL 33520
(813) 536-9427

Family Counseling Center,
St. Petersburg Office
928 22nd Ave. S.
St. Petersburg, FL 33733
(813) 822-3961

Family Counseling Center,
Tyrone Office
1400 66th St. N.
St. Petersburg, FL 33702
(813) 344-1686

Family Service Agency
1300 S. Andrews Ave.
Fort Lauderdale, FL 33335
(305) 524-8286

Family Consultation Service of
Jacksonville and Duval County
1639 Atlantic Blvd.
Jacksonville, FL 32207
(904) 396-4846

Jewish Family and Children's
Service
1790 S.W. 27th Ave.
Miami, FL 33145
(305) 445-0555

Jewish Family and Children's
Service, Miami Beach Offices
420 Lincoln Rd., Room 350
Miami Beach, FL 33139
(305) 531-2363

Jewish Family and Children's
Service, Miami Beach Offices
850 Washington Ave.
Miami Beach, FL 33101
(305) 538-1661

Jewish Family and Children's
Service, North District Office
2040 N.E. 163rd St.
North Miami Beach, FL 33160
(305) 949-6186

Jewish Family and Children's
Service, South District Office
8905 S.W. 87th Ave.
Miami, FL 33143
(305) 279-6611

United Family and Children's
Services
2190 N.W. Seventh St.
Miami, FL 33125
(305) 643-5700

United Family and Children's
Services, South Dade Office
18861 S. Dixie Highway
Miami, FL 33141
(305) 232-1610

United Family and Children's
Services, West Dade Office
9380 Sunset Dr.
Miami, FL 33101
(305) 643-5700

Family Counseling Center of
Brevard County
220 Coral Sands Dr.
Rockledge, FL 32955
(305) 632-5792

Family Counseling Center of
  Sarasota County
3205 S. Gate Circle
Sarasota, FL 33579
(813) 955-7017

Family Counseling Center,
  South County Office
800 S. Tamiami Trail
Venice, FL 33595
(813) 484-2681

Family Service Association of
  Greater Tampa
205 W. Brorein St., Suite 24
Tampa, FL 33606
(813) 251-8477

Family Service Association,
  Inner City Office
St. Paul's AME Church
506 Harrison
Tampa, FL 33601
(813) 248-6328

Family Service Association,
  Temple Terrace Office
United Methodist Church
5030 Busch Blvd.
Tampa, FL 33602
(813) 251-8477

Georgia

Child Service and Family
  Counseling Center
1105 W. Peachtree St. N.E.
Atlanta, GA 30357
(404) 873-6916

Child Service and Family
  Counseling Center
  Bankhead Courts
Building 3513, Apt. 418
Bankhead Highway
Atlanta, GA 30305
(404) 696-2471

Child Service and Family
  Counseling Center, Cobb Office
2050 Austell Rd.
Marietta, GA 30060
(404) 436-1567

Child Service and Family
  Counseling Center, Decatur
  Office
525 Marshall St.
Decatur, GA 30030
(404) 378-2543

Domestic Crisis Intervention Project
Georgia Hill Office
250 Georgia Ave.
Atlanta, GA 30301
(404) 658-6074

Child Service and Family
  Counseling Center
Martin Luther King, Jr. Office
2001 Martin Luther King, Jr.,
  Dr. N.W.
Atlanta, GA 30304
(404) 758-8511

Child Service and Family
  Counseling Center, Ponce de
  Leon Office
650 Ponce de Leon Ave.
Atlanta, GA 30301
(404) 873-4949

Child Service and Family
  Counseling Center,
  Douglas County Office
6707 E. Church St., Room D
Douglasville, GA 30134
(404) 949-5200

Child Service and Family
  Counseling Center, Fairburn
  City Office
18-A W. Broad St.
Fairburn, GA 30213
(404) 964-9863

Child Service and Family
  Counseling Center, Kirkwood
  Office
1599½-B Memorial Dr.
Atlanta, GA 30301
(404) 373-4596

Child Service and Family Counseling Center, Lakewood Office
215 Lakewood Way, Suite 201
Atlanta, GA 30315
(404) 624-1226

Child Service and Family Counseling Center, Rockdale Office
1131 West Ave.
Rockdale Plaza
Conyers, GA 30207
(404) 922-7228

Child Service and Family Counseling Center, West End Office
1128 Gordon Rd. S.W.
Atlanta, GA 30301
(404) 755-1510

Family Counseling Center
102 7th St.
Columbus, GA 31902
(404) 327-3238

Family Counseling Center of Macon and Bibb County
309 Robert E. Lee Building
830 Mulberry St.
Macon, GA 31201
(912) 745-2811

Family Counseling Center of Savannah
428 Bull St.
Savannah, GA 31401
(912) 233-5729

Hawaii

Child and Family Service
200 N. Vineyard Blvd., Building B
Honolulu, HI 96817
(808) 521-2377

Idaho

Community Mental Health Center
150 Schoup Avenue
Idaho Falls, Idaho 84301
(208) 525-7129
Boise Hotline
(208) 345-7888

Illinois

Family Service Association of the Alton-Wood River Region
211 E. Broadway
Alton, IL 62002
(618) 463-5959

Family Counseling Center
5109 N. Illinois St.
Belleville, IL 62221
(618) 235-5656

Family Counseling Center
McBarnes Memorial Building, Suite 200
201 E. Grove
Bloomington, IL 61701
(309) 828-4343

Family Service of Champaign County
608 W. Green
Urbana, IL 61801
(217) 384-1911

Family Service of Champaign County, Rantoul Office
117 N. Ohio
Rantoul, IL 61866
(217) 893-1530

Jewish Family and Community Service
1 S. Franklin St.
Chicago, IL 60606
(312) FI 6-6700

Jewish Family and Community Service, Niles Township Office
5050 Church St.
Skokie, IL 60076
(312) 675-2200

Jewish Family and Community Service, North Suburban Office
210 Skokie Valley Rd.
Highland Park, IL 60035
(312) 831-4225

Jewish Family and Community Service, Northern District Office
2710 W. Devon Ave.
Chicago, IL 60645
(312) 274-1324

Jewish Family and Community
Service, Northwest Surburban
Office
120 W. Eastman St.
Arlington Heights, IL 60004
(312) 255-4410

Jewish Family and Community
Service, South Suburban Office
18250 Harwood
Homewood, IL 60430
(312) 799-1869

Virginia Frank Child Development
Center
3033 W. Touhy Ave.
Chicago, IL 60607
(312) 761-4550

United Charities of Chicago
64 E. Jackson Blvd.
Chicago, IL 60604
(312) 939-5930

Calumet Family Center
235 E. 103rd St.
Chicago, IL 60617
(312) 264-3010

Family and Mental Health Services
of Southwestern Cook County
6401 W. 111th St.
Worth, IL 60482
(312) 448-5700

Blue Island Center
York Street Professional Building
2340 York St.
Blue Island, IL 60406
(312) 371-5170

Grady B. Murdock Family Center
734 S. Springfield Ave.
Chicago, IL 60607
(312) 638-2114

Loop Family Center
64 E. Jackson Blvd.
Chicago, IL 60637
(312) 939-1300

Near North Family Center
800 N. Clark, Suite 219
Chicago, IL 60645
(312) 337-0922

Near South Family Center
2105 S. Michigan
Chicago, IL 60617
(312) 225-7400

Northern Family Center
3354 N. Paulina St.
Chicago, IL 60645
(312) 327-3100

Family Service Association of
Greater Elgin Area
164 Division St., Room 808
Elgin, IL 60102
(312) 695-3680

Family Service Association of
Greater Elgin Area
Streamwood-Hanover Park Office
7421 Astor Ave.
Hanover Park, IL 60103
(312) 837-8553

Counseling and Family Service
1821 N. Knoxville Ave.
Peoria, IL 61603
(309) 685-5287

Counseling and Family Service,
Morton Office
Community United Church of
Christ
300 N. Main St.
Morton, IL 61550
(309) 266-7263

Counseling and Family Service,
Northside Outreach Office
800 N.E. Madison
Peoria, IL 61603
(309) 671-5230

Counseling and Family Service,
Pekin Office
St. Paul's United Church of Christ
101 N. Eighth St.
Pekin, IL 61554
(309) 346-5890

Counseling and Family Service,
Washington-Eureka Office
Evangelical United Methodist
Church
410 Walnut St.
Washington, IL 61571
(309) 444-9445

Family Service Center of
Sangamon County
1308 S. 7th St.
Springfield, IL 62703
(217) 528-8406

Indiana

Family Counseling Service of
Elkart County
101 E. Hively Ave.
Elkhart, IN 46514
(219) 295-6596

Family Counseling Service,
Goshen Office
Spohn Building
109 E. Clinton
Goshen, IN 46426
(219) 533-0862

Family and Children's Service
Mid-Town Center
305 S. Third Ave.
Evansville, IN 47708
(812) 425-5181

Family and Children's Services
2712 S. Calhoun
Fort Wayne, IN 46807
(219) 744-4326

Lutheran Social Services
330 Madison St.
Fort Wayne, IN 46802
(219) 743-3347

Family Service Association
615 N. Alabama St.
Indianapolis, IN 46204
(317) 634-6341

Family Service Association,
Hancock County Office
Memorial Building
Greenfield, IN 46140
(317) 462-3733

Jewish Family and Children's
Services
1717 W. 86th St., Suite 450
Indianapolis, IN 46260
(317) 872-6641

Family Service Agency of
Tippecanoe County
225 N. 4th St.
Lafayette, IN 47901
(317) 423-5361

Family and Children's Center
1411 Lincoln Way W.
Mishawaka, IN 46544
(219) 259-5666

Family Counseling Service
615 E. Washington St.
Muncie, IN 47305
(317) 284-7789

Family Service Association of
Wayne County
42 S. 9th St.
Richmond, IN 47374
(317) 935-2195

Family Service Association in
Terre Haute
620 Eighth Ave.
Terre Haute, IN 47804
(812) 232-4349

Iowa

Family Service Agency
400 Third Avenue S.E.
Cedar Rapids, IA 52401
(319) 398-3574

Family and Children's Service of
Davenport
115 W. Sixth St.
Davenport, IA 52803

Family and Children's Service of
Davenport
Anchorage House
1204 Iowa St.
Davenport, IA 52802
(319) 324-8298

Family and Children's Service,
Bettendorf Office
Bettendorf Bank Building, Suite 220
Duck Creek Plaza
Bettendorf, IA 52722
(319) 359-8216

Family and Children's Service,
Muscatine Office
116 Medical Arts Building
Muscatine, IA 52761
(319) 263-0067

Quad City Children's Center
2800 Eastern Avenue
Davenport, IA 52802
(319) 326-6431

Trinity House
305 W. 6th St.
Muscatine, IA 52761
(319) 264-8703

Family Counseling Center
1321 Walnut, Suite 200
Des Moines, IA 50309
(515) 288-9020

Family Service Center
Boys and Girls Home and
Family Service
2601 Douglas St.
Sioux City, IA 51101
(712) 277-4031

Family Service League
2530 University Ave.
Waterloo, IA 50701
(319) 235-6271

Kansas
Family and Children's Service
5424 State Ave.
Kansas City, KS 66102
(912) 287-1300

(See "Missouri" listings for Overland
Park and Shawnee Mission)

Kentucky
Family Counseling Service
620 Euclid Ave.
Lexington, KY 40502
(606) 266-0425

Family and Children's Agency
1115 Garvin Place
Louisville, KY 40201
(502) 583-1741
(See "Ohio" for Covington listing)

Louisiana
Family Counseling Agency
1545-B Jackson St.
Alexandria, LA 71301
(318) 448-0284

Family Counseling Service of East
Baton Rouge Parish
544 Colonial Dr.
Baton Rouge, LA 70806
(504) 926-5083

Family Service Society
535 Gravier St.
New Orleans, LA 71030
(504) 524-7471

Maine
Community Counseling Center
187 Middle St.
Portland, ME 04101
(207) 774-5727

Maryland
Family and Children's Society
204 W. Lanvale St.
Baltimore, MD 21217
(301) 669-9000

Family and Children's Society,
Annapolis Office
934 West St.
Annapolis, MD 21401
(301) 263-5743

Family and Children's Society,
Eastern Office
2502 St. Paul St.
Baltimore, MD 21233
(301) 366-1430

Family and Children's Society,
Southern Office
1310 S. Charles St.
Baltimore, MD 21230
(301) 752-0445

Jewish Family and Children's
Service
5750 Park Heights Ave.
Baltimore, MD 21215
(301) 466-9200

Jewish Family and Children's
Service
5310 Old Court Rd.
Randallstown, MD 21133
(301) 466-9200

Family Service of Montgomery
County
One W. Deer Park Rd., Suite 201
Gaithersburg, MD 20760
(301) 840-2000

Family Service Agency
208 Antietam Professional Center
138 E. Antietam St.
Hagerstown, MD 21740
(301) 733-5858

Family Service of Prince George's
County
7580 Annapolis Rd.
Lanham, MD 20801
(301) 459-2121

Family Service
Eastern Building
5010 Sunnyside Ave.
Beltsville, MD 20705
(301) 345-9100, 345-8822

Family Service
Route 3, Box 224
Baden, MD 21013
(301) 888-1444

Family Service
Marlow Square, Suite 200
4305 St. Barnabas Rd.
Marlow Heights, MD 20031
(301) 423-4800

Maryland Children's Aid and
Family Service Society
303 W. Chesapeake Ave.
Towson, MD 21204
(301) 825-3700
Toll free number from Maryland
communities: 800-492-4704

Massachusetts

Family Service Association of
Greater Boston
34½ Beacon St.
Boston, MA 02108
(617) 523-6400

Family Service Association,
Northeast Office
Family Service of Malden
29 Concord St.
Malden, MA 02148
(617) 324-8181

Family Service Association,
Northwest Office
131 Highland Ave.
Somerville, MA 02143
(617) 625-5638

Lexington Counseling Service
20 Muzzey St.
Lexington, MA 02173
(617) 862-2128

Family Service Association,
South Shore Office
1 Cliveden St.
Quincy, MA 02169
(617) 471-0630

Family Service Association,
Southwest Office
39 Grant St.
Needham, MA 02192
(617) 444-9303

Cambridge Family and Children's
Services
99 Bishop Richard Allen Dr.
Cambridge, MA 02139
(617) 876-4210

Concord Family Service Society
Community Agencies Building
Concord, MA 01742
(617) 369-4909

Family Service of Dedham
18 Norfolk St.
Dedham, MA 02026
(617) 326-0400

Family Service Association
101 Rock St.
Fall River, MA 02720
(617) 678-7541

Children's Aid and Family Service
47 Holt St.
Fitchburg, MA 01420
(617) 345-4147

Family Service Association of
Greater Lawrence
430 N. Canal St.
Lawrence, MA 01840
(617) 683-9505

Family Service of Greater Lowell
170 Merrimack St., Room 314
Lowell, MA 01852
(617) 459-9326

Cape Cod Family and Children's
Service
81 Old Colony Way
Orleans, MA 02653
(617) 255-2980

Cape Cod Family and Children's
Service, Hyannis Office
76 Enterprise Rd.
Hyannis, MA 02601
(617) 775-8605

Jewish Family Service of the
North Shore
Vinnin Square Professional Building
564 Loring Ave.
Salem, MA 01970
(617) 745-9760, 745-9761

Family Service Organization of
Worcester
31 Harvard St.
Worcester, MA 01608
(617) 756-4646

Jewish Family Service of Worcester
646 Salisbury St.
Worcester, MA 01609
(617) 755-3101

Michigan

Catholic Social Services of
Wayne County
9851 Hamilton Ave.
Detroit, MI 48202
(313) 883-2100

Catholic Social Services,
Eastside Office
17108 Mack Ave.
Grosse Pointe, MI 48236
(313) 881-6645

Catholic Social Services,
Northwest Office
17332 Farmington Rd.
Livonia, MI 48150
(313) 421-3730

Catholic Social Services,
Western Wayne Office
24331 Van Born Rd.
Taylor, MI 48180
(313) 292-5690

Family Service of Detroit and
Wayne County
51 W. Warren Ave.
Detroit, MI 48201
(313) 833-3733

Family Service, East District
9740 Chalmers Ave.
Detroit, MI 48233
(313) 839-3800

Family Service, Northwest District
15800 W. McNichols Rd.
Detroit, MI 48201
(313) 272-1760

Family Trouble Clinic
11000 W. McNicols, Suite 303
Detroit, MI 48226
(313) 862-0330,31,32

Family Service, Out-County District
16755 Middlebelt Rd.
Livonia, MI 48150
(313) 427-9310

Family Service, Southwest District
3042 First St.
Wyandotte, MI 48192
(313) 284-7171

Family Service, West District
22371 Newman Ave.
Dearborn, MI 48120
(313) 274-5840

Family Service Agency of
  Genesee County
202 E. Boulevard Dr., Room 310
Flint, MI 48503
(313) 767-4014

Family Service Association of
  Kent County
1122 Leonard N.E.
Grand Rapids, MI 49503
(616) 774-0633

Family Service and Children's Aid
of Jackson County
729 W. Michigan Ave.
Jackson, MI 49204
(517) 782-8191

Children's Aid and Family Service
of Macomb County
57 Church St.
Mount Clemens, MI 48043
(313) 468-2656

Family and Children Services of
Oakland
50 Wayne St.
Pontiac, MI 48058
(313) 332-8352

Catholic Social Services of
  Oakland County
1424 E. Eleven Mile Rd.
Royal Oak, MI 48067
(313) 548-4044

Jewish Family Service
24123 Greenfield
Southfield, MI 48075
(313) 559-1500

Minnesota
Family Service of Duluth
600 Ordean Building
424 Superior St.
Duluth, MN 55802
(218) 722-7766

Family and Children's Service
414 S. Eighth St.
Minneapolis, MN 55404
(612) 340-7444

South Hennepin Family and
  Children's Service
9301 Bryant Avenue S., Suite 101
Bloomington, MN 55420
(612) 884-7353

Family Service of Greater
  St. Paul Area
Nalpak Building, Suite 500
333 On-Sibley St.
St. Paul, MN 55101
(612) 222-0311

Family Service at Martin Luther
  King Center
270 N. Kent St.
St. Paul, MN 55101
(612) 224-4601

Family Service at Northwest Area
  Youth Service Bureau
Lake Owassa Community Center
934 Woodhill Dr., No. 121
Roseville, MN 55113
(612) 439-4840

South Suburban Family Service
Drovers State Bank Building
633 S. Concord
South St. Paul, MN 55075
(612) 451-1434

Mississippi
Family Service Association of
  Greater Jackson
1510 N. State St., Suite 201
Jackson, MS 39202
(601) 353-3891

Missouri
Family and Children Services of
  Kansas City
3515 Broadway, Suite 300
Kansas City, MO 64111
(816) 753-5280

Family and Children Services,
East Jackson County Office
300 N. Osage
Independence, MO 64050
(816) 254-4343

Family and Children Services,
Johnson County, Kansas Office
6300 W. 95th St., Suite 101
Overland Park, KS 66204
(913) 642-4300

Family and Children Services,
Northland Office
6317 N.E. Antioch Rd.
Kansas City, MO 64108
(816) 454-4819

The Living Center for Family
Enrichment
3515 Broadway, Suite 203
Kansas City, MO 64111
(816) 753-5325

Jewish Family and Children
Services
1115 E. 65th St.
Kansas City, MO 64131
(816) 333-1172

Jewish Family and Children
Services
Johnson County Office
4550 W. 90th Terrace
Shawnee Mission, KS 66203
(913) 649-1056

Family Guidance Center
200 Corby Building
Fifth and Felix
St. Joseph, MO 64501
(816) 364-1501

Catholic Family Service
4140 Lindell Blvd.
St. Louis, MO 63108
(314) 371-4980

Family and Children's Service of
Greater St. Louis
2650 Olive St.
St. Louis, MO 63103
(314) 371-6500

Jewish Family and Children's
Service
9385 Olive Blvd.
St. Louis, MO 63132
(314) 993-1000

Lutheran Family and Children's
Services
4625 Lindell Blvd.
St. Louis, MO 63108
(314) 361-2121

Montana
Eastern Montana Counseling
Association
928 Broadwater Avenue
Billings, Montana 59101
(406) 259-6918

Billings Mental Health Center
Emergency Line
(406) 252-5650

Nebraska
Family Service of Lincoln
1133 H St.
Lincoln, NB 68508
(402) 476-3327

Family Service
2240 Landon Court
Omaha, NB 68102
(402) 345-9118

Family Service, Bellevue
Multi-Service Center
1912 Hancock
Bellevue, NB 69101
(402) 291-6065

Family Service, Hilltop-
Pleasantview Multi-Service
Center
3012 Grant St.
Omaha, NB 68108
(402) 451-3483

Family Service, Logan-Fontenelle
Multi-Service Center
2211 Paul St.
Omaha, NB 68108
(402) 341-9186

Family Service, Papillon
Multi-Service Center
City Municipal Building
122 E. 3rd St.
Papillon, NB 59467
(712) 339-2544

Nevada

Family Counseling Service of
Northern Nevada
106 East Adams
Carson City, Nevada 89701
(702) 882-0884

Focus Adolescent Services
1916 Gold Ring Avenue
Las Vegas, Nevada 89106
(702) 382-4762

New Hampshire

Derry Counseling Services
Derry, New Hampshire 03038
(603) 434-5672

Manchester Counseling Services
Manchester, New Hampshire
03101
(603) 668-4079

New Jersey

Family Service of West Essex
9 Park Ave.
Caldwell, NJ 07006
(201) 228-5585

Family Service, Livingston Branch
Office
185 S. Livingston Ave.
Livingston, NJ 07039
(201) 992-9040

Jewish Family Service of
Southern New Jersey
2393 W. Marlton Pike
Cherry Hill, NJ 08002
(609) 662-8611

Family Counseling Service
10 Banta Place
Hackensack, NJ 07601
(201) 342-9200

Jewish Family Service
20 Banta Place
Hackensack, NJ 07601
(201) 488-8340

Family Service Association of
Middlesex County
901 Raritan Ave.
Highland Park, NJ 08904
(201) 572-0300

Family Service of Morris County
62 Elm St.
Morristown, NJ 07960
(201) 538-5260

Family Service Bureau of Newark
15 Fulton St.
Newark, NJ 07102
(201) 624-0913

Family Service Bureau,
Belleville Office
103 Belleville Ave.
Belleville, NJ 07109
(201) 759-1090

Family Service Bureau,
West Hudson Office
545 Kearny Ave.
Kearny, NJ 07032
(201) 991-1467

Nutley Family Service Bureau
155 Chestnut St.
Nutley, NJ 07110
(201) 667-1884

Family Counseling Service of
Paterson and Vicinity
49 Colfax Ave.
Pompton Lakes, NJ 07442
(201) 839-2234

Family Service Agency of Princeton
120 John St.
Princeton, NJ 08540
(609) 924-2098

Family Service Association of
Summit
43 Franklin Place
Summit, NJ 07901
(201) 273-1414

Jewish Family Service of
Greater Mercer County
51 Walter St.
Trenton, NJ 08628
(609) 882-9317
(Note: This office also serves the
Lower Makefield, Morrisville and
Yardley areas of Pennsylvania.)

Family Service Association
143 E. State St., M-5
Trenton, NJ 08608
(609) 393-1626

Jewish Family Service of
North Jersey
One Pike Dr.
Wayne, NJ 07470

Family Service Association of
Atlantic County
4000 Black Horse Pike
West Atlantic City, NJ 08232
(609) 645-2942

Mamora Family Practice Center
Box 617
Wayside Village
Mamora, NJ 08223
(609) 398-6610

Memorial Park Medical Center
Route 50
Belcoville, NJ 07109
(609) 625-9146

New Mexico
Family Counseling Service
4011 Silver Ave. S.E.
Albuquerque, NM 87108
(505) 265-8596

New York
Family and Children's Service of
Albany
12 S. Lake Ave.
Albany, NY 12203
(518) 462-6531

Child and Family Services
330 Delaware Ave.
Buffalo, NY 14202
(716) 842-2750

Child and Family Services,
Amherst Regional Office
5449 Main St.
Williamsville, NY 14221
(716) 632-5500

Connors Children's Center
824 Delaware Avenue
Buffalo, NY 14224
(716) 884-3802

Child and Family Services,
East Regional Office
45 Anderson Rd.
Cheektowaga, NY 10514
(716) 896-7485

Child and Family Services,
North Branch Office
4 Webster St.
North Tonawanda, NY 14120
(716) 693-5344

Child and Family Services,
North Regional Office
3407 Delaware Ave.
Kenmore, NY 14217
(716) 876-8174

Reach-Out Ellicott
344 Perry St.
Buffalo, NY 14206
(716) 852-7398

Reach-Out Kenfield
41 Tower
Buffalo, NY 14240
(716) 835-4571

Reach-Out Masten
1490 Jefferson Ave.
Buffalo, NY 14240
(716) 883-1973

Reach-Out Perry
344 Perry St.
Buffalo, NY 14240
(716) 852-7396

Child and Family Services,
South Regional Office
585 Ridge Rd.
Lackawanna, NY 14218
(716) 823-2531

Jewish Family Service of
   Erie County
615 Sidway Building
775 Main St.
Buffalo, NY 14203
(716) 853-9956

Jewish Board of Family and
   Children's Services
120 W. 57th St.
New York, NY 10019
(212) 582-9100

Jewish Board, Pelham Parkway
   Office
990 Pelham Parkway S.
Bronx, NY 10451
(212) 931-2600

Jewish Board, J. W. Beatman
   Counseling Center
4049 Henry Hudson Parkway
Riverdale, NY 10471
(212) 549-6900

Jewish Board, Montague Street
   Office
186 Montague St.
Brooklyn, NY 11201
(212) 855-6900

Jewish Board, Mid-Brooklyn Office
1113 Avenue J
Brooklyn, NY 11201
(212) 258-7700

Jewish Board, Coney Island Mental
   Health Services for Youth
2857 W. 8th St.
Brooklyn, NY 11201
(212) 266-5300

Jewish Board, Thomas Askin Youth
   Project (TAYP)
307 Brighton Beach Ave.
Brooklyn, NY 11201
(212) 769-0500

Jewish Board, Manhattan East
   Office
1651 Third Ave.
New York, NY 10028
(212) 860-3500

Jewish Board, Manhattan West
   Office
33 W. 60th St.
New York, NY 10023
(212) 586-2900

Jewish Board, Staten Island Office
3974 Amboy Rd.
Staten Island, NY 10308
(212) 948-0050

Jewish Board, Midwood Adolescent
   Project
1484 Flatbush Ave.
Brooklyn, NY 11210
(212) 434-4158

Family Service Association of
   America
44 E. 23rd St.
New York, NY 10010
(212) 674-6100

Family and Children's Service of
   Niagara
826 Chilton Ave.
Niagara Falls, NY 14301
(716) 285-6984

Family Services of Dutchess County
50 N. Hamilton St.
Poughkeepsie, NY 12601
(914) 452-1110

Family Service of Rochester
30 N. Clinton Ave.
Rochester, NY 14604
(716) 232-1840

Family Service, Avon Office
93 High St.
Avon, NY 14414
(716) 226-2360

Family Service, Brockport Office
1 Clinton St.
Brockport, NY 14420
(716) 637-6841

Family Service, Greece Office
51 Maiden Lane
Rochester, NY 14616
(716) 663-3001

Family Service, Henrietta Office
2025 Lehigh Station Rd.
Henrietta, NY 14467
(716) 334-6520

Family Service, Irondequoit Office
2400 Oakview Dr.
Rochester, NY 14617
(716) 266-2200

Family Service, Webster Office
27 W. Main St.
Webster, NY 14580
(716) 872-4420

North Carolina
Family and Children's Service
301 S. Brevard St.
Charlotte, NC 28202
(704) 332-9034

Family Counseling Service
Allen Center
331 College St.
Asheville, NC 28801
(704) 253-9314

Family Counseling Service of
Durham
1200 Broad St.
Durham, NC 27705
(919) 286-3757

Family Counseling Service of
Gaston County
318 South St.
Gastonia, NC 28052
(704) 864-7704

Family Services of Greater
Greensboro
1301 N. Elm St.
Greensboro, NC 27401
(919) 373-1341

Family Guidance Center
#17 Highway 64-70 S.E.
Hickory, NC 28601
(704) 322-1400

Family Service Bureau
410 Gatewood Ave.
High Point, NC 27260
(919) 889-6161

Family Services of Wake County
3803 Computer Dr., Suite 101
Raleigh, NC 27609
(919) 781-9317

Family Services
610 Coliseum Dr.
Winston-Salem, NC 27106
(919) 722-8173

Ohio
Catholic Service League
640 N. Main St.
Akron, OH 44310
(216) 762-7481

Family Services of Summit County
212 Exchange St.
Akron, OH 44304
(216) 376-9494

ABC Teenage Parent Center
220 S. Broadway
Akron, OH 44304
(216) 535-3117

Jewish Family Service
3085 W. Market St. #102
Akron, OH 44313
(216) 867-3388

Family Counseling Services
618 Second St. N.W.
Canton, OH 44703
(216) 454-7066

Family Service of the Cincinnati
Area
2343 Auburn Ave.
Cincinnati, OH 45219
(513) 381-6300

Family Service, Clermont County
Office
285 Main St.
Batavia, OH 45103
(513) 732-2070

Family Service, North Surburban
Office
4100 Executive Park Dr.
Cincinnati, OH 45239
(513) 733-3232

Family Service, Northern Kentucky Office
615 Greenup St.
Covington, KY 41011
(606) 291-1121

Family Service, Western Office
3907 Northbend Rd.
Cincinnati, OH 45238
(513) 661-0241

Jewish Family Service
1710 Section Rd.
Cincinnati, OH 45237
(513) 351-3680

Catholic Counseling Center
1001 Huron Rd.
Cleveland, OH 44115
(216) 696-6650

Center for Human Services
1001 Huron Rd.
Cleveland, OH 44115
(216) 241-6400

Jewish Family Service Association of Cleveland
2060 S. Taylor Rd.
Cleveland, OH 44118
(216) 371-2600

Family Counseling and Crittenton Services
199 S. Fifth St.
Columbus, OH 43215
(614) 221-7608

Family Counseling Center East
3901 E. Livingston Ave.
Columbus, OH 43215
(614) 236-8733

Family Counseling Center North
4770 Indianola Ave.
Columbus, OH 43216
(614) 885-8259

Family Counseling Northwest
1560 Fishinger Rd.
Columbus, OH 43216
(614) 457-8237

The Family Life Center
1229 Sunbury Rd.
Columbus, OH 43216
(614) 252-0901

Jewish Family Service
1175 College Ave.
Columbus, OH 43209

Family Service of Cuyahoga Falls
507 Portage Trail
Cuyahoga Falls, OH 44221
(216) 928-1159

Family Service Association
184 Salem Ave.
Dayton, OH 45406
(513) 222-9481

Family Service Association, East Side Office
734 Watervliet Ave.
Dayton, OH 45401
(513) 222-9481

Family Service, Eaton Office
209½ E. Main St., 2nd floor
Eaton, OH 45320
(513) 456-4697

Family Service, Fairborn Office
1164 S. Maple St.
Fairborn, OH 45324
(513) 879-2061

Family Service, South Office
2513-15 Centerville Rd.
Dayton, OH 45401
(513) 222-9481

Family Service, Xenia Office
50 S. Detroit St., Room 303
Xenia, OH 45385
(513) 372-4611

Family Service of Butler County
111 Buckeye St.
Hamilton, OH 45011
(513) 868-3245

Child and Family Service
616 S. Collett St.
Lima, OH 45805
(419) 225-1040

Family Service Association of
Lorain County
4370 Oberlin Ave.
Lorain, OH 44053
(216) 282-4273

Family Service Association of Elyria
351 4th St.
Elyria, OH 44035
(216) 322-6209

Family Counseling Services of
Western Stark County
11 Lincoln Way W., Suite 612
Massillon, OH 44646
(216) 832-5043

Family Service Association of
Licking County
122 W. Church St.
Newark, OH 43055
(614) 345-4920

Counseling and Growth Center
412 Jackson St.
Sandusky, OH 44870
(419) 627-0712

Family Service Agency of
Springfield and Clark County
Tecumseh Building, 10th floor
34 W. High St.
Springfield, OH 45502
(513) 325-5564

Family Service Association
248 N. Fifth St.
Steubenville, OH 43952
(614) 283-4763

Family Service Association,
Weirton Office
3354 Main St.
Weirton, WV 26062
(304) 797-1383

Family Services of Greater Toledo
1 Stranahan Square
Toledo, OH 43604
(419) 244-5511

Family Services, Ottawa County
Office
126 W. Third St.
Port Clinton, OH 43452
(419) 732-3569

Family Services, Wood County
Office
306 Huntington Bank Building
130 S. Main St.
Bowling Green, OH 43402
(419) 352-4624

Family Service Association
455 Elm Rd. N.E.
Warren, OH 44483
(216) 399-1847

Children's and Family Service
The Family Center
535 Marmion
Youngstown, OH 44502
(216) 782-5664

Oklahoma

Sunbeam Family Services
616 N.W. 21st St.
Oklahoma City, OK 73103
(405) 528-7721

Family and Children's Service
650 S. Peoria
Tulsa, OK 74120
(918) 587-9471

East Tulsa Family and Children's
Services
11322 "E" E. 21st St.
Tulsa, OK 74101
(918) 939-5409

Westside Family and Children's
Services
4965 S. Union
Tulsa, OK 74107
(918) 446-4549

Oregon

Metropolitan Family Service
2281 N.W. Everett St.
Portland, OR 97210
(503) 228-7238

Metropolitan Family Service,
Washington County Office
245 S.E. 5th
Hillsboro, OR 97123
(503) 648-0753

Pennsylvania
Family and Children's Service of
     Lehigh County
411 Walnut St.
Allentown, PA 18102
(215) 435-9651

Family Service of Beaver County
1445 Market St. (W.B.)
Beaver, PA 15009
(412) 775-8390

Family Counseling Service of
     Northampton County
520 E. Broad St.
Bethlehem, PA 18018
(215) 867-3946

Family Service Association of
     Bucks County
20 W. Oakland Ave.
Doylestown, PA 18901
(215) 345-0550

Family Counseling Service
Sumner E. Nichols Building,
     Suite 216
155 W. 8th St.
Erie, PA 16501
(814) 454-6478, 453-3623

Family and Children's Service
121 Locust St.
Harrisburg, PA 17101
(717) 238-8118

Family and Children's Service of
     Lancaster County
630 Janet Ave.
Lancaster, PA 17601
(717) 397-5241

Family and Community Service of
     Delaware County
100 W. Front St.
Media, PA 19063
(215) LO 6-7540

Family Service of Montgomery
     County
1904-06 Swede St.
Norristown, PA 19401
(215) 272-1520

Family Service, Eastern
     Montgomery Branch
1603 Old York Rd.
Abington, PA 19001
(215) 886-3636

Family Service, Main Line Branch
18 Simpson Rd.
Ardmore, PA 19003
(215) MI 2-5354

Family Service, North Penn Branch
713 W. Main St.
Lansdale, PA 19446
(215) 368-0985

Family Service, Pottstown Branch
933 N. Charlotte St.
Pottstown, PA 19464
(215) 326-1610

Family Service, Upper Perkiomen
     Branch
517 Main St.
East Greenville, PA 18041
(215) 679-6949

Family Service and Children's Aid
     of Venango County
202 W. First St.
Oil City, PA 16301
(814) 646-1283

Center For Human Services of
     Episcopal Community Services
225 S. Third St.
Philadelphia, PA 19106
(215) WA 5-8110

Family Service of Philadelphia
311 S. Juniper St.
Philadelphia, PA 19107
(215) 875-3300

Jewish Family Service of
     Philadelphia
1610 Spruce St.
Philadelphia, PA 19103
(215) KI 5-3290

Family and Children's Service
Clark Building, 18th floor
717 Liberty Ave.
Pittsburgh, PA 15222
(412) 261-3623

Jewish Family and Children's Sercie
234 McKee Place
Pittsburgh, PA 15213
(412) 683-4900

Family Service of Lackawanna
County
615 Jefferson Ave.
Scranton, PA 18510
(717) 342-3149

Family Service of Warren County
8 Pennsylvania Ave. W.
Warren, PA 16365
(814) 723-1330

Family Service of Chester County
310 N. Matlack St.
West Chester, PA 19380
(215) 696-4900

Family Service, Coatesville Office
103 N. Third Ave.
Coatesville, PA 19320
(215) 384-1926

Family Service, Kennett Square
Office
209 E. State St.
Kennett Square, PA 19348
(215) 444-5652

Family Service, Oxford
Neighborhood Center
35 N. Third St.
Oxford, PA 19363
(215) 932-8557

Family Service Association of
Wyoming Valley
73 W. Union St.
Wilkes-Barre, PA 18702
(717) 823-5144

Family Service of York and
York County
800 E. King St.
York, PA 17403
(717) 845-6624

(See "New Jersey" for Lower
Makefield, Morrisville and
Yardley areas listings)

Rhode Island

Child and Family Services of
Newport County
24 School St.
Newport, RI 02840
(401) 849-2300

Family Service Society of
Pawtucket and Vicinity
33 Summer St.
Pawtucket, RI 02860
(401) 723-2124

Family Service, Center Annex
Family Life Education Unit
25 N. Union St.
Pawtucket, RI 02860
(401) 728-6540

Family Service Center
Adolescent and Drug Counseling
Unit
35 Summer St.
Pawtucket, RI 02860
(401) 728-3260

Family Service
75 Charlesfield St.
Providence, RI 02906
(401) 331-1350

Jewish Family and Children's
Service
229 Waterman St.
Providence, RI 02906
(401) 331-1244

South Carolina

Charleston County Department of
Social Services
409 County Center
Charleston, SC 29403
(803) 792-7290

Family Service of Charleston
County
Community Services Building
30 Lockwood Blvd.
Charleston, SC 29401
(803) 723-4566

Family Service Center
1800 Main St.
Columbia, SC 29201
(803) 779-3250

Family Counseling Service
108 Three Hundred Building
300 University Ridge
Greenville, SC 29603
(803) 232-2434

Services to Families
830 N. Church St.
Spartanburg, SC 29303
(803) 573-6762

South Dakota
Helpline
(605) 673-2819

Family Service
1728 S. Cliff Ave.
Sioux Falls, SD 57105
(605) 336-1974

Tennessee
Family and Children's Services of
    Chattanooga
323 High St.
Chattanooga, TN 37401
(615) 267-0021

Child and Family Services of
    Knox County
114 Dameron Ave.
Knoxville, TN 37917
(615) 524-7483

Family Crisis Center and Runaway
    Shelter
2535 Magnolia Ave.
Knoxville, TN 37901
(615) 637-8000

Family Service of Memphis
2400 Poplar Building, Suite 500
Memphis, TN 38112
(901) 324-3637

Family and Children's Service
201 23rd Ave. N.
Nashville, TN 37203
(615) 327-0833

Texas
Family Service of Amarillo
900 S. Lincoln
Amarillo, TX 79101
(806) 372-3202

Child and Family Service
419 W. Sixth St.
Austin, TX 78701
(512) 478-1648

Family Services Association
650 Main St.
Beaumont, TX 77701
(713) 833-2668

Family Counseling Service
507 S. Water St.
Corpus Christi, TX 78401
(512) 882-2546

Family Guidance Center
2200 Main St.
Dallas, TX 75201
(214) 747-8331

Family Guidance Center,
    Garland Office
318 S. 9th St.
Garland, TX 75040
(214) 747-8331

Family Guidance Center,
    Irving Office
Southwest Bank and Trust Building,
    Suite 302
2520 W. Irving Blvd.
Irving, TX 75060
(214) 253-8879

Family Guidance Center,
    Lewisville Office
223 Kay Lane
Lewisville, TX 75067
(214) 221-4541

Family Guidance Center,
    Mesquite Office
Mesquite Social Services Center
207 W. Main St.
Mesquite, TX 75149
(214) 747-8331

Family Service of El Paso
2930 N. Stanton St.
El Paso, TX 79902
(915) 533-2491

Family and Individual Services
Association of Tarrant County
716 W. Magnolia
Fort Worth, TX 76104
(817) 335-2401
Crisis Intervention Service: 24-hour
caller service—(817) 336-3355

Family Service Center of Galveston
County
926 Broadway
Galveston, TX 77550
(713) 762-8636

Family Service Center
5049 39th St., Suite C
Groves, TX 77619
(713) 963-0159

Family Service Center
3635 West Dallas
Houston, TX 77019
(713) 524-3881

Family Service Center, Youth
Services Program
6425 Chimney Rock
Houston, TX 77002
(713) 667-9626

Family Service Center, Youth
Services Program
5530 Van Fleet
Houston, TX 77002
(713) 738-8211

Family Service Center, Youth
Services Program
7700 Fulton, Suite 206
Houston, TX 77002
(713) 694-5521

Jewish Family Service
4131 S. Braeswood Blvd.
Houston, TX 77025
(713) 667-9336

Family Service Association
1220 Broadway, Suite 1406
Lubbock, TX 79401
(806) 747-3488

Family Services of Midland
9 Rivercrest Building
2101 W. Wall
Midland, TX 79701
(915) 683-4241

Family Service Association of
San Antonio
230 Pereida St.
San Antonio, TX 78210
(512) 226-3391

Jewish Family Service
8438 Ahern Dr.
San Antonio, TX 78216
(512) 349-5481

Family Counseling and Children's
Services
213 Community Services Building
201 W. Waco Dr.
Waco, TX 76703
(817) 753-1509

Utah
Davis County Mental Health
Center
175 East 2100 South
Salt Lake City, Utah 84101
(801) 487-5841

Family Counseling Center
420 North 200 West
Provo, Utah 84601
(801) 375-6736

Virginia
Social Service Bureau
Municipal Building
Danville, VA 24541
(804) 799-6537

Northern Virginia Family Service
100 N. Washington St.
Falls Church, VA 22046
(703) 533-9727

Northern Virginia Family Service,
Alexandria Office
206 N. Washington St.
Alexandria, VA 22313
(703) 549-3814

Peninsula Family Service
1520 Aberdeen Rd.
Hampton, VA 23666
(804) 838-1960

Family Service of Central Virginia
1010 Miller Park Square
Lynchburg, VA 24501
(804) 845-5944

Family Service
222 19th St. W.
Norfolk, VA 23517
(804) 622-7017

Jewish Family Service of Tidewater
7300 Newport Ave.
Norfolk, VA 23505
(804) 489-3111

Child and Family Service
355 Crawford St.
Portsmouth, VA 23704
(804) 397-2121, 397-3311,
  399-8008

Family and Children's Service of
  Richmond
1518 Willion Lawn Dr.
Richmond, VA 23230
(804) 282-4255

Oasis House (for runaways)
2213 W. Grace Ave.
Richmond, VA 23219
(804) 359-1647

Park School (for adolescent
  parents)
100 W. Baker St.
Richmond, VA 23219
(804) 780-4641

Jewish Family Services
7027 Three Chopt Rd.
Richmond, VA 23226
(804) 282-5644

Family Service of Roanoke Valley
518 Carlton Terrace Building
920 S. Jefferson St.
Roanoke, VA 24016
(703) 344-3253

Washington, D.C.
Family Service Association
1819 H Street Northwest
Washington, DC 20006
(202) 785-2438

Family Stress Hot Line
(202) 628-3228

Family and Child Services
  of Washington
929 L St., N.W.
Washington, DC 20001
(202) 232-6510

Washington
Family Services of King County
500 Lowman Building
107 Cherry St.
Seattle, WA 98104
(206) 447-3883

Family Services, East Side Office
1101 N.E. 8th, Suite 201
Bellevue, WA 98004
(206) 447-3871

Family Services, East Valley Office
305 S. 43rd St.
Renton, WA 98055
(206) 226-1253

Family Services, Enumclaw Office
1705 Wells
Enumclaw, WA 98022
(206) 825-7154

Family Services, Federal Way
  Office
31003-18th S.
Federal Way, WA 98002
(206) 839-5015

Family Counseling Service
1008 S. Yakima Ave.
Tacoma, WA 98405
(206) 627-6105

Family Counseling Service,
  Gig Harbor Office
6318-38th Ave. N.W.
Gig Harbor, WA 98335
(206) 858-9938

Family Counseling Service,
Lakewood Office
Little Church on the Prairie
6310 Motor Ave. S.W.
Lakewood, WA 98259
(206) 588-6631

Family Counseling Service,
Puyallup Valley Office
2208 E. Main
Puyallup, WA 98371
(206) 848-7217

West Virginia
Family Service of Marion and
Harrison Counties
201 Virginia Ave.
Fairmont, WV 26545
(304) 366-4750

Family Service, Harrison County
Office
115 S. 4th St.
Clarksburg, WV 26301
(304) 624-7587

Children and Family Service
Association
Multi-Service Center
109 N. Main St.
Wheeling, WV 26003
(304) 233-6300

(See "Ohio" for Weirton, WV
listing)

Wisconsin
Family Service Association of Beloit
423 Bluff St.
Beloit, WI 53511
(608) 365-1244

Family Service Association of
Brown County
1546 Dousman St.
Green Bay, WI 54303
(414) 499-8768

Crisis Intervention Center
929 Cass St.
Green Bay, WI 54301
(414) 432-8832

Family Service Association,
East Side Office
529 Greene Ave.
Green Bay, WI 54301
(414) 437-7071

Family Service Association
2350 South Ave.
La Crosse, WI 54601
(608) 788-6762

Family Service
214 N. Hamilton St.
Madison, WI 53703
(608) 251-7611

Family Service Association of the
Fox Valley
929 Midway Rd.
Menasha, WI 54952
(414) 739-4226

Family Service of Milwaukee
2819 W. Highland Blvd.
Milwaukee, WI 53208
(414) 342-4558

Jewish Family and Children's
Service
1360 N. Prospect Ave.
Milwaukee, WI 53202
(414) 273-6515

Family Service of Racine
420 Seventh St.
Racine, WI 53403
(414) 634-2391

Family Service of Waukesha County
414 W. Moreland Blvd.
Waukesha, WI 53186
(414) 547-5567

Canada

Alberta

Catholic Social Services
9518-102 A Ave.
Edmonton, Alta. T5H 0G1
(403) 424-0651

Family Service Association of
  Edmunton
Family Service Building
9919 106th St.
Edmunton, Alta. T5K 1E2
(403) 423-2831

Centre for Personal and
  Community Development
205 Professional Building
740-4th Ave. S.
Lethbridge, Alta. T1J 0N9
(403) 327-5724

British Columbia

Family Services of Greater
  Vancouver
1616 W. Seventh Ave.
Vancouver, B.C. V6J 1S5
(604) 731-4951

Manitoba

Family Services of Winnipeg
287 Broadway Ave., 4th floor
Winnipeg, Man. R3C 0R9
(204) 947-1401

Ontario

Family Services of Hamilton-
  Wentworth
First Place
350 King St. E., Suite 201
Hamilton, Ont. L8N 3Y3
(416) 523-5640

Family Service Association of
  Metropolitan Toronto
22 Wellesley St. E.
Toronto, Ont. M4Y 1G3
(416) 922-3126

Family Service Bureau of Windsor
450 Victoria Ave.
Windsor, Ont. N9A 6T7
(519) 256-1831

Quebec

Ville Marie Social Service Centre
4018 St. Catherine St. W.
Montreal, Que. H3Z 1P2
(514) 989-1885

Saskatchewan

Catholic Family Services
635 Main St.
Saskatoon, Sask. S7H 0J8
(306) 244-7773

Family Service Bureau
200-245 3rd Ave. S.
Saskatoon, Sask. S7K 1M4
(306) 244-0127

Information and Special Help Resources

Alcohol and Drug Abuse

National Federation of Parents for
  Drug-Free Youth
P.O. Box 57217
Washington, DC 20037
(Send $1.00 for NFD starter kit
with information on how to start a
local parent group.)

National Institute on Drug Abuse
P.O. Box 2305
Rockville, MD 20852
(Ask for free books: "Parents, Peers
and Pot" and "For Parents Only:
What You Need to Know About
Marijuana.")

Parent Resources and Information on Drug Education (PRIDE)
Georgia State University
University Plaza
Atlanta, GA 30303
(Send $5.00 for packet of information on drugs and an action plan for parents. A subscription to the quarterly newsletter is $2.00.)

Straight Talk
c/o Drug Fair, Inc.
6295 Edsall Rd.
Alexandria, VA 22314
(Send $1.00 for 5 pamphlets on how to spot drug abuse in your child and what to do about it.)

Palmer Drug Abuse Program
(213) 989-0902
(PDAP, which has helped over 20,000 young people overcome drug habits, has centers in Houston and Los Angeles which accept youngsters from all over the country for treatment.)

National Clearinghouse for Alcohol Information
P.O. Box 2345
Rockville, MD 20853
(Write for list of alcohol treatment facilities and programs in your area and a free copy of "The Drinking Question: Honest Answers to Questions Teenagers Ask About Drinking.")

National Highway Traffic Safety Administration
General Services Division
400 7th St. N.W.
Washington, DC 20590
(Ask for free booklet "How to Talk to Your Teenager About Drinking and Driving.")

Alcoholics Anonymous World Services, Inc.
Box 459
Grand Central Station
New York, NY 10017

(Send 25¢ for the booklet "Too Young?" on the issue of teenage alcoholism.)

Medical Problems

National Association of Anorexia Nervosa and Associated Disorders
P.O. Box 271
Highland Park, IL 60035
(312) 831-3438

American Anorexia Nervosa Association
101 Cedar Lane
Teaneck, NJ 07666
(201) 836-1800

Juvenile Diabetes Foundation
2200 Benjamin Franklin Parkway
Philadelphia, PA 19104
(215) LO 7-4307

American Diabetes Association
600 Fifth Ave.
New York, NY 10020

VD National Hotline
In California: (800) 982-5833
Outside California: (800) 227-8922

Pregnancy and Parenting Services for Adolescents

For Abortion Referral
Check the white pages of your telephone directory for local listings of:
    The Clergy Counseling Service
    Planned Parenthood
    National Organization of Women
    Or call the National Abortion Federation Hotline at
        (800) 223-0618

For Alternatives to Abortion
Check the white pages of your telephone directory for local listings of:
    Birthright
    Florence Crittenden Association (or Crittenden Services)
    Children's Home Society (in California)

*Parenting Support Group for
Adolescents*
National Association Concerned
   With School-Age Parents
7315 Wisconsin Ave.
Suite 211-W
Washington, DC 20014
(Write to the above address for the
group nearest you.)

Parenting Education (for Parents of Teenagers)

Parenting classes are sponsored by
many community and national organizations such as the YMCA, Red
Cross and PTA as well as private
groups. These classes are designed
to help clarify values, improve communication skills and help you in
your efforts to understand your teenager and to set firm guidelines for
him or her. Some of these classes
include Dr. Thomas Gordon's "Parenting Effectiveness" (classes $25
to $65), the YMCA's "Positive Par-
enting" (a maximum total fee of
$25 is charged) and STEP (the
complete kit—for class or independent study—is $77).

To get more information on parenting courses, write to:

The Parent/Early Childhood and
   Special Programs Office
U.S. Department of Education
400 Maryland Avenue S.W.
Washington, DC 20202

Effectiveness Training, Inc.
531 Stevens Ave.
Solona Beach, CA 92075
(Ask for descriptive literature or location of the "Parenting Effectiveness" course nearest you.)

Institute for Adolescent Studies
311 South San Gabriel Blvd.
Pasadena, CA 91107
(213) 795-0208
(You can write to this main office

for the address of the institute in
your area. These institutes, located
nationwide, offer counseling and
classes for parents on how to live
with teenagers.)

Self-Help Groups for Parents of Troubled Teenagers

Toughlove
Community Service Foundation
P.O. Box 70
Sellersville, PA 18960
(215) 766-8022
(This program helps parents develop new strengths to give a sense
of support and firm directions to
troubled teens who may be acting
out in school, within the family,
with drugs, alcohol or trouble with
the law.)

Parents Anonymous
22330 Hawthorne Blvd. #208
Torrance, CA 90505
Hotline (crisis counseling and information available 24 hours a day,
seven days a week):
   California: (800) 352-0386
   Outside California:
      (800) 421-0353
(Parents Anonymous is a national
organization with over 1,000 chapters in the United States. All services, which include working with
volunteer professionals to solve
problems with children and getting
support in weekly meetings with
professionals and other parents, are
free.)

Al-Anon
World Service Office
P.O. Box 182
Madison Square Station
New York, NY 10159
(212) 481-6565
(Al-Anon helps relatives of alcohol-
ics learn to deal with the problem
drinker more effectively and to make
their own lives more manageable

whether or not the alcoholic stops drinking. You can usually find your local chapter in your telephone directory, but can get literature about the organization and the location of the group nearest you by writing to the above address.)

Parents and Friends of Gays
P.O. Box 24528
Los Angeles, CA 90024
(You can write to this address for information about the group in your area. The reply will be confidential and arrive in a plain envelope.)

Parental Stress Line
In Massachusetts: (800) 632-8188
Outside Massachusetts:
   (617) 742-7573
(This is a 24-hour service for parents experiencing crises with their children. Out-of-state callers may ask for a referral to their local Stress Line.)

Runaway Services

National Youth Work Alliance
1346 Connecticut Avenue N.W.
Washington, DC 20036
(For name of runaway/teen crisis shelter in your area.)

National Runaway Switchboard
(800) 621-4000
(This is a toll-free service offering crisis help and referrals to runaway shelters, counseling and supportive services nationwide.)

Operation Peace of Mind
In Texas: (800) 392-3352
Elsewhere in continental U.S.:
   (800) 231-6946
In Alaska and Hawaii:
   (800) 231-6762
(This is a toll-free message and information service for teenage runaways and their families.)

Therapy—Information and Referral Sources

If you're looking for a qualified marriage or family counselor, a psychiatrist or psychologist, you might seek referrals from professional organizations. Some of these include:

The American Association for
   Marriage and Family Therapy
924 W. 9th St.
Upland, CA 91786
(714) 981-0888
(This organization has over 7,500 members in the U.S. and Canada. You can write or call for free referrals to qualified marriage/family counselors.)

American Psychiatric Association
1700 18th St. N.W.
Washington, DC 20009
(202) 797-4900

American Psychological Association
1200 17th St. N.W.
Washington, DC 20036
(202) 833-7600

Medical Clinics for Adolescents

The following list is used with the permission of The Society for Adolescent Medicine.

Alabama

Adolescent Clinic
Department of Pediatrics
University of Alabama Medical
    Center
Birmingham, AL 35294
(205) 934-4961

Arizona

Adolescent Clinic
Arizona Health Services
University of Arizona
1501 N. Campbell Ave.
Tucson, AZ 85724

California

Leo J. Ryan Teen Clinic
Guadalupe Health Center
75 Willington St.
Daly City, CA 94014
(415) 755-7740

Adolescent Clinic
445 S. Cedar St.
Fresno, CA 93702
(209) 453-5201

Adolescent Clinic
Children's Hospital of Los Angeles
4650 Sunset Blvd.
Los Angeles, CA 90027
(213) 669-2153

Adolescent Clinic
Kaiser Foundation Hospital
12500 S. Hoxie Ave.
Norwalk, CA 90650
(213) 920-4881

Teen Clinic
Oakland Children's Hospital
51st at Grove Ave.
Oakland, CA 94609
(415) 654-8363

Adolescent Clinic
Kaiser Foundation Hospital
13652 Cantara St.
Panorama City, CA 91402
(213) 781-2361

Adolescent Medical Clinic
UCSD Medical Center
225 W. Dickinson St.
San Diego, CA 92103
(714) 294-6786

Adolescent Clinic
Child and Youth Project
Mt. Zion Hospital
1600 Divisadero St.
San Francisco, CA 94120
(415) 567-6600

Adolescent and Youth Clinics
University of California Medical
    Center
400 Parnassus Ave.
San Francisco, CA 94143
(415) 666-2184

Youth Clinic
San Francisco General Hospital
1001 Potrero Ave.
San Francisco, CA 94110
(415) 821-8376

Adolescent Clinic
Children's Hospital
3700 California St.
San Francisco, CA 94119
(415) 387-8700

Adolescent Youth Clinic
Children's Hospital
520 Willow Rd.
Stanford, CA 94304
(415) 327-4800

Adolescent Clinic
Harbor UCLA Medical Center
1000 West Carson St.
Torrance, CA 90509
(213) 533-2317

Colorado
Adolescent Clinic
University of Colorado Medical
    Center
4200 E. 9th Ave.
Denver, CO 80220
(303) 394-8461

Westside Teen Connection
990 Federal Blvd., 2nd floor
Denver, CO 80204
(303) 292-9690

Valley Wide Health Service
P.O. Box 778
Alamosa, CO 81101
(303) 589-3658

Connecticut
Child and Adolescent Service
Mount Sinai Hospital
500 Blue Hills Ave.
Hartford, CT 06112
(203) 242-4431

Adolescent Clinic
Yale New Haven Hospital
789 Howard Ave.
New Haven, CT 06510
(203) 436-3616

Adolescent Unit
Bridgeport Hospital
267 Grant St.
Bridgeport, CT 06602
(203) 384-3064

District of Columbia
Adolescent Medicine Clinic
Howard University Hospital
2041 Georgia Ave. N.W.
Washington, DC 20060
(202) 745-1376

Adolescent Medicine
Children's Hospital, National
111 Michigan Ave. N.W.
Washington, DC 20010
(202) 745-5464

Child and Youth Ambulatory
    Services
Georgetown University Medical
    Center
3800 Reservoir Rd.
Washington, DC 20012
(202) 576-1107

Hawaii
Adolescent Program
Kapiolani Children's Medical Center
1319 Punahou St.
Honolulu, HI 96826

Adolescent Unit
Straub Clinic and Hospital
888 S. King St.
Honolulu, HI 96813
(808) 523-2311

Idaho
Nampa Clinic
1515 Third St. N.
Nampa, ID 83651
(208) 466-7869

Parma Clinic
311 Grove
Parma, ID 83660
(208) 722-5147

Homedale Clinic
116 E. Idaho St.
Homedale, ID 83628
(208) 337-3189

Illinois
Adolescent Clinic
Rush Presbyterian Hospital
1753 W. Congress Parkway
Chicago, IL 60612
(312) 942-5000

Doc's Corner
500 Racine
Chicago, IL 60607
(312) 829-0046

Adolescent Medical Clinic
Michael Reese Hospital
29th St. at Ellis Ave.
Chicago, IL 60616
(312) 791-2000

Iowa

Adolescent Clinic
Departments of Medicine and
    Pediatrics
University of Iowa Hospitals
Iowa City, IA 52242
(319) 356-2229

Kentucky

Adolescent Clinic/GYN Clinic
Division of Adolescent Medicine
Norton Children's Hospital
Louisville, KY 40202
(502) 589-8750

Maryland

Adolescent Clinic
Montgomery County Health
    Department
8500 Colesville Rd.
Silver Spring, MD 20910
(301) 565-7729

Adolescent Clinic
Wing 5-C
University of Maryland Hospital
22 S. Greene St.
Baltimore, MD 21201
(301) 528-5400

Massachusetts

Adolescent and Young Adult
    Medicine
Children's Hospital Medical Center
300 Longwood Ave.
Boston, MA 02115
(617) 734-6000

Adolescent Clinic
Tufts New England Medical Center
171 Harrison Ave.
Boston, MA 02111
(617) 956-5000

Adolescent Center
Boston City Hospital
818 Harrison Ave.
Boston, MA 02118
(617) 424-6086

Adolescent Clinic
Kennedy Memorial Hospital
Brighton, MA 02135
(617) 254-3800

Teen Health Services
St. John's Hospital
Hospital Dr.
Lowell, MA 01852

Michigan

Internal/Adolescent Medicine
Out-Patient Building, 3rd floor
University Hospital
Ann Arbor, MI 48109

Adolescent Ambulatory Services
Children's Hospital of Michigan
3901 Beaubien Blvd.
Detroit, MI 48201
(313) 494-5762

Adolescent Clinic
Hurley Medical Center
1 Hurley Plaza
Flint, MI 48502
(313) 766-0193

Minnesota

Community University Health Care
    Center
2016 16th Ave., S.
Minneapolis, MN 55404
(612) 376-4774

Teenage Medical Services
2425 Chicago Ave.
Minneapolis, MN 55404
(612) 874-6125

Face-to-Face
716 Mendota St.
St. Paul, MN 55101
(612) 772-2557

Mississippi

Rush Clinic
1314 19th Ave.
Meridian, MS 39301
(601) 483-0011

Missouri
Adolescent Clinic
Children's Hospital
240 Gillham Rd.
Kansas City, MO 64108
(816) 471-0626

Nebraska
Adolescent Clinic
Omaha Children's Hospital
12808 Augusta Ave.
Omaha, NB 68144
(402) 330-5690

Weight Loss Clinic
Children's Memorial Hospital
44th at Dewey Ave.
Omaha, NB 68105
(402) 553-5400

New Jersey
Adolescent Clinic
Monmouth Medical Center
Long Branch, NJ 07740
(201) 222-5200

Adolescent Services and Clinic
Morristown Memorial Hospital
100 Madison Ave.
Morristown, NJ 07960
(201) 540-5199

Adolescent Clinic
Martland Hospital
100 Bergen St.
Newark, NJ 07103
(201) 456-5779

New York
Adolescent Medical Program
Brookdale Hospital Medical Center
Linden Blvd. at Brookdale Plaza
Brooklyn, NY 11212
(212) 240-6452

Division of Adolescent Medicine
Montefiore Hospital and Medical
   Center
111 E. 210th St.
Bronx, NY 10467
(212) 920-4045

Adolescent Medicine
Long Island-Jewish Hillside
   Medical Center
New Hyde Park, NY 11042
(212) 470-2756

Adolescent Medical Unit
Pediatric Project
550 First Ave.
New York, NY 10016
(212) 561-6321

Child and Youth Project
Roosevelt Hospital
428 W. 59th St.
New York, NY 10019
(212) 554-7475

Adolescent Health Center
The Door
618 Avenue of the Americas
New York, NY 10011
(212) 691-6161

Adolescent Health Center
Mt. Sinai Medical Center
19 E. 101st St.
New York, NY 10029
(212) 831-1127

Adolescent Clinic
New York Hospital-Cornell Medical
   Center
525 E. 68th St.
New York, NY 10021
(212) 472-5454

W. F. Ryan Teen Center
160 W. 100th St.
New York, NY 10025
(212) 865-7661

Adolescent Clinic
601 Elmwood Ave.
Rochester, NY 14642
(716) 275-2962

Threshold
115 Clinton Ave. S.
Rochester, NY 14604
(716) 454-7530

General Adolescent Clinic
Onondago County Health
  Department
Family Planning
Civic Center
Syracuse, NY 13210

Adolescent Services
Westchester County Medical
  Center
Valhalla, NY 10595
(914) 347-7570

North Dakota
Fargo Clinic
737 Broadway
Fargo, ND 58102
(701) 237-2431

Ohio
Adolescent Clinic
Pavilion Building
Children's Hospital Medical Center
Elland and Bethesda Aves.
Cincinnati, OH 45229
(513) 559-4681

Price Hill Clinic
741 State Ave.
Cincinnati, OH 45202
(513) 251-4600

Mt. Auburn Health Center
1947 Auburn Ave.
Cincinnati, OH 45202
(513) 241-4949

Millvale Clinic
3301 Beekman
Cincinnati, OH 45202
(513) 681-3855

Lincoln Heights Health Center
1171 Adams Ave.
Cincinnati, OH 45202
(513) 771-7801

Findlay Market Clinic
19 West Elder
Cincinnati, OH 45202
(513) 621-4400

Adolescent Clinic
Cleveland Metropolitan General
  Hospital
3395 Scranton Rd.
Cleveland, OH 44109
(216) 398-6000

Adolescent Diagnostic Center
Cleveland Clinic Foundation
9500 Euclid St.
Cleveland, OH 44118
(214) 444-5616

Teen Health Center
St. Vincent Hospital and Medical
  Center
2213 Cherry St.
Toledo, OH 43608
(419) 259-4795

Oklahoma
Adolescent Medicine Clinic
Children's Memorial Hospital
940 N.E. 13th St., Room 1B511
Oklahoma City, OK 73190
(405) 271-6208

Pennsylvania
Adolescent and Youth Center
801 Old York Rd., Suite 222
Jenkintown, PA 19046
(215) 887-1678

Adolescent Medical Center
1723 Woodbourne Rd., #10
Levittown, PA 19057
(215) 946-8353

Adolescent Clinic
Children's Hospital
34th St. and Civic Center Blvd.
Philadelphia, PA 19104
(215) 387-6311

South Carolina
Medical Park Pediatrics and
  Adolescent Clinic
3321 Medical Park Rd.
Columbia, SC 29203
(803) 779-7380

Adolescent Clinic
Greenville General Hospital
701 Grove Rd.
Greenville, SC 29605
(803) 242-8625

Texas
Adolescent Clinic
Children's Medical Center
1935 Amelia St.
Dallas, TX 75235
(214) 637-3820

Adolescent Clinic
Robert B. Green Hospital
527 N. Leona St.
San Antonio, TX 78207
(512) 223-6361

Adolescent Referral Clinic
University of Texas
Health Services Center
7703 Floyd Curl Dr.
San Antonio, TX 78284
(512) 691-6551

Adolescent Clinic
University of Texas, Medical
  Branch
Galveston, TX 77550
(713) 765-1444

Adolescent Clinic
Ben Taub Hospital
Ben Taub Loop
Houston, TX 77071
(713) 791-7000

Chimney Rock Center
6425 Chimney Rock Rd.
Houston, TX 77071
(713) 667-9626

Virginia
Adolescent Medicine
Children's Hospital of the King's
  Daughters
800 W. Olney Rd.
Norfolk, VA 23507
(804) 622-1381

Adolescent Medical Clinic
Medical College of Virginia
Box 151-MCV Station
Richmond, VA 23298
(804) 786-9408

Washington
Adolescent Clinic
Group Health Co-Op of Puget
  Sound
10200 First St. N.E.
Seattle, WA 98123
(206) 545-7138

Rainier Youth Clinic
Child and Youth Project
3722 S. Hudson St.
Seattle, WA 98118

Adolescent Clinic
University of Washington
Division of Adolescent Medicine
Seattle, WA 98105
(206) 545-1274

Adolescent Health Clinic
Tacoma Pierce County Health
  Department
Tacoma, WA 98405
(206) 593-4813

Wisconsin
Beaumont Clinic
1821 S. Webster Ave.
Green Bay, WI 54301
(414) 437-9051

Teenage Clinic
Clinical Sciences Center
600 Highland Ave.
Madison, WI 53792
(608) 263-6406

Marshfield Clinic
Adolescent Section and Clinic
100 North Oak
Marshfield, WI 65549
(715) 387-5413

Child and Adolescent Health Center
Milwaukee Children's Hospital
1700 West Wisconsin Ave.
Milwaukee, WI 53233
(414) 931-4105

Canada

I.O.D.E. Children's Centre
North York General Hospital
4001 Leslie St.
Willowdale, Ont. M2K 1E1
(416) 492-3836

Adolescent Clinic
Hospital for Sick Children
555 University Ave.
Toronto, Ont. M5G 1X8
(416) 597-1500

Child and Adolescent Services
3666 McTavish St.
Montreal, Que. H3A 1YA
(514) 392-5022

Adolescent Unit
Montreal Children's Hospital
2300 Tupper St.
Montreal, Que. H3H 1P3
(514) 937-8511

Miriam Kennedy Child and Family
   Clinic
509 Pine Ave. W.
Montreal, Que. H2W 1S4
(514) 849-1315

Adolescent Clinic
Ste-Justin Hospital
3175 Côte Ste-Catherine
Montreal, Que. H3T 1C5
(514) 731-4931

Suicide Prevention Centers and Hot Lines

All listed centers are members of the American Association of Suicidology.
(See **Additional Suicide-Crisis Intervention Centers** following this section.)

Alaska

Suicide Prevention and Crisis
   Center
P.O. Box 2863
Anchorage, AK 99510

Arizona

Information and Referral Service
2302 E. Speedway, Suite 210
Tucson, AZ 85719
(602) 323-1303

Arkansas

Hope Line
3807 McCain Park Dr., Suite 110
North Little Rock, AR 72116
(501) 758-6922

California

Suicide Prevention and Crisis
   Center of San Mateo County
1811 Trousdale Dr.
Burlingame, CA 94010
(415) 877-5604

Monterey County Suicide
   Prevention Center
P.O. Box 3241
Carmel, CA 93921
(408) 375-6966

Suicide Prevention of Yolo County
P.O. Box 672
Davis, CA 95616
(916) 756-7542

Suicide Prevention Center
1041 S. Menlo Ave.
Los Angeles, CA 90006
(213) 386-5111

Suicide Prevention Service of
   Sacramento County, Inc.
P.O. Box 449
Sacramento, CA 95802
(916) 441-1138

Defy Counseling Line
2870 4th Ave.
San Diego, CA 92103
(714) 236-3339

Suicide and Crisis Service
2221 Enborg Lane
San Jose, CA 95128
(408) 279-6250

Colorado
Pueblo Suicide Prevention Center
229 Colorado Ave.
Pueblo, CO 81004
(303) 545-2477

Connecticut
Info Line of Southwestern
 Connecticut
7 Academy St.
Norwalk, CT 06850
(203) 853-9109

The Wheeler Clinic—Emergency
 Services
91 Northwest Dr.
Plainville, CT 06062
(203) 747-6801

Florida
Alachua County Crisis Center
606 S.W. 3rd Ave.
Gainesville, FL 32601
(904) 372-3659

Central Crisis Center of Jacksonville
P.O. Box 6393
Jacksonville, FL 32205
(904) 387-5641

Suicide and Crisis Center
2214 E. Henry Ave.
Tampa, FL 33610
(813) 238-8411

Hawaii
Suicide and Crisis Center
200 N. Vineyard Blvd., Suite 601-3
Honolulu, HI 96817
(808) 521-4555

Illinois
Call For Help—Suicide and Crisis
 Intervention Services, Inc.
7623 (Rear) W. Main St.
Belleville, IL 62223
(618) 397-0968

Indiana
Suicide Prevention Center of
 St. Joseph County
532 S. Michigan St.
South Bend, IN 46601
(219) 288-4842

Louisiana
Baton Rouge Crisis Intervention
 Center, Inc.
P.O. Box 23273
Baton Rouge, LA 70893
(504) 344-0319

Education and Treatment Council,
 Inc.
200 W. Eleventh St.
Lake Charles, LA 70601
(504) 433-1062

Crisis Line
1528 Jackson Ave.
New Orleans, LA 70130
(504) 523-4146

Massachusetts
Bath-Brunswick Area Rescue, Inc.
P.O. Box 534
Brunswick, MA 04011
(207) 729-4168

The Samaritans
802 Boylston St.
Boston, MA 02199
(617) 536-2460

Greater Lawrence Psychiatric
 Associates
42 Franklin St.
Lawrence, MA 01840
(617) 682-7442

South Norfolk Screening and
 Emergency Team
45 Hospital Rd.
Medfield, MA 02052
(617) 359-4966

Maryland
Montgomery County Hotline
10920 Connecticut Ave.
Kensington, MD 20795
(301) 949-1255

Michigan

Suicide Prevention and Drug
   Information Center
220 Bagley, Room 618
Detroit, MI 48226
(313) 875-5466

Lapeer County Community Mental
   Health Center
1575 Suncrest Dr.
Lapeer, MI 48446

Missouri

Crisis Intervention, Inc.
P.O. Box 582
Joplin, MO 64801
(417) 781-2255

Life Crisis Services, Inc.
7438 Forsyth, Suite 210
St. Louis, MO 63105
(314) 721-4310

Nevada

Growth Foundation—Suicide
   Prevention Center, Inc.
2408 Santa Clara Dr.
Las Vegas, NV 89104
(702) 732-1622

New Hampshire

Emergency Services—Central New
   Hampshire Community Mental
   Health
5 Market Lane
Concord, NH 03301
(603) 228-1551

Mental Health Center for Southern
   New Hampshire
Medical Arts Building
Derry Professional Park
Birch St.
Derry, NH 03038
(603) 434-1577

Intake And Emergency Services
787 Central Ave.
Dover, NH 03820
(603) 742-0630

New Jersey

Screening and Crisis Intervention
   Program
Zurbrugg Memorial Hospital
Riverside, NJ 08075
(609) 764-1100

New York

Suicide Prevention and Crisis
   Service
Box 312
Ithaca, NY 14850
(607) 272-1505

North Carolina

Suicide and Crisis Service of
   Alamance County, Inc.
P.O. Box 2573
Burlington, NC 27215
(919) 228-1720

Ohio

Support, Inc.
1361 W. Market
Akron, OH 44313
(216) 864-7743

Crisis Center
425 Chestnut St.
Chillicothe, OH 45601
(614) 773-0760

Psychiatric Emergency Evaluation
   and Referral Service
10900 Carnegie Ave., Room 400
Cleveland, OH 44106
(216) 229-4547

Suicide Prevention Service
1515 E. Broad St.
Columbus, OH 43205
(614) 252-0354

Suicide Prevention Center
184 Salem Ave.
Dayton, OH 45406
(513) 225-3093

South Carolina

Contact-Help, Inc.
P.O. Box 6336
Columbia, S.C. 29260

Tennessee
Suicide and Crisis Intervention
Service
P.O. Box 4068
Memphis, TN 38104
(901) 726-5534

Crisis Intervention Center
P.O. Box 120934
Nashville, TN 37212
(615) 298-3359

Texas
Crisis Intervention Service
P.O. Box 3075
Corpus Christi, TX 78404
(512) 883-0271

Suicide Prevention of Dallas, Inc.
P.O. Box 19651
Dallas, TX 75219
(214) 521-9111

Crisis Intervention of Houston, Inc.
P.O. Box 4123
Houston, TX 77210
(713) 527-9864

Crisis Intervention Service
406 W. Market St.
San Antonio, TX 78205
(512) 227-4357

Virginia
Northern Virginia Hotline
P.O. Box 187
Arlington, VA 22210

Suicide-Crisis Center, Inc.
P.O. Box 1493
Portsmouth, VA 23705
(804) 399-6395

Washington
Crisis Clinic
1530 Eastlake East
Seattle, WA 98102
(206) 329-1882

Wisconsin
Eau Claire Suicide Prevention
Center
Luther Hospital
1221 Whipple St.
Eau Claire, WI 54701
(715) 834-6040

Emergency Services—Dane County
MHC
31 S. Henry St.
Madison, WI 53703
(608) 251-2341

Additional Suicide-Crisis Intervention Centers

The following are not listed as members of the American Association of
Suicidology but are established services nonetheless.

Arizona
Mental Health Services—Suicide
Prevention Center
1825 E. Roosevelt
Phoenix, AZ 85006
(602) 258-6301

California
Suicide Prevention Center of
Bakersfield, Inc.
800 Eleventh St.
Bakersfield, CA 93304
(805) 325-1232

Suicide Prevention of Alameda
County, Inc.
P.O. Box 9102
Berkeley, CA 94709
North County: (415) 849-2212
South County: (415) 537-1323

Saddleback Valley Help Line
El Toro, CA 92630
(714) 830-2522

Help in Emotional Trouble
P.O. Box 468
Fresno, CA 93721
(805) 485-1432

Hot-Line Garden Grove
12345 Euclid St.
Garden Grove, CA 92640
(714) 636-2424

"Help Now" Line
2750 Bellflower Blvd., Suite 204
Long Beach, CA 90815
(213) 435-7669

North Bay Suicide Prevention, Inc.
P.O. Box 2444
Napa, CA 94558
Vallejo: (707) 643-2555
Napa: (707) 255-2555
St. Helena: (707) 963-2555

Suicide Prevention and Crisis
    Intervention Center
101 S. Manchester Ave.
Orange, CA 92668
(714) 633-9393, ext. 856, 857,
    858, 859

Suicide Crisis Intervention Center
c/o Palm Springs Mental Health
    Clinic
1720 E. Vista Chino
Palm Springs, CA 92262
(714) 346-9502

Suicide and Crisis Intervention
1999 N. D St.
San Bernardino, CA 92405
(714) 886-4880

San Francisco Suicide Prevention,
    Inc.
307 Twelfth Ave.
San Francisco, CA 94118
(415) 221-1424

Ventura County Suicide Prevention
    Service
33 Chrisman St.
Ventura, CA 93003
(805) 648-2444

Contra Costa Suicide Prevention
P.O. Box 4852
Walnut Creek, CA 94596
(415) 939-3232

Colorado
Suicide Referral Service
P.O. Box 1351
Colorado Springs, CO 80901
(303) 471-4357

Suicide and Crisis Control
2459 S. Ash
Denver, CO 80222
(303) 746-8485; 757-0988;
    789-3073

Delaware
Psychiatric Emergency Service
Farnurst
2001 North DuPont Parkway
New Castle, DE 19720
(302) 656-4428

District of Columbia
Suicide Prevention Service
801 North Capitol St. N.E.,
    Room 423
Washington, DC 20002
(202) 629-5222

Florida
Personal Crisis Service
30 S.E. Eighth St.
Miami, FL 33131
(305) 379-2611

We Care, Inc.
610 Mariposa
Orlando, FL 32801
(305) 241-3329

Georgia
Fulton County Emergency Mental
    Health Service
99 Butler St. S.E.
Atlanta, GA 30303
(404) 572-2626

Helpline
1512 Bull St.
Savannah, GA 31401
(912) 232-3383

Illinois

Suicide Prevention and Crisis
    Service
1206 S. Randolph
Champaign, IL 61820
(217) 359-4141

Crisis Intervention Program
4200 N. Oak Park Ave.
Chicago, IL 60634
(312) 794-3609

Call for Help
320 E. Armstrong Ave.
Peoria, IL 61603
(309) 691-7373/7374

Indiana

Suicide Prevention Service
1433 N. Meridian St.
Indianapolis, IN 46202
(317) 632-7575

Iowa

Lee County Mental Health Center
110 N. Eighth St.
Keokuk, IA 52632
(319) 524-3873

Kansas

Area Mental Health Center
156 Gardendale
Garden City, KS 67846
(316) 276-7689

Suicide Prevention Center
250 N. Seventeenth
Kansas City, KS 66102
(913) 371-7171

Can Help
P.O. Box 4253
Topeka, KS 66604
(913) 235-3434/3435

Suicide Prevention Service
1045 N. Minneapolis
Wichita, KS 67214
(316) 268-8251

Minnesota

Crisis Intervention Center
Hennepin County General Hospital
Minneapolis, MN 55415
(612) 330-7777/7780

Emergency Social Service
413 Auditorium St.
St. Paul, MN 55102
(612) 225-1515

Mississippi

Listening Post
P.O. Box 2072
Meridian, MS 39301
(601) 693-1001

Missouri

Western Missouri Suicide
    Prevention Center
600 E. 22nd St.
Kansas City, MO 64108
(816) 471-3000

Montana

Great Falls Crisis Center
P.O. Box 124
Great Falls, MT 59401
(406) 453-6511

Nebraska

Omaha Personal Crisis Service
P.O. Box 1491
Omaha, NB 68101
(402) 342-6290

Nevada

Suicide Prevention and Crisis Call
    Center
Mack SS Building, Room 206
University of Nevada
Reno, NV 89501
(702) 323-6111

New Jersey

Crisis Referral and Information
232 E. Front St.
Plainfield, NJ 07060
(201) 561-4800

New Mexico

Suicide Prevention and Crisis
  Center, Inc.
P.O. Box 4511, Station A
Albuquerque, NM 87106
(505) 265-7557

New York

Suicide Prevention Service
Kings County Hospital Center
600 Winthrop St.
Brooklyn, NY 11203
(212) 462-3322

Lifeline
Nassau County Medical Center
2201 Hempstead Turnpike
East Meadow, NY 11554
(516) 538-3111

Help Line Telephone Center
1 W. 29th St.
New York, NY 10016
(212) 686-3061

National Save-A-Life League, Inc.
815 Second Ave.
New York, NY 10017
(212) 736-6191

North Carolina

Durham County Mental Health
  Center
300 E. Main St.
Durham, NC 27701
(919) 688-5504

Crisis Help and Suicide Prevention
  Service
805 W. Main Ave.
Gastonia, NC 28052
(704) 867-6373

North Dakota

Suicide Prevention and Emergency
  Service
Ninth and Thayer
Bismarck, ND 58501
(701) 255-4124

Suicide Prevention and Mental
  Health Center
700 First Ave. S.
Fargo, ND 58102
(701) 323-4357

Northeast Region Mental Health
  Center
509 S. Third St.
Grand Forks, ND 58201
(701) 772-7258

St. Joseph's Hospital Suicide
  Prevention Center
Minot, ND 58701
(701) 838-5555

Oregon

Crisis Service
127 N.W. Sixth St.
Corvallis, OR 97330
(503) 752-7030

Crisis Center
University of Oregon Counseling
  Center
Eugene, OR 97403
(503) 686-4488

Pennsylvania

Lifeline
520 E. Broad St.
Bethleham, PA 18018
(215) 691-0660

Suicide Prevention Center
City Hall Annex, Room 430
Philadelphia, PA 19107
(215) 686-4420

South Carolina

Crisis Intervention Service
715 Grove Rd.
Greenville, SC 29605
(803) 239-1021

Utah

Granite Community Mental Health
  Center
156 Westminster Ave.
Salt Lake City, UT 84115
(801) 484-8761

West Virginia
Suicide Prevention Service
418 Morrison Building
815 Quarrier St.
Charleston, WV 25301
(304) 346-3332

Wisconsin
Milwaukee County Mental Health
    Center
8700 W. Wisconsin Ave.
Milwaukee, WI 53226
(414) 258-2040, ext. 3143

Wyoming
Help Line, Inc.
Cheyenne, WY 82001
(307) 634-4469

Church-Related Hot Lines
(Contact Teleministries USA)

Contact hot lines, staffed by volunteers, respond compassionately to callers
with a variety of problems and crises. The following is the most current
available list of services nationwide. New centers are being established all
the time; if you don't find your area listed, look for a Contact Tele-
ministries number in the white pages of your telephone book. Many, but
not all centers, provide full, 24-hour-a-day service.

Alabama
Foley
(205) 943-5675
Mobile
(205) 342-0711

Arkansas
Hot Springs
(501) 623-2515
Little Rock
(501) 666-0234
Pine Bluff
(501) 536-4226
Searcy
(501) 268-4109

California
Fresno
(209) 298-2022
Garden Grove
(714) 639-4673

Lafayette
(415) 284-2273
Lake Arrowhead
(714) 337-4300
Los Angeles
(213) 482-8000
Pasadena
(213) 449-4500
Sacramento
(916) 452-8255
San Jose
(408) 266-8228

Colorado
Denver
(303) 458-7777

Delaware
Wilmington
(302) 575-1112

Florida
Miami
(305) 754-3369

Tampa
(813) 932-1976

Georgia
Atlanta
(404) 261-3644

Columbus
(404) 327-3999

Gainesville
(404) 534-0617

Illinois
Rockford
(815) 964-4044

Indiana
Anderson
(317) 649-5211

Greencastle
(317) 653-2645

Merrillville
(219) 769-3141

Monticello
(219) 583-4357

Maryland
Baltimore
(301) 332-1114

Michigan
Detroit
(313) 894-5555

Minnesota
Minneapolis
(612) 341-2896

Owatonna
(507) 451-9100

Mississippi
Columbus
(601) 328-0200

Jackson
(601) 969-7272

Missouri
St. Louis
(314) 725-3022

Nebraska
Lincoln
(402) 474-5683

New Jersey
Atlantic City
(609) 646-6616

Bridgeton
(609) 455-3280

Colt's Neck
(201) 544-1444

Cherry Hill
(609) 667-3000

Glassboro
(609) 881-6200

Moorestown
(609) 234-8888

Roselle
(201) 527-0555

Salem
(609) 935-4357

Scotch Plains
(201) 232-2880

Toms River
(201) 240-6100

Trenton
(609) 888-2111

New York
New York City
(212) 532-2400

Syracuse
(315) 445-1500

North Carolina
Charlotte
(704) 333-6121

Durham
(919) 683-1595

Fayetteville
(919) 485-4134

High Point
(919) 882-8121

Lexington
(704) 249-8974

Rocky Mount
(919) 443-5144

Smithfield
(919) 934-6161

Winston-Salem
(919) 722-5153

Ohio
Ashtabula
(216) 998-2607

Bucyrus
(419) 562-9010

Cincinnati
(513) 791-4673

Dayton
(513) 434-6684

Warren
(216) 393-1565

Wooster
(216) 345-6618

Oklahoma
Clinton
(405) 323-1064

Enid
(405) 234-1111

Oklahoma City
(405) 848-2273

Weatherford
(405) 772-7867

Pennsylvania
Beaver
(412) 728-3650

Bensalem
(215) 245-1442

Chambersburg
(717) 264-7799

Harrisburg
(717) 652-4400

Lancaster
(717) 299-4855

New Castle
(412) 658-5529

Philadelphia
(215) 879-4402

Pittsburgh
(412) 782-4024

York
(717) 845-3656

South Carolina
Columbia
(803) 782-9222

Tennessee
Athens
(615) 745-9111

Chattanooga
(615) 622-5193

Cleveland
(615) 479-9666

Johnson City
(615) 926-0144

Kingsport
(615) 246-2273

Knoxville
(615) 523-9124

Oak Ridge
(615) 482-4949

Texas
Arlington
(817) 277-2233

Dallas
(214) 361-6624

Lubbock
(806) 765-8393

San Antonio
(512) 736-1876

Virginia
Martinsville
(703) 632-7295

Newport News
(804) 245-0041

Petersburg
(804) 733-1100

Richmond
(804) 257-7373

Virginia Beach
(804) 428-2211

Washington
Richland
(509) 943-6606

Renton
(206) 226-2273

West Virginia
Beckley
(304) 877-3535

Charleston
(304) 346-0826

Huntington
(304) 523-3448

Lewisburg
(304) 645-7557

Oak Hill
(304) 877-3535